JOAN SLABBERT

BWANA
KAKULI

Note for Librarians: A cataloguing record for this book is available from Library and Archives
Canada at www.collectionscanada.ca/amicus/index-e.html
ISBN 1-4120-6156-3

TRAFFORD
P U B L I S H I N G™
Offices in Canada, USA, Ireland and UK
This book was published *on-demand* in cooperation with Trafford Publishing. On-demand
publishing is a unique process and service of making a book available for retail sale to the
public taking advantage of on-demand manufacturing and Internet marketing. On-demand
publishing includes promotions, retail sales, manufacturing, order fulfilment, accounting and
collecting royalties on behalf of the author.

Book sales for North America and international:
Trafford Publishing, 6E–2333 Government St.,
Victoria, BC v8t 4p4 CANADA
phone 250 383 6864 (toll-free 1 888 232 4444)
fax 250 383 6804; email to orders@trafford.com
Book sales in Europe:
Trafford Publishing (uk) Ltd., Enterprise House, Wistaston Road Business Centre,
Wistaston Road, Crewe, Cheshire cw2 7rp UNITED KINGDOM
phone 01270 251 396 (local rate 0845 230 9601)
facsimile 01270 254 983; orders.uk@trafford.com
Order online at:
trafford.com/05-1057

10 9 8 7 6 5 4 3 2 1

NOTE FROM THE AUTHOR

Some time after my husband's death, I wrote an article recalling some of our adventures in the African bush and submitted it to the editor of a hunting magazine. His three-page reply simultaneously instilled in me both joy and utter dismay. He was unable to use it in its present form for a hunting magazine, but considered it too good to go unpublished. There were two options, he very kindly explained. The first was to shorten the story and submit it to more suitable magazines or, and here came the dismay, to expand on it and write a book. The latter, he wrote, was a far better option, as if the story were shortened, then it would lose its impact. He encouraged me to relate my life story in great detail and even provided me with examples of how each adventure could be expanded upon by describing more emotion and animating the characters involved in each instance.

This editor expressed such genuine interest in my story and adeptly awoke in me a sense of challenge. I realised that a huge task loomed ahead, yet felt utterly alive with enthusiasm. And so, at the age of seventy seven, I began to write for the first time in my life.

PREFACE

As wild as the buffalo after which he was nicknamed, as steadfast as the trunk of the great baobab, as gentle as the gazelle nudging her newborn, he was Kakuli. He was my love.

As a spoilt, demanding young woman, I married this man and he took me to wildest Africa. It was here that he taught me the magnitude of love, the harsh lessons of humility and the raw instinct to survive.

This book tells of passion, humour, adventure, dangerous encounters, but most of all, it is the story of a love that endured challenges beyond belief. It is my story.

My heartfelt thanks to the Hunting Editor of Magnum Magazine, Mr Gregor Woods, for his encouragement, it is through him that I write this book.

My special thanks to my daughter, Jeni, for her typing, editing and cover design. To Ethné, Francois and Shirley – your proof-reading helped tremendously and to dear Norman, thank you for patience while I was so preoccupied with my book.

I dedicate this book to Kakuli, who was the head of my herd. Powerful and decisive, he led the way throughout our lives and kept us safe always. Like any bull, there were times we thought him arrogant and intimidating, but it was those very qualities that made him such a leader and teacher and I thank God that he filled my life for so many years. It was an honour to be his wife.

To Kakuli...

Hamba Kahle, Bwana.

CHAPTER ONE

Meeting Kakuli....

I looked across at the elephant. He was a magnificent animal with two enormous ivory tusks, feeding quite a way from the track that we were on. His lower body was clean and shining from wading through the Lafupa River, the top half full of red dust and mud. It was just before the rainy season and the surrounding landscape was dry and brown. Everywhere was quiet, even the birds seemed to have stopped singing. It was just after midday and most animals at that time were resting, in whatever shade they could find. The grass each side of the bakkie appeared listless, just as we felt, due to the intense heat beating down onto the metal roof of the vehicle. The countryside still had a beauty all of its own, but one wasn't conscious of it. The elephant stopped feeding and as he looked our way, he threw up his trunk and shook his head violently.

I turned to Cecil, who was fondly known as 'Kakuli' by the locals, and pleaded with him. "Please drive on, I've had all I can take of wild animals and this elephant is getting restless."
Cecil tried unsuccessfully to start the bakkie, (an LDV, known in Rhodesia as a 'vanette' and in South Africa as a 'bakkie'), then turned to me and matter-of-factly stated "The bendix is stuck, we're not going anywhere".
He spoke quietly to the two labourers on the back, asking them to get off the bakkie on the far side of the elephant and rock the vehicle to release the bendix. As the bakkie began to rock back and forth, the elephant spread its ears, fanning them menacingly as he watched. Almost hoarse with fear, I whispered to Cecil "It's going to charge!"
Cecil replied "It won't come the whole way; it will make a feint charge first."
My nerves were shattered and I glared at him as I retorted "It's alright for you, it's on my side of the bakkie."

7

Cecil laughed teasingly, his eyes twinkling with excitement, as he looked at my angry face.

Wherever danger lurked, or when Cecil faced a challenge, he was in his element, but this was one situation I was quietly wishing he could face alone. Even though we had lived in the bush among the wild animals for years, I had never got rid of my fear, nor did I underestimate them. I sat there, utterly terrified at the monstrous size of the animal, as it flapped its ears and trumpeted in rage. My heart was pounding so fast that it made my chest ache. My mouth was dry and my body shook uncontrollably.

The elephant's trunk flew skywards, his ears flapping in earnest, as he let out a shrill, threatening trumpet. He charged swiftly towards the bakkie, dust flying from his thundering feet as the distance between us closed rapidly. True to Cecil's word, the elephant stopped short a few yards from the bakkie, then it pretended to pick at a nearby tree, but its beady eyes never left us for a second. I heard a click as the bendix slipped into place, just as the monstrous mammal again threw its trunk up, shaking its head violently from side to side, preparing to charge at us yet again. The bakkie thankfully started and the labourers scrambled onto the back as Cecil pulled away, leaving the enraged animal in a cloud of dust.

On our arrival back in camp, I sat down under the baobab tree while Cecil collected extra wood for the fire, which we would keep burning all night for protection from the animals. Leaning against the old, gnarled trunk, I looked across and studied this man of mine. He was tall, dark haired, with a lock of hair always falling loosely onto his forehead. He was exceptionally lean from all the manual work and sported a golden tan. His eyes were brown and, although normally quite serene in appearance, I had also seen those same eyes wrinkle up in laughter, shining mischievously when he teased someone and blaze brilliantly with the prospect of danger. He was a man of great presence and if he felt wronged, or became angry, those same eyes would grow cold, with a yellow hue that could intimidate anyone. He was wearing a khaki shirt and his longs were tucked into his hunting boots. Khaki was the bush attire, for it blended in so well with the surroundings. We had been in the bush for three months and his hair now fell on his broad shoulders in soft waves. In the prime of his life, he was an extremely attractive man who oozed self confidence. Watching him in the early twilight, my mind wandered back to how we had met and then even further back, to my parents.

My mother was a tiny woman, with light brown hair and beautiful blue eyes. Extremely slim and always smiling, she was very active and seemed to do everything in a hurry. My father was small in stature, with dark hair and blue eyes, but like most small men, he was quick to anger and always appeared to be on the defensive. They emigrated from United Kingdom when my brother was eleven and I was but a year old. They had hoped to give us a better life in Africa. My mother had lost a little girl before my birth and I think she was afraid of being hurt again, so kisses and cuddles were rare. My father was a rolling stone, so I attended ten different schools in eight years, some in South Africa and others in Southern Rhodesia. We spent a short time in the Transkei, in a little place called Emjinyana, which was a leper institution. It was here that my parents hired a servant by the name of Lily.

Lily, a young seventeen year old and oh, so tiny, lived in our outbuildings. She had such a happy disposition and was always singing and laughing. She was lighter in colour than the other people of that area and I wonder perhaps if she had a little of the Koi people in her. I was such a lonely young girl and Lily became my friend. We spent many evenings in her room, eating gnush (a mixture of mealies and beans), while Lily patiently taught me to crochet. This was my first lesson that race and colour meant nothing between friends and I was devastated when my father decided to move once again, resulting in me having to say goodbye to Lily.

With all our travelling around, I learned to admire beauty at an early age. There were not many tarred roads and cars were forced to travel at a rather slow pace, so we would jog along at about twenty miles an hour, which literally felt as though we were low-flying. One of the cars we owned was known as a 'Tourer' and this car did not have windows. If it rained, you could clip in sides of clear celluloid, at least I think it was called celluloid in those days, as there was no such thing as plastic. The sides didn't close up the area completely and the cold still crept in, so we always had blankets to warm ourselves. On sunny days, when the sides were open, one could sit and watch the birds singing their hearts out in the trees as they enjoyed the warm sunshine. At other times, you would see a tree full of vultures, watching for some animal to die, or waiting for lions to finish feeding on their kill, so they could pick on the remains. The changing scenery from South Africa to Southern Rhodesia was remarkable. How does one describe the beauty of the bush, the changing colours of green, beige and brown on the banks, either side of the car as one travelled. There would be bursts of blue, red and yellow flowers, creating a wondrous kaleidoscope rushing past the moving vehicle. If we stopped to eat our picnic lunch, I would look up into the heavens and admire the deep blue of the sky, with fluffy white clouds slowly drifting past. It was at times like these that one realised that there is a designing force out there somewhere that is far superior to any man-made designs.

A little rhyme ends 'You are closer to God in the garden, than anywhere else on earth', but believe me, if you go into the wilder parts of Africa; you are even closer to God than in any man-created garden. The peace you feel within when you stand alone in these areas is indescribable. I only had to sit quietly in the Kafue Game Park, for there was all of God's beauty and the stillness of those days made one want to humbly kneel and say 'Lord, how great Thou art'.
My father always planned our travelling to make sure that we stayed in hotels at night, so I was still very much a 'townie' until I moved to Northern Rhodesia, after my marriage to Cecil. I had no idea what 'roughing it' meant, or what was in store for me.

At the age of twelve, we moved to Port Elizabeth. Next door, but one, to our home lived a family with six sons and no daughters. In the innocence of my youth, I watched in disgust as they played football in the street in their bare feet. They tried hard to make friends, but I ignored them completely until they eventually gave up any efforts to get to know me. Little did I know that one of those boys was my future husband. The only thing I knew about them was that their surname was Slabbert.

On turning thirteen and passing standard six with an almighty kick in the pants, I ran away from school and went in search of work without telling my parents. I managed to convince the owner of a printing works that I was sixteen and he signed me up as an apprentice. He insisted that I let him have my birth certificate and my excuse for not having it, was that I was born in England and was not able to get a reply from the authorities over there.

I loved going to work each day and my salary was nine shillings and six pence (ninety five cents) per week. I bought my mom a bunch of flowers and gave her half a crown for boarding. My father was still furious with me, as he had always wanted me to be a draughtswoman. However, to my utmost relief, he was too proud to admit to the printing firm that his daughter had lied in her application and so, once again, I had my way.

Originally I was hired as the printer's assistant. The factory was very old and most of the machines came out of the ark. Collating was done by hand, as was numbering. Some days it felt like my hand was about to fall off with all the manual work. If we did wedding invitations in silver or gold, which was not available in paint, we printed them in black and then patted silver or gold dust into the wet ink.

In 1939 England declared war on Germany. The war did not affect us very much in South Africa, apart from the families whose sons and husbands signed up, with many of them never coming back. Certain items of food became very scarce and flour was unobtainable. The available substitute, brown meal, could be sifted into flour, but this was forbidden, with heavy fines payable if you were caught. I remember standing in queues with my mother at a huge army truck to get a little rice and some eggs. It was at this time that four of the six Slabbert boys, together with their father, disappeared to fight in the war.

A few months later all the English Royal Air Force troops arrived in our country and my family, being English, had open-house for many of them. Most evenings were spent around the piano, one RAF playing and eight or nine of us singing all the latest war songs, such as Jealousy, Long & the Short & the Tall and Run Rabbit Run. They were happy evenings with lots of laughter. So many of these boys never made it through the war and I like to think that they had a few happy hours in my mother's home.

My brother, Charles, was a short chap, very stocky and fair-haired who constantly smiled. He joined the army, but was recalled from active service for special duties. He went fishing one weekend and stepped onto a rusty nail. There were no antibiotics those days and his foot became steadily worse, until they even considered amputation, but my mother would not authorise this procedure. Eventually the foot was saved, but at the cost of Charlie being permanently semi-crippled.

I was fifteen when he got engaged to a local girl by the name of Joyce. She was very pretty and seemed to flirt with every RAF boy that looked my way. Unfortunately it was at this stage that I lost every ounce of self confidence I had ever possessed. Being proud, I refused to try and compete with her, so would simply walk away and lick my wounds in private. I became quite introvert and even to this day find it difficult to express my feelings with anyone. Whether it was deliberate on Joyce's part or not is no longer relevant, but it did change a part of my personality forever.

I was still thoroughly spoilt and when Joyce and Charlie finally married and moved away, I started flirting with the RAF boys and loved being the centre of attention, with everyone giving in to my demands and slowly became more selfish until my entire world revolved around 'me'.

I was about sixteen years old when my father decided to move to Queenstown. I couldn't find employment in my trade, but was offered a position with a bakery, packing bread and serving in the shop. I also assisted with bookwork from time to time and earned the princely sum of ten pounds a month. I loved the work and, strangely enough, I have baked more than most people in my lifetime.

Once a week they would hold a dance in the drill hall, which we had nicknamed the Mealie Patch, for the airmen and any South African soldiers who wished to attend. Sadly, our soldiers never patronised the place, so it was always RAF boys. Most of the girls would arrive in groups of three or four and would enjoy a lovely evening. Those that befriended a special boy would drop out of the group and he would escort her home. The girls wore full-length dresses and looked breathtakingly beautiful in a rainbow of colours, twirling gracefully on the dance floor. Slowly this fashion changed and short dresses became increasingly popular, with some girls even arriving in uniform, as many of them had joined the Forces. Eventually even dancing changed from waltzing and the quickstep, to jiving and rock. Older people who read this book will recall doing the Lambeth Walk, the Palais Glide and even the fun of the Elimination Dance, where they would call out various instructions, such as 'any lady wearing a watch, please leave the floor'. There was always a prize for the last couple left.

Every Wednesday afternoon the shops and offices would close early so that the women could take on some form of war work. I attended all the First Aid classes run by the Red Cross and we even had a mock air raid. We were all instructed to be on duty at seven in the evening. The air raid siren sounded and we rushed off individually to look for survivors. I found an elderly man lying on the road with his arm full of mock blood, a huge piece of putty stuck into this mess with a large piece of glass in it. Fortunately for me, the ambulance arrived before I was able to treat him. My second patient was a man who appeared unharmed, but literally just lay there with his eyes closed. I asked him what was wrong with him, but he never replied. Again I asked him and still got no response. The ambulance arrived and I shouted "Take this one to the morgue, he's dead."
An indignant voice from behind me said "Hey, I'm supposed to be unconscious. I'm glad you're not my nurse, you'll bury all your patients alive!"

After the air raid we all gathered together for tea and discussed our cases with the senior. I cannot stress how much I was teased about my dead hero.

Every afternoon after work, I used to take our little fox terrier, Micky, for a walk along a road that was not often used and I noticed a lot of buildings being erected, with a huge barbed wire fence around them. On one particular day, I saw a large group of soldiers on the premises and realised that they were Italian prisoners of war who had been captured in North Africa.

They noticed Micky and they would call to him as he walked on his leash, speaking words of endearment as they did so. I was extremely heart-sore for these men and realised just how cruel the war actually was. They were all so far away from their wives and families and were now trapped indefinitely behind a barbed wire fence, like wild animals. I always smiled and waved as Micky and I walked past and would let Micky off the leash so that they could play with him. Micky naturally loved all the attention as much as they enjoyed his visits. One soldier stood apart from the others and called to me to approach the fence. Checking to see whether anyone was looking, I walked up to the fence as he approached. In broken English, he said "For you" as he pushed his hand towards me. "You a nice lady." He handed me a tiny heart, carved in perspex, with a small metal ring in the top so it could be worn as a pendant on a chain. It must have taken him hours to carve and it had been polished to a brilliant, clear finish. I smiled and thanked him, called my dog and walked away with tears in my eyes. When my dad heard what had happened, he forbade me to take that road again and lectured me on prisoners of war. "They are your enemy and you must have absolutely nothing to do with them", he scolded.

However, in my heart I knew these men were not my enemies; they were flesh and blood, the same as me. The next day, I sneaked away with the dog and went back to the fence. I gestured to them that I would not be coming back along that road and blew them a kiss as I walked away, never to return.

I met a Flight Lieutenant by the name of Bruce. He was a dark-haired, very handsome man, but had been in a plane accident in North Africa. His legs had been terribly burned inside his sheepskin boots, resulting in dreadful scarring, so he never wore shorts. Sadly, he also had a drinking problem, but when our relationship started getting serious, he stopped drinking completely. I was very much in love with him, but knew that deep down he was a rebel. Even my mother kept saying, "A leopard doesn't change his spots and once Bruce knows that you belong to him, he will start drinking again." Needless to say, these remarks fell on deaf ears.

After a few months, we got engaged on my nineteenth birthday. A short while later Bruce had to return to England. I can still recall how afraid I was when he left and how sad I felt as the train pulled away from the station. Quite a few of my friends had married, but my mother felt that I was still too young. Weeks went by and my friends would visit with letters from their loved ones, but no letters arrived for me. Inwardly, I fretted terribly, but never let on to anyone how hollow words can be when friends look at you with pity, saying "Perhaps he isn't in a position to get a letter to you."

After about five months with no news from Bruce, I guessed I had heard the last of him. I had lost weight and had forgotten how to smile. Eventually my father suggested I take a month's leave to accompany them to Port Elizabeth. Peace had been declared, lots of our soldiers were home and many were waiting for demobilisation. When we arrived in Port Elizabeth, accommodation was impossible to find, there wasn't even a room to let and hotels were full. We visited the friends who had taken over our house when we left for Queenstown and mentioned our predicament as regards a place to stay. Aunt Winnie, as I called her, said her husband and son had returned and her home was full, but that a Mrs Slabbert two doors away still had two sons away and her husband was a prisoner of war in Italy. To her knowledge, Mrs Slabbert had one room to spare. My dad rushed off to see her and returned smiling, announcing that we could move in for a month.

Mrs Slabbert was a short, plump woman, with dark hair, blue eyes and a gentle smile. She got on very well with my folks, as she also came from England. A wonderful cook, she prepared a lot of her meals in the traditional South African manner, which we all enjoyed very much, as it had a far more concentrated flavour than the English way.

We moved in with Mrs Slabbert later that day. My parents took the spare room and I was to sleep in Mrs Slabbert's double bed with her. It was early evening when a young sailor walked in and Mrs Slabbert introduced him as her son, Cecil. He was tall, slim and extremely good looking, with little laughter lines starting to show around his eyes. He sported a lovely bronze tan from the long days on board ship and walked with the sailor's roll from months at sea. His hat was tilted on the back of his head, one dark curl licking his forehead, and he had the loveliest brown eyes. I took one look at this man and thought 'This is the one you have been looking for all these years, while you have been flirting with one man after another' and even Bruce faded from my mind, despite the fact that I still wore his ring. Mrs Slabbert introduced us and he looked at me and said "I know you. You're the girl who lived down the road a while back and drank Eau de Cologne!"
Well! I was terribly embarrassed and I know I blushed furiously, but started to laugh and retorted, "At least I have grown up a little since then."

I tried to flirt with him and get to know him better, but this was one man who never jumped at my request and actually was very cool most of the time. He gave me the impression that I bored him to tears. This was a hard lesson to learn, because by this time, I was head over heels in love with him and wasn't at all sure how to deal with the situation. I would put on my sweetest smile and he would look right through me, sometimes with a hint of contempt.

My father was a keen fisherman and before leaving one morning for the harbour, he asked me if I would take him sandwiches later in the day. Once he had left, I asked Cecil how to get to the harbour. Cecil was ready to return to his ship and offered to show me, but hardly spoke to me as we walked along together. He walked at such a fast pace, I had the feeling he wanted to bid me farewell as quickly as possible. Later in life I realised that he always walked fast and was never a very talkative man, but on that particular day I felt really unhappy as we parted. I so wanted him to like me, but I didn't have any idea how to attract his interest.

A couple of days passed without seeing very much of Cecil, he always seemed to be in a hurry, until one night it appeared as though he had decided to stay at home. I dressed in my very best dress, not that I had anywhere to go, but I intended to impress him. His mother had a large mirror in the lounge and I stood in front of it to put on some perfume. Cecil was sitting in a chair behind me and I knew he was watching.
"Going on a date?" he asked.
"Yes, of course." Attempting to be flippant, I hoped to spark some jealousy, but my hands were shaking uncontrollably as I attempted to put the cap back on the bottle.
"I suppose you think you smell nice?" Sarcasm was evident in his tone.
My flashing temper reared its ugly head as I shouted, "Yes, have some!" as I hurled the bottle at him. Naturally, the lid came off and the entire bottle of perfume emptied all over him. I flew out of the lounge and up the street before he could move and spent a few hours window shopping. Those days it was safe to walk around at night, one didn't fear anything at all. I often met up with the Black or Coloured fishermen, sometimes blind drunk, but their greeting always remained the same. "Good evening, ma'am" or "Isn't it a lovely evening?" These fishermen were a tough bunch, but still perfect gentlemen when addressing the opposite sex. By half past ten I realised I had to go home, but I was terrified. I thought I had spoiled all my chances of ever getting him to like me.

As I opened the garden gate, I saw Cecil sitting alone on the verandah. I knelt beside his chair and, with as much sincerity as I could muster, I said "Cecil, I am so sorry. I honestly thought the lid was on. I would never have done that to anyone, particularly a man."

17

He patted me on the head and said, "I hope you had a nice time. I had to cancel my date, as it took three baths to get that smell off me." When I realised that he was serious and really had been going on a date, my heart froze. I knew that whoever she was, she could be something special to this man whom I now loved very deeply.

"Would you like some tea?" I asked in a tiny voice.

"No thanks."

"Well, I think I'll go to bed. Goodnight."

"Goodnight." His voice was polite, but curt and I hardly slept a wink that entire night, cursing myself for having allowed my temper to get the better of me.

Strangely enough, it seemed after that night that we had arrived at some sort of truce. Although we didn't talk often, he didn't seem quite so cold after my apology and this small improvement in our relationship gladdened my heart. My pretence of going on dates now a thing of the past, I stayed in every night and it was Cecil who went out most nights. One evening he walked in unexpectedly and announced, "I'm going to visit my cousin in Walmer, would you like to walk with me?"

I got the feeling that he felt sorry for me, but pushed my pride as far back as I could and accepted. We walked about eight blocks, which took half an hour and talked about trivial things, avoiding personal issues. When we arrived, Cecil introduced me to Alice and Bill and the two men disappeared to work on an engine in the garage.

Alice was a fair-haired mother of two. She had the most beautiful smile and was one of the kindest people I have ever met. She later had twins, but we had already moved away and I never saw them. Bill, Cecil's cousin, was a small man with lovely brown eyes and he and Cecil were great fishing buddies. Bill loved toast and tea and, no matter what his mood, if you offered him toast, a smile would appear on his face. Alice and I got on well and she told me a little about Cecil.

"I love him to bits," she said, "He's the finest man I know."

"I do too, Alice, but he hardly knows that I exist. In fact, I am shocked that he actually asked me to accompany him tonight."

We chatted for about two hours, when the men returned to wash their greasy hands. Alice made tea and we left at about ten thirty. Those days there were only street lights on the corners of each block. Half way home, beneath one of these street lights, just opposite a family sitting on their verandah, Cecil suddenly grabbed me and kissed me thoroughly. Taken aback and shaken beyond all belief, I felt him wrap his arm around me and we walked in silence. Not once was I aware of touching the ground, I seemed to be floating and the joy I felt was overwhelming. 'He likes me' I thought. I didn't dare think that he may love me at that stage.

Our first date was on the harbour and as the wartime security was still on, Cecil bribed the guard at the gate to allow me through. He took me aboard the ship that he had spent a little while on, as most of the time he had been on a minesweeper. I was amazed at how small the bunks and hammocks were and the galley, although minute, was well organised. Getting onto the boat was bad enough, as you had to go down a ladder off the quay and then wait for the boat to come close enough in order to jump on board. Cecil leaped like a monkey, and kept shouting 'jump' but hesitation prevailed. I eventually got on board and met some of his shipmates, enjoying the virtual tour tremendously. Finally it was time to leave and this proved even more daunting. I had to wait for the ship to move closer to the quay, jump at that moment and grab hold of the ladder. Quite convinced that I would land in the water and drown, I jumped successfully, but only started breathing again when I was on the quay. Walking home that evening there was piece of tin on the quayside with the words 'Dreadnaught Wire' on it. I picked it up as a souvenir and today, sixty years later, it lies, still treasured, in my jewellery box.

Our month was soon up and it was time to return to Queenstown. Cecil and I were chatting and I said, "Tomorrow is goodbye."
"You can't leave. What about us?"
My heart skipped a beat. I realised I did not want to return to Queenstown and answered, "I will find work down here and somehow I will find accommodation". Quite a brave statement from someone who knew the accommodation situation, but I was

19

determined to remain with him, no matter what, as now I knew that he was serious about me.

There were temper tantrums and intense drama from my parents, until eventually my mother approached Aunt Winnie, who arranged to put our caravan, which had to be brought from Queenstown, in her yard. My mother announced that she was staying on as well to look after me, but I could see that she wasn't happy about my decision and kept bringing up Bruce's name, reminding me that I was still engaged. I eventually decided to send Bruce's ring to his parents' address with a letter enclosed to tell them that Bruce had not contacted me and as far as I was concerned, I was no longer engaged. I received a letter back advising me that he had got married a few months previously and that he had informed his parents that he had already broken off our engagement.

Cecil's demob came around and the government gave him thirty pounds and a bicycle. He spent his money on two tailor-made suits, a couple of shirts, a sports jacket and shoes. When Cecil was given his bicycle, I went out and bought one for myself. Every Sunday we would cycle along the coastal road, now called Marine Drive. The scenery around the Marine Drive was really pretty. On the one side of the road one saw masses of trees, mainly Port Jackson Willows, but on the opposite side the scenery changed with the weather. There was a steep bank which ended on the beach and if it was a sunny day, the sea would be calm and an exquisite green in colour. However, if the wind blew, or it was overcast and cold, the sea would be pounding onto the beach in huge, angry grey waves, white foam splashing into the cool air. Irrespective of the weather, we would set out every weekend on our bicycles and always met many other couples doing the same. No one could afford motor cars, so you either walked or owned a bicycle, but the atmosphere was wonderful as you passed others and greeted them pleasantly.

At some point on our trip we would stop and make a small fire. With us we carried an empty tin in which to boil water. We would then make ourselves a cup of tea before continuing on our journey. On this particular day I was wearing a new dress that my mom had bought for me, instead of the usual shorts. It was made of a revolutionary new fabric called 'crepe'. The dress was black with blue, red, yellow and green dots and it looked absolutely beautiful on. During our trip it started raining quite heavily and we were drenched. I can still see Cecil sitting on the rocks, the waves crashing behind him, trying to make a fire and boil water in a tin that now had a hole in from being used so much. To my horror, I looked down and realised that my crepe dress had shrunk and made the mini skirts of today appear quite modest. The back was dryer than the front and had not shrunk quite as much, but the front was the length of a shirt. Thank goodness I wore a decent petticoat, but the dress was ruined. To this day I have never trusted any garment that is made from crepe.

I managed to find work at a printing firm and each day Cecil and I would walk together as far as Fry's Furnishers where Cecil was employed, and I would then catch a bus to work. One memory of that time that comes to mind was the day he arrived at my work early in the morning and, with a serious expression, said, "Your mom asked me to fetch you. She's not feeling well." I took the rest of the day off and as we left the premises, Cecil smiled and said, "Your mom's fine. I hurt my hand at work this morning and they've given me the day off. Where shall we go?"
We spent a lovely day together, sitting in Happy Valley, a glorified park near the ocean, holding hands and gazing into each other's eyes. However, even on a week day, there were dozens of people about, soldiers waiting for demob and older people sitting enjoying the sunshine.

Cecil's two younger brothers were aged ten and thirteen and I spent many early evenings playing Kick the Tin with them, believe it or not, barefoot in the street. Slowly I was losing some of my high and mighty ways and becoming more down to earth, but I was still spoilt and liked getting my own way.

Our era was so very different compared with today's way of life. We were raised completely brainwashed into considering what the neighbours would say, or that good girls never go beyond a certain point in petting. There was no privacy to have a little time together alone. You lived at home and there was just no way that your parents would allow anyone of the opposite sex into your bedroom, so you went out. There was no such thing as television and very little money to go anywhere special. Any couple who were considering marriage saved all their spare cash to buy furnishings for their home, so no matter where you went, you had company. If you went onto the harbour, there were fishermen trying to catch tomorrow's breakfast. If you took a walk along the beach, dozens of other couples had the same idea.

As a result, our courting was mainly sharing a packet of chips (served in newspaper) and window shopping. It was quite safe to walk around with no fear of being attacked. On the few occasions that we found ourselves alone and began kissing and cuddling, our own brainwashing would take over and Cecil would jump up and say, "Come on, let's get out of here."
Yes, I will admit it was frustrating, but it taught us both control and respect for each other. It was because of these circumstances that on the day of our wedding, I could look into Cecil's eyes with complete honesty and love and for fifty four years, he was my only lover.

I see the youngsters of today, going in and out of relationships, sleeping around quite happily. Whether they are right or we were, doesn't matter, I only know our way was difficult, but left me with a sense of accomplishment and if I had that time over, I wouldn't have wanted it any other way.

CHAPTER TWO

I'll always be at your side…..

In March Cecil proposed, but I insisted on an engagement first and immediately said I should go and look at rings. Cecil quietly took hold of my chin, lifted my face to look at him and said, "You have two choices. One, we buy an engagement ring and wait for two years while I pay it off, or two, we get married now with practically nothing except our love for each other."
I chose to go without an engagement ring, as I had no intention of giving this man two years to think about it. Cecil then approached my family to ask whether we could get married on my twentieth birthday in May. I had met him in the November, so we had only known each other for five months. However love knows no time and I felt that I had known this man for an eternity. A direct "No" from my mother brought a flood of tears from me.

My father was visiting from Queenstown at the time and she asked him to persuade me to wait. I think, secretly, that she was afraid of losing me if I married Cecil. Finally, my father consented on the condition that we first find accommodation. His reasoning was fair, as more and more soldiers were coming home, including the POW's from Italy and accommodation was almost unobtainable anywhere in PE. My father insisted that the accommodation be decent and up to standard, or no wedding would take place. Cecil grabbed my arm, uttering, "Let's go". I asked him where we were going.
"To Bill and Alice. They have two rooms in their back yard with a private entrance"
Needless to say, Bill and Alice were delighted to help, but this was only the first hurdle overcome. Having my parents' permission at last, I started collecting items for our home, even to tins of food and rice.

23

Rice was another item in short supply and my mother began collecting some for me, but I was worried that weevils would get into it. Aunt Winnie told me to go to the chemist and buy Copper Sulphate to preserve the rice. I duly popped in to the chemist and asked the gentleman behind the counter for Copper Sulphate. He looked at me for a minute, frowning through his dark-rimmed spectacles and then asked, "What exactly do you want it for?"

"I'm getting married soon and want to put it into my rice to preserve it."

He burst into laughter and replied, "No, my dear, I don't advise you to use that in your rice, particularly if you're getting married."

I was teased for years about this, after Cecil had explained that it is used mainly to prevent sexual urges.

One of my first tasks was to go in search of a wedding dress. The dress I fell in love with was in Garlicks, an upmarket store in the city centre and it was frightfully expensive. It was even beyond my parents' means and we had to look for an alternative. Every dress I tried on was either too big or too outlandish for my mother's taste. Several of them were really nice and I liked them, but the neckline was either too low or it didn't have the traditional long sleeve with the point over the hand. Eventually we found a tiny shop advertising wedding dresses. The woman looked at me and said "I don't think I have anything so small, but I do have a dress here that has been cancelled, so if it too large, we can alter it for you. I also have a little sailor outfit to fit a six year old boy and a dress for a flower girl of the same age in pale blue."

I looked at the dress and my heart still remained with the one in Garlicks. I had loved the Crinoline skirt and yards and yards of lace, but these setbacks couldn't make me throw a tantrum. I loved Cecil far too much for that. Quietly, I picked up the dress and headed for the fitting room. The dress had about thirty tiny mirrors around the neck and top of the bodice. It was pretty, not my first choice, but it fitted and we got all three outfits for seven pounds ten shillings. The veil had orange blossoms around the head and we ordered a deep-blue bridesmaids dress for Sancia, Aunt Winnie's daughter. She was also a redhead and just as full of fun as her mother, so I had a bridesmaid, flower-girl and page-boy.

We placed an announcement in the newspaper advising that the wedding would take place at three in the afternoon and a few days later two men appeared at our door. They were from some department that controlled meal and flour and were there to advise us that nothing containing meal or flour could be served in the afternoon. No cakes, breads or biscuits were allowed. So, another announcement was placed in the paper, advising that the wedding would be at eleven. Four days before the wedding they were back to tell us that a new law had been passed and nothing containing meal or flour could be served in any form, at any time of the day, if there were more than ten people. We had invited thirty guests, but my mother and Cecil's mother were wonderful. They decided to serve savouries such as crisps, meat slices, sausages and lots of puddings and jellies.

The night before the wedding, Cecil and I were out walking and we had a terrible argument. My parting words to him were "Don't be too sure I'll be at the church tomorrow" and he retorted, "What makes you think I'm going to be there?"
I cried all night long and as we were following the tradition of the bride not seeing the groom before the wedding, I couldn't contact him to apologise and there was no word from him the next day. I had hoped for a message via one of his younger brothers, but nothing came.

I was all dressed up in my finery when there was a knock at the door and one of the prettiest women I had ever seen stepped in. "May I come in? I am to be your sister-in-law, Phyllis from Mossel Bay, where you are coming for your honeymoon."
Phyllis was married to Cecil's eldest brother, Bill, and this couple remained favourites of mine all my life. Bill was a small man, but had the same brown eyes as Cecil. Phyllis had long, wavy hair and the smile of an angel. Bill had got a piece of steel in his eye and had come to Port Elizabeth for an operation to remove it. They gave us the keys to their home in Mossel Bay, telling us to go ahead and they would join us when Bill was discharged from hospital.

Aunt Winnie insisted on dressing me and was really angry when she had finished and I told her I needed the toilet. My nerves were shattered and I was still frantically worried about whether Cecil would turn up. When I got into the car I was amazed to see the people from every house in the neighbourhood standing in the street to cheer me and wish me well. They were all plain, middle class people with hearts of gold and they left me with some very precious memories. In those days there was no apartheid, so every race, from white to black, Indian and Chinese, lived in harmony in our street.

On the way to the church, my father leaned over and said, "It's still not too late to change your mind. Don't you want to think it over?" Hell, it had taken me this long to charm my way into Cecil's heart and here was my father trying to talk me out of it! We arrived at the church and my dad helped me out of the car. They started the wedding march and as I entered the church and walked down the aisle, I couldn't tell you today if there were dozens of people, or none at all. My eyes were on the man I loved and as I looked at him I saw that love reflected in his own dark eyes. He was dressed in full sailor uniform. Where the ordinary sailor wore a navy blue ribbon on the front of his top, on their wedding day they wore a white one. The uniform made him appear so proud and he seemed to stand taller than usual as I walked towards him. There was a tenderness there that I very seldom saw in the years to come, but whenever it showed itself, I loved him even more. Standing next to him was his Best Man, also in full uniform.

I stood beside Cecil in front of the altar and a woman began to sing 'I'll walk beside you'. It sounded so beautiful, I have no idea who she was, but her voice was sweet and crystal clear. At last the minister pronounced us man and wife and I felt utterly at peace. I had married the man that I had loved since I set eyes on him and my heart swelled with joy. Our life together was about to begin.

After the service we had photographs taken and then moved on to the reception. This was held at Aunt Winnie's home and someone had put our wedding presents on display in her dining room.

Mentioning some of them will bring a smile. Bearing in mind that the war was just over, there was very little in the shops. Plastic was, at that stage, unheard of. Someone had bought four cups and saucers in the new heat-resistant glass, which promptly exploded with the first cup of tea made in them. Another tea set was made of Bakelite, but when you poured boiling water into these, the smell of the hot Bakelite was awful enough to put you off tea forever. Right in front of all the other gifts was a small side plate and in the centre of the plate was a black-lettered price sticker, marked 1/8 ½. It was from Cecil's younger brother, George. Next to it were two suckers and a little card from Albert, his youngest brother. I kept these gifts for many years and never rubbed the price off the plate but, when moving one day, they were unfortunately in a box of articles that went missing. One of the highlights of my day was to see Uncle Martin at the wedding and he kindly acted as barman.

He was not actually my real uncle, but a friend of my family from Enjimyana days and he had become very precious to me, as he always found time to play with a lonely little girl and I learned to love him dearly. Although I never saw him again after the wedding, I was later to meet his son, who also became a dear friend when we were living in Rhodesia.

In the middle of the table stood our three-tier wedding cake and two small side cakes with ships on. The two mothers had truly outdone themselves, the table looked lovely and Cecil and I were thrilled. The wedding cake had been ordered before we had been advised of the new law. Sitting among our guests were the two food controllers and due to the fact that no food containing flour could be consumed, Cecil and I begged them to allow us to follow tradition by just pushing the knife into the cake. They sat through the entire reception and actually fitted in quite well, enjoying the festivities as much as the invited guests.

By three that afternoon all the men were quite inebriated, including the two controllers. We managed to drag the reception out until five and then I quietly left to change into my going-away outfit. I had a tailor-made green suit with a tiny Russian fur hat in brown, with gloves, shoes and handbag to match. I draped my brown fur coat over my arm as I inspected my appearance in the mirror and smiled with satisfaction. Cecil asked my father to take us to the Cenotaph to lay my bouquet there in memory of the boys who never came home from the war. Guests started to leave and at six-thirty we thankfully left for the Cenotaph. On arrival, we stood quietly for a few minutes to pay our respects and then I lay the bouquet of lilies and roses down. It was a poignant moment, remembering all those young men who were cruelly snatched away from their families in the prime of their lives. We left for the station to catch the train, which was leaving for Mossel Bay at seven-thirty. En route we were stopped by a traffic officer for speeding and I am so grateful that there were no breathalysers those days, or my dad would have been arrested and jailed for life! On being told about the wedding, the police officer smiled, wished us lots of happiness and turned to my dad and said "Take it easy with your speed if you want to get these two safely to the train".

Quite a few of our guests were waiting at the station and the noise was deafening from the happy group of inebriated men, as they wrote rude remarks on the outside of our compartment with chalk. My mother had been very quiet and, as I looked at her, she appeared so tiny and lost. She stood alone under one of the station lights, crying softly. Naturally by the time the train pulled out of the station, the stress of the wedding and seeing my mom crying brought a sudden gush of tears from me. Cecil sat and watched me for a few minutes, then looked at his watch. A little later he looked at his watch again and said "Listen, we will be arriving at Swartkops station in ten minutes. If you are still crying then, we will get off the train and I will take you home to your mother!" Needless to say, my tears dried up very quickly, particularly when he said "I will hold your legs and I want you to lean out of the window as far as possible and wipe all the chalk remarks off the side of the carriage." There was certainly no romance or dignity in leaning dangerously out of the train with Cecil hanging onto my legs. Little did I know at the time, but this was one of many lessons in trust, and that it would be of vital importance in our lives in the bush.

Some time later the train inspector popped his head through the door to tell us that we were in the wrong compartment and helped us move to another. Once we had settled in, we went into the dining car for dinner. The dining cars in those days were as pretty as a picture, with white tablecloths and serviettes, sparkling silver and waiters donned in white. On each newly laid table were vases of lovely fresh flowers.

Finally, it was time for bed and, feeling extremely awkward, I began to change, while Cecil lay there laughing at my discomfort. Once I had slipped between the covers beside him, which was no easy feat on a train bunk, my fears slipped away as he took me in his strong arms and held me close. He was a gentle, compassionate lover and made me feel that I was his entire universe as we discovered each other long into the cool night.

By eight the next morning Cecil looked out of the door for a steward and one just happened to be walking towards our compartment. Those days one got coffee in the mornings, served on a little silver tray, together with the cutest glass jug and sugar basin.
"Good morning, sir, coffee has already been served, but we don't bother newly-weds on the train."
Cecil retorted "I only got married; I didn't have my throat cut!" This brought a peal of laughter from the understanding steward, who rushed off to get our coffee. As we sat sipping the welcome, hot coffee we enjoyed the magnificent scenery of the Garden Route. Perhaps my incredible happiness had something to do with it, but it seemed that every flower had put on a show just for me that morning and I was captivated by the beauty of nature yet once again.

I kept thinking to myself how perfect everything was and that life was going to be one happy dream. I had been getting my own way most of the time until now and thought it would go on forever. That spoilt, selfish streak was there and the most important person in my life was still me at that stage.

On arriving in Mossel Bay, we went straight to Bill's house and Cecil's first words were "I'm starving."

There were tins of meat in the cupboard and plenty of fresh vegetables in the rack. There I stood. I didn't even know how to boil an egg, let alone cook an entire meal. Cecil looked at me for a moment and then sweetly said, "I did quite a bit of cooking in the Navy, so I'll cook and you unpack". I could have kissed him as the relief welled up inside me and I rushed off to unpack our suitcases. As I opened mine and took out four ounces of wool and a pair of knitting needles, Cecil entered the room and asked, "What's that?"
"Baby wool." I replied innocently.
He appeared completely dumbstruck and then asked "What for?"
Smiling at him knowingly, I asked, "Well, we do want a baby, don't we?"
Laughing as he shook his head, he said "Very much so, but do you mind if we have a honeymoon first?"

Our honeymoon was one lovely experience after another as we found each other and started to learn each other's ways, except for one small drawback. The toilet at Bill's house was situated at the very far end of Bill's yard. I was used to outside toilets, as most houses had them those days, but they were usually built fairly close to the house and yards were normally quite small. The toilet in Bill's yard, however, was quite a walk from the house, because this property was what we now refer to as a 'double-plot' and it was at the far end of the property. I would wake Cecil in the middle of the night and tell him "I need to go, please walk with me".

For the first two nights he complied without any complaint, but on the third night he got the mutters. Bill and Phyllis arrived home, the operation having been a complete success and Bill was back to his old self. Cecil very casually asked Phyllis for a bucket, explaining that Joan needed it at night. Phyllis dragged one out from somewhere, but I was cringing with embarrassment. Don't forget, I had only met these people once on my wedding day and I was not used to this type of thing at all, having been treated as an absolute lady all my life. I had always been taught that some subjects were taboo and speaking about toilets was an embarrassing subject to say the least.

That night I was too afraid to go back to sleep, as I desperately needed to go, but refused to use the bucket and certainly wasn't going to walk outside alone. The next night Cecil told me to use the bucket, which got him a very obstinate refusal from my end of the bed. Without another word, Cecil got up and used the bucket himself, making as much noise as he possibly could, then on the top of his voice, he said, "Joan, not so much noise, you'll wake Bill and Phyllis".

Chagrined, and as red as a stoplight, I heard hysterical giggles from Bill and Phyllis' bedroom. I realised much later on that Cecil was humanising me, bringing me down to size and teaching me a little humility, but for this spoilt little lady it was one tough lesson to learn.

I noticed when we went into town to do some shopping that Cecil would often cross the road, instead of going up one side and down the other. I remarked on this and he sheepishly acknowledged that he was dodging various girls he had met during his several dockings in Mossel Bay. I might add that he must have had a good time during these dockings, because we crossed the road several times on each shopping spree!

One incident on our honeymoon that has always stuck in my mind was a visit from one of Bill's friends. His fiancée was with him and she had obviously met Cecil on his visits to the area. She was the complete opposite of me, being very tall, slim, a pretty face and exquisite long hair, whereas I was short and easily lost in a crowd. It was not long before she had him cornered, talking of all things, rugby. Feeling left out, I made some remark about rugby and she turned to look at me, a sickly sweet smile across her face, as she replied, "My dear, you obviously don't follow rugby, as you don't know what you're talking about."

Low esteem engulfing me instantly, I sat in silence and then followed Phyllis to the kitchen to make tea. Phyl, as I called her, tried not to laugh at my woebegone face and attempted to console me. I didn't realise then just how many women would try to coax my handsome, rugged man away from me in our lifetime together, as even in our old age, I saw female eyes sparkle when he entered a room, then look at me, enviously implying how lucky I was.

We had been back off honeymoon for a couple of weeks when Bill and Alice suggested we all go to Krom River and do some fishing for the weekend. We took two tents and left after work on the Friday night. By the time we had erected the tents and eaten the food we had prepared before leaving home, it was already dark. Cecil and Bill had hired a boat and, as they preferred night fishing, they bade us goodnight and disappeared onto the river. Alice and I eventually decided to go to bed. It was the first time I had ever slept on the ground with just a couple of blankets and oh, how I missed my bed. Every tiny stone under me felt as large as a fowl's egg and I was most uncomfortable. To make matters worse, it began to get really cold and I lay in a little ball all night, shivering, until finally dawn broke. What a joy to feel the warmth of the sun! I was just starting to relax and doze off, when a slab of ice, with the most dreadful smell of fish around it, crept under the blankets beside me. "Bill and I are frozen, it was so cold on the river, but at least we have some fish for breakfast. He cuddled up against me and fell asleep as I lay there shivering again, wondering where the fun was in fishing. Nevertheless, there was always a gleam of excitement in the men's' eyes when they said 'let's go fishing!' I personally could think of many better things to do, but it usually ended up with the men getting their own way.

The next six months were the worst of our entire lives. When I couldn't have my own way, I would throw a tantrum and if Cecil couldn't have his way, he would sulk. The first argument came about a couple of days after we got home. We had given each other a Cyma Sports watch as wedding gifts and during this argument, I took off my watch and threw it at the wall, at which point it shattered. Staring at the shattered watch in disbelief, Cecil took off his watch and acted accordingly, resulting in two useless watches lying on the floor.

Cecil bought me a Slim Whitman record called 'Don't Fence Me In', because I had told him that I liked it so much and that night we had another argument. I went over to our little record player and played my song, feeling very sorry for myself, but enjoying the music anyway. Cecil promptly grabbed the record and broke it, walking angrily from the room. Later, once we had resolved our differences, I asked him why he had broken my record and he replied, "I thought you were being sarcastic, telling me not to fence you in!"

I was very fond of slamming doors during arguments, making sure I was on the opposite side to Cecil when I did so. I once slammed a door that had a glass panel and Cecil, attempting to stop it, put his hand out. To my horror, his hand went through the glass and was very badly lacerated. It goes without saying that this was the end of the argument, as I frantically bandaged his hand and forgot all about what I had been so angry about. Most of the arguments were stupid and childish; we were both so young.

Being a qualified French Polisher, Cecil was busy polishing a friend's radio, when he knocked a bottle of Spirit Green onto my floral Lino square, which was very much like today's Novilon flooring. I was furious and shouted, "Now you've gone and ruined my Lino".

Cecil retorted "Oh, don't worry, I'll fix it now." To my utter disbelief, he wiped Spirit Green over the entire floor to blend it in with the spill and my lovely red roses turned green.

One of the last childish rows that we ever had began late one night, over something really silly. In those days our nightgowns were not made from the flimsy fabrics of today, but looked rather like evening dresses. I took my wedding ring off my finger and threw it out of the window into the garden, shouting angrily "I will not stay married to you, I'm going home to my mother". My father had been transferred back to Port Elizabeth and also lived in the caravan in Aunt Winnie's yard, while he sought alternative accommodation. Beside myself with emotion, I stormed out of the flat in my nightie, heading up the dark street. Walking barefoot, it was about eight blocks to reach my parents' caravan, but none of these factors even entered my angry mind. Having walked a full block, I heard footsteps behind me and started walking a little faster, my heart beating wildly. Suddenly the realisation of where I was and what I was dressed in, hit me and I was truly afraid of who was following me. No matter how fast I walked, the footsteps kept gaining on me, but I was too afraid to turn around and look, so I began to run. No sooner had I done so, an arm closed around my waist and I was lifted effortlessly into the air, my head dangling on one end and my feet on the other. I realised that it was Cecil and tried to fight him, but to no avail. He carried me in this fashion back to our flat, dropped me on the bed and walked out, locking the door behind him. As my anger subsided and rational thought returned, I was ashamed. I realised, beyond all doubt, that my insistence on getting my own way was taking away Cecil's masculinity. All he wanted from me was my respect and acceptance that he was the man of the house. This realisation proved correct, as I slowly began to discover in the wilds, that my husband was all man. He feared nothing or anyone and was admired all his life, by men and women alike.

Putting my pride aside, I began to try being more reasonable and taught myself to use the words 'this is my opinion, but I will abide by your decision'. Slowly, but surely, the arguments became less and, although they never came to a complete end, (my will sometimes being unable to remain silent); they were never as violent as in the early days.

After eight months of marriage, Cecil began to look thin, had little energy and after some coaxing, I went with him to a doctor. Tests for Tuberculosis were negative, but after a number of alternative tests, the doctor came up with a diagnosis I had never heard before. He said that Cecil, being subjected to the wet and cold for a prolonged period in the Navy, had developed a Rheumatic Globule between his heart and his ribcage. He told us that if we did not leave the coast, Cecil would eventually die. By this time Cecil's father had returned home from being a Prisoner of War in Italy and had moved his family to Bloemfontein, where he bought a smallholding with a four-bedroom house, eight miles out of the city. We immediately wrote to his father, asking if we could stay with them for a while and he agreed.

We boarded the train with nothing but our clothes and Cecil's bicycle, (I had sold mine), no spare money at all, and arrived in

Bloemfontein the following morning. Cecil's dad met us at the station. He was quite a tall man, slim in build, in fact a fine looking man, but kept very much to himself, although he had a tremendous sense of humour, playing many tricks on the family. He took us through to his smallholding and all he could talk about was his garden. The old man loved gardening and was truly in his element on the plot, which consisted of approximately four morgan of land. It never occurred to him that the house had no inner doors, not even the bathroom. All he could see at that stage was the land, the house being of no importance at all. He would come home from work; have his coffee, then disappear into his garden, preparing the soil for planting, staying out sometimes until midnight. He was no company for mom and I secretly knew that she was happy to have Cecil and me staying there.

When we arrived, the first thing I did was to hang a curtain over our door to give us a little privacy. George and Albert were still living at home, so the house was relatively full. The two young boys, who were responsible for milking the cow and other chores after school, unknowingly became my allies while we stayed there. George had grown tall and skinny, remaining that way all his life. Albert was of medium height, with dark hair like Cecil. We would play games together and even had competitions to see who could eat the most watermelon. Often we would have watermelon fights like naughty children and, once we were sticky from head to toe, we would simply jump into the reservoir and wash off. Dad had a little Mini, but it was only used on Sundays, except for every fortnight when we went to market. The boys and I would wash the car and, after lunch, we would go for our Sunday drive, then the car was put away until the following Sunday. Dad and Cecil cycled to work each day, even in the middle of a Bloemfontein winter, travelling eight miles each way. Mom and I walked the eight miles to town to apply for a ration card for sugar, because although the war was over, sugar was still in short supply. It took us all day, as Mom tired very easily, but we managed. On market days, we would leave at five in the morning in order to beat the crowds, so the prices were cheaper, with less people bidding. We often saw an old lady picking up scrap cabbage leaves that had fallen, or a carrot that had broken from the bunch and we felt terribly sorry for her. Mom always gave her a bunch of carrots, or a little of whatever we had purchased that day, until we read in the paper that she had died, with two million pounds in the bank.

We had only been on the smallholding a few weeks when Dad received a phone call from Cecil's brother, Bill. He had been transferred to Bloemfontein and they needed a place to stay. Their children were aged five, four and three. We had loved these children while we honeymooned in Mossel Bay, Cecil and I playing with them for hours on end. When they arrived, we truly had a full house and Phyllis and I became very close. One day the radio played a piece of classical music and mom stopped sweeping the floor, leaned on her broom and began to sing. Never before had I heard such an exquisite, perfect voice. I waited for her to finish, then asked her where she had learned to sing like that and she sat down and told me the story about her and dad.

It seems that in World War One, Dad was one of the South Africans that had signed up and was one of the men who survived Delville Wood. Dad and his cousin, who was a much smaller man, were stretcher bearers in the same regiment. Dad was standing on a mound when a sniper's bullet passed between his legs and hit his cousin in the stomach. As he lay there dying, he asked Dad to go to England before returning home. He had fallen in love with a girl who sang in Sadler's Wells while on leave there and had asked her to wait for him, to which she had agreed. As soon as the opportunity arose, Dad headed for London and found Jessie Morris at Sadler's Wells. He gently broke the news to her of his cousin's death and, during the time that he was there, they became friends. After a while they realised that they had fallen in love, soon got married and she followed him to South Africa. I believe that her sister, Rose Morris, sang in Sadler's Wells for many years after Jessie left.

It was while living on the plot that I saw my first hail storm, with chunks of ice the size of bantam eggs falling relentlessly on the ground. It killed at least half of the chickens, flattened the garden, knocked all the peaches from the trees and broke quite a few windows. It was frightening, to say the least, but also extremely fascinating to watch. The noise on the roof was deafening, leaving me in absolute awe. When Cecil came home, I excitedly began to tell him of the storm and he started to laugh. He told me that when he and his brothers had lived in Bloemfontein, when they were very young, they would walk to school five miles away and were often caught in similar storms. They would huddle together and hold their satchels above their heads until it was over. Yet, despite the adversities, Cecil and one of his brothers were awarded medals from Brebner School for full attendance from grade one to grade eight, having not missed one day during all those years.

Phyllis announced that she was, once again, pregnant and I was so envious. As the months passed we were still trying and hoping for a miracle, but in the meantime I made baby clothes for Phyllis. Around this time I bought myself another bicycle and Cecil and I cycled into town one day. We passed a shop and I smelled chips cooking and begged Cecil to buy me some. The shop owner apologised, but said that they were actually cooking their own supper and they were not for sale. When we got home, I asked Mom to make chips for supper, but she had just boiled the last of the potatoes for mash.

I must mention that Dad's garden was an Eden, with peach trees, and all kinds of vegetables, including potatoes. However, no-one would dare pick a peach without his permission and if you did, somehow he knew and boy, would there be trouble. Mom and Dad left for market the next morning and Bill and Cecil were down in the work shed. I told Phyllis I was really longing for a few chips and that I knew there were potatoes in Dad's garden. I suddenly had a brainwave, put on Dad's gumboots and sneaked into the vegetable garden to pick a few potatoes. Very cleverly, or so I thought, I pinched the potatoes from the bottoms of a few plants and then carefully replanted them. With no visible evidence and only Dad's boot prints, I thought I was well and truly in the clear. Returning to the kitchen, I washed the potatoes and made a few chips, which I savoured tremendously.

A few days later, Dad stormed into the house, as mad as a snake. "I noticed that a few of my plants were dying and when I pulled them up, not a potato in sight. These damned moles are a curse."

Sitting there, hoping that a look of sheer innocence would mask my guilt, I watched Phyllis suffer a sudden coughing attack as she ran from the room. It was only a few days later that I discovered that I, too, was pregnant, hence the sudden cravings.

A few weeks later, Bill and Phyllis took a railway house at a place called Kloof End, which was closer to Bill's work and, as he worked for the railways, he got it at a good rental. They moved out shortly afterwards. A letter arrived from my mom to say that my dad had resigned and was going back to Rhodesia. They spent a couple of days with us before they left. I was quite content as the months passed, having bought a little cane crib, I spent my days covering it with voile and making baby clothes, when another letter arrived from my father. He had bought a business called Ndola Saw Mills and asked Cecil to consider moving to Northern Rhodesia to manage it for him. My dad had taken a job with African Housing, so did not have time to supervise at the mill. Cecil asked me how I felt about moving, but I insisted that the decision lay entirely with him. This was one decision that I was glad not to make.

After a few days, Cecil announced that he had made a decision. "I don't like Bloemfontein, I'm in a dead-end job, I miss my fishing and I'm tired of living with family because my salary isn't big enough to get a place of our own. We are going to Ndola to make a better life for ourselves"
He took me in his arms and reassuringly said, "We'll be alright."
I smiled up at him and said, "I know."
It was at this time that Cecil was so gentle and understanding. Our love just grew and grew and when he offered to go on ahead to Northern Rhodesia, saying that I could follow after the baby's birth, I said, "Where you are, my sweetheart, that's where I'll be. I will always be at your side."
The respect and love that shone in his eyes that day were worth any sacrifice I had to make in the future and believe me, there were many. The next few days were spent applying for passports, having yellow fever injections and being vaccinated against smallpox. By this time I was six months pregnant and in good health. Cecil's father was very

upset and tried hard to change our minds, but the decision was made and our train tickets were booked.

CHAPTER THREE

Hello, Northern Rhodesia….

I sold my bicycle and once again, we packed our clothes and placed Cecil's bicycle in the guard's van. On leaving Bloemfontein, the first couple of stations were large and quite close together, but as we travelled further north, they became quite small and many miles apart. The mountains were rugged and the bush so wild. It was a couple of months before rainy season and although the scenery was magnificent, everywhere was dry and dusty and the heat oppressive. One felt listless all day long. Despite the discomfort of the heat, the beauty of the surroundings truly made one gasp at times. The sense of anticipation, waiting to see which animal may be coming into view as the train snaked on its course, kept the journey interesting from sunrise to sunset. The familiar expression 'Rhodesia is God's own country' is so very true. The diversity of the countryside, from flat plains, to bushveld, to lush forests of majestic trees, kept one captivated every mile of the trip.

One could only gasp in pleasure as a herd of buffalo stood close to the tracks with the bulls on the flanks, the cows and calves grazing between them. They were huge in size, their curved horns held so proudly on their foreheads as they gazed fearlessly at us. They made me realise just how dangerous they were. A little further on, one would view a herd of wildebeest grazing in the distance. They were smaller than buffalo and lacked the sturdiness and almighty power, but were fascinating all the same. Elephant would be walking along with babies at their mothers' sides and one could only smile as the babies' trunks flapped around, having no control over them yet. Various antelope, from the large ones such as kudu, sable and eland, down to the duiker and little dik-dik all appeared at various locations during our trip. The dik-dik's ears were huge and had the most exquisite markings inside. Now and then my eyes would be drawn to a baobab tree and I would marvel at the size of the trunk, the sparse branches reaching skywards and resembling roots, making the tree appear inverted.

As we travelled further into the Rhodesias, one could see hundreds of anthills, some standing as tall as a grown man. The base of the anthill would be the size of a tree trunk and it slowly tapered off to a blunt point. They reminded me of sentinels amongst the grass and bushes. Once or twice I attempted to lean out of the train window, but on each occasion I got a piece of coal in my eye, as those days there were only steam trains and when the stoker opened the door to add more coal, tiny sparks and pieces of coal would blow up the chimney, past the coaches.

I had not been aware of just how I had neglected myself while living on the plot. After all, who needed to dress up when you lived eight miles from town? My hair was long and straight, I hadn't had a perm since I got married and Cecil had said that he didn't like women who permed their hair and wore makeup. My dresses had never been bought to accommodate a pregnant belly; (I called it my mosquito bite). When I stepped off the train in Ndola, my mother nearly had a heart attack. She waited until Cecil was out of earshot and then I got the lecture of my life. I kept saying that Cecil preferred me this way, and she retorted "Just how long do you think you'll keep him? The woman he fell in love with was well-groomed and was everything that he supposedly didn't like. Get wise and get pretty again, or you'll lose him."

We moved into my parents' home in Ndola, which was a beautiful town, but there was more news awaiting us. My dad had bought a business with a lot of problems, so he had put it back on the market, but Cecil would run it until it was sold. Cecil's old bicycle came in handy for him to get to work and back and when I needed to go to town, he would sit me on the bar and pedal me wherever I asked, big tummy and all. How he got his arms around my belly I will never know, but I trusted him completely and we never fell.

One of the first things we were told to do was buy a Topi. This was a cumbersome pith helmet that most people wore because of the intense sun beating down on their heads. We only wore them a couple of months, finding them most uncomfortable and then bought softer hats, which worked just as well. I was told that you get sunstroke through your eyes, not through the top of your head, but as no-one in my family ever got sunstroke, even when the youngsters refused to wear hats at all, I do not know whether this was true or not.

My mom had four servants, so there was very little for me to do. I spent my time making baby clothes and mom bought a home-perm, which was new on the market at that time. We waited for Cecil to leave for work and then I permed my hair. Since then I have never had a perm in a salon, as I always do my own. Mom managed to get a couple of maternity outfits from a friend for me, I bought some makeup and I was once again back to my old self.

At the weekend, Cecil borrowed a .22 rifle from my father and headed for the bush. He got back quite late that night, saying that he had thoroughly enjoyed walking in the open spaces looking for game and he knew he was going to love Rhodesia. I will give him his due; he never shot anything that we did not eat, except for a few occasions where he needed to shoot a rogue animal or one that was destroying villagers' crops. Cecil told us that on his way home that evening he had seen three lions, but they had thankfully ignored him, as his .22 rifle would not have been much good against three lions. From that day on, Cecil referred to lions as 'the gentlemen of the bush'. He explained that they never killed unless they were hungry or found themselves in a threatening situation that caused them fear, otherwise they would simply move away rather than confront you. In all Cecil's days in the bush, he only went after one lion, which had killed cattle on a farm near Mazabuka. He and a friend, Koen, went out together that night and shot the lion as it returned to the kraal after another kill. Both men shot at it, so we never knew exactly who had killed it. Someone once asked him to shoot one for its hide. Cecil's reply was "Why destroy such a beautiful animal for someone to walk on its skin? They deserve far more respect than that."

We heard that Northern Rhodesia was handing out farms free to ex-servicemen, but you had to have sufficient capital to run the farm. We went to look at one a few miles from Ndola. It was just bush and I mean dense vegetation and trees. The house was wattle and daub (mud and sticks), the front door a piece of corrugated iron which you lifted up from the bottom and swivelled on two little bolts. The windows were open holes in the building, with no cover whatsoever. We were sorely tempted, but knew that we didn't have any capital to run the farm. I might also mention that the thought of holes in the outer walls left me terrified at the thought of animals coming into the house. At that stage I was still living in town and was not used to the wilds at all.

We had only been in Ndola for three weeks when my father was transferred to Fort Jameson and he went down for a week to see what it was like. The Government notified my mother that she had to vacate the house immediately, as my dad's replacement had already arrived and wanted to move in. The only house we could find was a derelict old place on the outskirts of town, with no electricity or water. Cecil arranged for a forty-five gallon drum of water to be delivered and we bought a couple of Coleman pressure lamps, a primus stove, a Beatrice stove, matches and candles. A primus stove was a round cylinder which was filled with paraffin. The top burner was lit and it had a small pump on the side, which would increase the heat. A Beatrice stove was also a cylinder, filled with paraffin, but the top had a large wick, which protruded from a metal casing, with Mica walls so you could check the height of the burning wick to prevent smoking. This little stove gave off a gentle heat, which was excellent for cooking soups and stews. The paraffin pump used to fill them was a long cylinder, with a spout and was pumped from the top. By this time I was over seven months pregnant and my 'mosquito bite' was a full size ant-hill. The servants, who had already been advised that we would be moving and could not keep them, helped us move to the new house.

A few days earlier, Cecil had caught his hand in a saw at work and it sliced his thumb nail through to the flesh. This wound had turned septic and he was in a lot of pain. I boiled some bread and water on the primus stove to use as a poultice, a home-made remedy for infected areas. It was nearly dark and the biggest spider I had ever seen ran inside, from under the front door. It was hairy, of reddish colour, about four inches long and one and a half inches wide. Its little red eyes gleamed in the lamplight and even Cecil was impressed by its size. He grabbed the flit spray (a round cylinder containing insecticide with a long handle which you pumped to spray) and took off the lid. As he poured the entire contents over the spider, another two came running under the door. We didn't know it then, but these spiders were known as 'hunting spiders' and are extremely common in Central Africa. That night I was terrified to put my foot to the floor, because the spiders were running in faster than Cecil could kill them by hitting them with my handbag, of all things.

I knew I was putting the poultices on the wound on his thumb straight out of the pot and he would cringe as he saw one coming, but I was honestly too concerned with spiders to care. My mother never got off her bed, shouting advice and yelling every time a spider entered her room. The next day we counted forty eight dead spiders but we were, in fact, very lucky that they never ran up into our bedclothes, as this is something they seemed to like doing. I know of one man who got a spider up his trouser leg and he was quite prepared to do a strip show right there and then, but fortunately it ran down again before he could remove his trousers. On another occasion I was sitting in the theatre with my sister in-law when she whispered, "There's something in my skirt. I'm holding it in my fist. Come with me to the ladies." When she let her skirt fall, a huge hunting spider dropped onto the floor. I never thought I would see the day when I would casually look at a spider and say, "It's getting near rainy season, the spiders are back." We eventually used to leave them well alone if they came into the house and they would leave again when they were ready.

My father arrived back from Fort Jimmy, as we called it, one week later to say that their accommodation was nearly ready and he had spoken to a Mister Gush who owned the Fort Jameson Garage and Milling Company. He had offered Cecil a job and my father encouraged him to accept. Although Cecil was a French Polisher and had never done any form of building work, Mr Gush wanted him to erect some buildings. My father assured us that he would advise and help Cecil, having once been clerk of works for the South African government and was a builder by trade. The decision was made to accompany my parents to Fort Jimmy immediately.

Dad bought a truck and mom insisted on taking most of her furniture. I bought a black Tansad Pram (the very best those days) and between us, the poor truck was completely overloaded. At the back of the truck was also a forty-five gallon drum of petrol and one servant, named Isaac, accompanied us to help with any heavy work and do some cooking. Early next morning, we headed for Lusaka and, if my memory serves me correctly, it was about two hundred miles. It was a good trip with tar roads all the way; lovely scenery and the sheer excitement of a new adventure kept us all in good spirits. As there were four of us and the truck cab only seated three, they had made a little nest between the furniture on the back for me, as mom felt it would be a less stressful journey if I could lie down. I quite happily read my book and rested when I wanted to. Isaac sat at the very back of the truck and appeared to sleep all the way.

On arriving in Lusaka, we booked into a hotel and Isaac slept on the truck to guard our belongings. Cecil's bicycle was lashed to the rear end of the truck, as he had refused to part with it. Next morning Cecil tied a piece of string to his finger and passed the other end to me on the back of the truck, saying, "If you want dad to stop, pull the string." We started off on the worst road in Africa, or at least it felt that bad. Deep corrugations in the road resulted in everything bouncing about on the back, furniture started to shift and my nest became smaller and smaller. I became very agitated when I realised that the wardrobe was loose and could topple over on top of me at any moment, so frantically began pulling the string. In my panic, I pulled so hard that Cecil hung half out of the truck window and had a sore finger for days afterwards.

The scenery was not impressive at this stage. There were miles of black earth where raging veld fires had swept through and one would see mounds of ash where smaller trees had burned completely. The larger trees were also badly scorched, but they would recover in time. Animal carcasses were strewn across the ashen landscape where poor creatures had been trapped by the inferno. In areas where the flames had not reached, the grass was yellow and limp. It was late October and Rhodesia was at its hottest. The Cicados (beetles) sat in their dozens in the trees and screamed all day long. It was a high, shrill sort of whistle. The Mopani Flies were around in their dozens, irritating beyond description. This was the month commonly called 'Suicide month', as so many Rhodesians committed suicide at this time of year, not being able to stand the heat and humidity. It also brought about major depression in many people.

I was being bounced about so badly on the back of the truck that I feared for my baby. We had to cover two hundred miles that day, so we ended up with mom, dad and Cecil sitting on the seat and I sat on a biscuit tin between Cecil's legs. Mom's dog, Micky, was on the floor as well, sitting near my feet. (The doctor was horrified when he saw my bruised back when we eventually got to Fort Jimmy.) At last we came to the end of our day's journey as we crossed the bridge over the Luangwa River and we headed straight for the Luangwa Rest Camp. These camps were primitive, to say the least. There were two beds to a room, they did have mosquito nets, but no bedding was provided. A cook was available in the camp to prepare any food that you had brought with you and as a side line if you had no food, he had chickens available for sale at a shilling each and eggs were 1 penny.

There was no bathroom, only a basin of cold water to wash in. We spent two days there for me to rest, as dad knew that the next two hundred miles were a sheer nightmare, with escarpments so high that it was like being in an aircraft and the road had such sharp bends that we had to stop and reverse once or twice to manoeuvre the vehicle around them. It was so bad that vehicles could only leave Lusaka between twelve midnight and twelve noon and vehicles from Fort Jimmy between twelve noon and twelve midnight. There just wasn't room for two vehicles to pass at any point on this journey.

There was still over a hundred and fifty miles to go and the heat beat down so fiercely onto the metal cab that one actually felt faint and suffered dull headaches. From the escarpment one could see for miles across the hills, the hot air shimmering and the horizon a smoky haze. In future travels I would see this same scenery in its utter splendour, so beautiful in fact, that it could take your breath away. The one thing that remained with me always, though, was my fear of our vehicle falling over the edge of the escarpment and I had to place all my faith in Cecil's driving skills for these journeys. However, on this journey my dad was driving.

We didn't make as much progress as we had hoped and it was late afternoon. Dad pulled over and asked Isaac to start making a fire, then turned to Cecil. "Let's see if we can get anything for supper before dark."
As the men left, Isaac disappeared into the bush to find firewood, leaving mom and I alone. We soon discovered that the men had accidentally locked the cab and taken the keys with them and dusk was closing in. Suddenly we spotted a shadowy shape approaching us from up the road and mom asked whether I could climb onto the back of the truck without help. I was so afraid that nothing could have stopped me. I scrambled almost effortlessly into the truck and mom climbed up behind me. The animal was getting quite close to the truck by this time and mom found one of dad's guns on the back of the truck. She leaned over and grabbed it. The animal was now right next to us and mom said, "If it comes any closer, I'll shoot."
I retorted, "Don't even try". She was shaking so badly that the gun was hitting the side of the truck and sounded like someone playing animatedly on a set of drums.

As last the animal moved away and just after that Isaac appeared with the wood, leaving us more than a little relieved. The men arrived shortly afterwards and immediately suffered a burst of anger from my mother about the keys. She told them about the dangerous animal that had scared us, but the men laughed, saying it was probably only a hyena. I realised at this stage that my husband and mother were not going to get on at all. Deep down my mom had a heart of gold, but I realised that since I had left home, she had

47

become a different person to the one I had known. She seemed to have lost a lot of her confidence and appeared to be on the defensive all the time. She did not smile as often as she had done when I was younger. Whether something had happened between her and my dad since I had moved away, or whether she resented Cecil for taking me away from her, I don't know. However, I only saw 'the old mom' on a few occasions in the many years we lived near each other from then on. The men had not managed to shoot anything, so we opened tins.

As soon as we had eaten, we continued our journey in the dark, but had only travelled about fifteen miles when we came to a rest camp, so we stopped and booked in for the night. We lazed around the next day until noon and then set off once again. We had only travelled a few miles when mom and dad started an argument. I realised that Cecil had also gone very quiet and we travelled for hours in complete silence. Suddenly the vehicle lunged into a skid and we slammed up against a bank on the side of the road. Dad tried to back up, but Cecil's bicycle wheels went under the truck and buckled so badly, that we untied it, and threw it down next to the trees. I honestly believe that my dad was so tired at this stage that he wasn't thinking clearly, because when we arrived in Fort Jimmy he reversed the truck into a tree, knocking off the back of the wardrobe. I watched all my beautiful baby clothes fluttering down into the red soil which, even after several washes, were permanently stained and had to be discarded. This brought another tirade from my mother and tempers flared dangerously, particularly when we were advised that our house was not ready and we had to travel a few more miles to a hotel, known as Rangely's Hotel, owned or managed by a Mrs Sequera.

On our arrival, Dad didn't notice a wire hanging between the hotel and an annexe, which was the source of power from a generator. As dad reversed, the wardrobe caught the wire and the entire hotel was plunged into darkness. My dad, who had obviously had enough, turned to Cecil with gritted teeth and spat out "Fix it."
Without answering, Cecil jumped from the truck and stormed off, his anger showing in the swing of his shoulders. It took him half an

hour, but thankfully he managed to get the lights back on. I was still sitting on my biscuit tin, very unhappy at the sight of my baby clothes and I was so dirty from the dusty trip. In fact, putting it bluntly, I was absolutely filthy. Mrs Sequera approached me and offered me a hot bath, at which time I could have kissed her. I felt so tired and sore from all the battering around on the corrugations and my back ached from the seat banging against it while sitting on the biscuit tin, even though Cecil had done his best to steady me between his legs.

Mrs Sequera showed us to our room and when I saw Cecil's face, and realised how upset he was, I told him to have his bath first, while I unpacked some clean clothes. On his return, Cecil was smiling and he casually informed me that my bath was ready. I scooped up my clean clothes and entered the bathroom with eager anticipation of a good, hot soaking. What awaited me brought sheer disbelief. It was an empty room, with a cold concrete floor which sloped to allow excess water to run through holes in the outer wall. In the middle of the room stood two paraffin tins, filled with hot water. A paraffin tin was about thirty five centimetres square and the same in depth. The idea was to place a foot in each tin and bathe yourself while standing. I knelt next to the one tin, put my head in the other and washed my hair before standing in the tins to bath. Nevertheless, it turned out to be a bath I would never forget and at least I was able to rid myself of the dust and grime from the long journey.

Later that evening we sat on the hotel verandah, enjoying a drink in the warm night air. Everyone had calmed down sufficiently to chat about the trip and share a few giggles. Mrs Sequera joined us for a while and told us that a leopard had jumped through her bedroom window a week before. It had seated itself on her dressing table and was looking at itself in the mirror. It was beyond my comprehension at that stage how she could laugh at the situation, knowing just how dangerous leopards were. She also warned us to watch mom's little dog, Micky, as Fort Jimmy was alive with wild animals, particularly leopard. This was the first time I realised what living in the bush could truly mean and I felt a thrill of fear course through me. However I also knew deep down that I would follow my man wherever he decided to go, animals or no animals. Only years later, after many similar narrow escapes, did I realise that laughter was a form of unwinding after the initial danger had passed and the adrenalin levels had returned to normal. At this stage in my life I was not only afraid of insects, spiders, snakes and wild animals. I was trying to get used to sweating all day, getting covered with dust every time you travelled in a vehicle. I had always been a fastidious person and now I felt dirty and smelly all the time. There were no deodorants to buy those days in Rhodesia. I had to become used to using the bush as a toilet when we travelled and it filled me with disgust every time I had to squat. I was not a very happy person at that stage.

Next morning we went to explore Fort Jimmy and, within ten minutes, had seen the entire place. What fascinated me most were a group of Indian shops, selling materials, hardware and so on, but only one shop in town (if my memory serves me correctly), called Mandala Stores, sold food. There was no electricity, so everyone used pressure lamps and candles. There was also no water laid on and it had to be brought in forty-five gallon drums to the house. I went to the doctor, the bruises on my back already fading, but he was terribly upset when he saw them. He had been an army doctor, so didn't have much experience with babies. He had built a house just outside Fort Jimmy and erected the outside toilet to face the road. When friends drove past his house in the morning, he would be sitting on the toilet, door wide open, so that he could wave to them and anyone else that passed by. He became a good friend and told me that my baby was due on Christmas Day.

We stayed in the hotel for four days and then moved into the house allocated to my dad. It had been left in quite a state after the builders were finished, so Cecil decided to create a few flower beds around the front garden. Being so heavily pregnant at this stage, I could not stand for very long, so sat myself down on the ground and worked alongside him. Mom's little dog, Micky, was running around behind me, when he suddenly started barking. Cecil looked back, then said "Joan, get up very slowly and walk towards me."

I knew by the tone of his voice that there was something wrong, so I got up as slowly as possible and moved towards him. As I said before, I trusted him completely and on reaching him, I turned around to see what the problem was. Right next to where I had been seated, was a huge snake. The head, rounded by the large hood, was swaying from side to side. Micky stood a little way from it, barking incessantly. Cecil grabbed the spade and killed it, then took me into his arms. I was trembling with absolute terror and said a quiet prayer of thanks for my safety and for this man I had married.

There was no bakery, nor butchery, so we made our own bread and shot for the pot. We slowly began making friends and Cecil became very close to Norman Carr, the game ranger for Luangwa. In fact, at one stage, Cecil considered joining Norman as a game ranger. He also got on very well with Mister Gush and seemed happy in his work, but could hardly wait for the weekends to go off on his own with a rifle. We had no form of transport, except for the big truck, so my dad arranged a trip to Lusaka to buy a bakkie, but it didn't materialise for over a year.

We heard someone knocking on the door one night at midnight and it turned out to be a couple who we had met a few days earlier. They were terribly excited and said, "Get in the car. We want you to see your first bushfire." We drove a short distance and stopped on the top of a hill. Ahead of us was the most spectacular sight of flames shooting heavenwards. It was quite a few miles away, but it looked as if half the world was burning. There was a deep red-orange glow against the black void of the night sky and the stars seemed to twinkle in competition with the dancing flames, as the colours blended, then once again broke apart. Sparks flew upwards and then died. I stood, fascinated, until Cecil touched my arm and said, "We must go, don't forget I have to work tomorrow."

CHAPTER FOUR

A buffalo claims our friend....

On Christmas Eve I sat with my parents in the lounge, Cecil having not yet returned from hunting since early afternoon. I was upset and feeling very neglected and asked, "What sort of guy doesn't spend Christmas Eve with his wife, when her baby is due the next day?"

My father angrily retorted, "You have to eat, don't you, and Cecil is only doing what any sensible, responsible man would do for his family".

Needless to say, Cecil arrived home at about nine that evening. The truck had given him trouble, but he came home with a big kudu. He would travel as far as possible with the truck and then walk through the bush, looking for game and thought nothing of doing about twenty-five miles in a day. If he shot an animal, he would simply put it over his shoulder and carry it back to the truck. He was exceptionally fit at this stage in his life and had fully recovered from the Rheumatic globule. He had also put on a little weight, but his torso and legs were firm from all the walking. He took out a five pound shooting licence, which gave him the right to shoot four elephant, two rhino and ten of each species of antelope.

Christmas Day came, but with it, no sign of baby. The rains had arrived late and with them came the mosquitoes, so it was a case of sleeping under nets and every house was sprayed inside and out with DDT by the government. It was a happy time, with less family arguments than usual and on the morning of the twenty eighth, a Sunday, I felt the first stirrings of labour.

The hospital had four beds in the female ward and four in the male ward, with no theatre. It was actually used mostly for malaria cases and had no facilities for labour patients or emergency surgical procedures. I sat around all day smiling, even though the smiles were a little strained eventually. As the pain progressed, I started to walk up and down the verandah, as a hyena walked up and down on the outside, whooping wildly all night with just the gauze between us. (Strangely enough, my baby's first imitation was the whooping of the hyena and people would laugh at this little mite whooping happily to herself.)

On Monday morning a strange man walked over to me and introduced himself as Doctor Davidson. "I'm relieving Doctor Taube, who has gone on leave" he explained.
He was a tall, elderly man and appeared to be very nice. By that night, I was still walking up and down, and by this time wishing I could die, when I heard Cecil and my mom approaching. I overheard my mom saying something about him bringing me four hundred miles to the back of beyond and couldn't he see that I needed a specialist? I never heard Cecil's reply, but I can just imagine what it might have been!

The sister wanted to bring Cecil in to help me with the labour, but there was no ways on earth I would have my husband see me in such an undignified position. On Tuesday morning the doctor came and said, "We are going to help you along". They wheeled me into a little store room they had prepared with a bed and pressure lamp. There was just enough room for the doctor to squeeze in next to the bed and, without any warning; the sister slapped a piece of cotton wool drenched in chloroform onto my face. In my panic, I thought they were trying to make my dying wish come true and suddenly realised I didn't intend dying just yet. I threw my arms up as I lost consciousness. I did come round once and heard the doctor and sister talking, but I couldn't make out what they were saying.

Eventually I awoke to no pain, much to my relief. The sister announced that I had a baby girl, weighing eight and a half pounds. I immediately asked to see her, but her reply took me by surprise. "Well, at the moment she's in the men's ward with your husband. He was admitted this morning with suspected malaria, but he seems much better now, so he's babysitting for us." I asked for a mirror, but she casually replied that I didn't need one yet. Naturally, being me, I

insisted. After all, I needed to put on my makeup before seeing my husband. The sister then explained that I had knocked the bottle of chloroform all over my face when I threw my arms up and it had burnt my face quite badly. "It's not permanent and won't leave scars, she assured me, but it does look rather awful right now."
Sure enough, I found my little mirror and my face and neck was badly blistered. I realised then that I should be grateful that it had not damaged my eyes.

The pain in my face miraculously disappeared when Cecil walked into the ward, my beautiful little girl in his arms. As I looked at the dark, curly hair, just like her daddy's, my heart swelled at the wonder that love between two people could produce something so perfect. I remained in hospital for fourteen days and each time Cecil visited, he came with dad's rifle, as during the previous week, the golfers had been chased off the golf course, which was on the way to the hospital, by four lions. In another incident, a gentleman had been walking his dog on a leash in the main street of Fort Jimmy, when a leopard had suddenly appeared and taken his dog, leash and all.

Doctor Taube finally returned and I started my endless visits to him with my daughter, Ethné. She cried incessantly, sleeping for half an hour and then waking and crying again. This continued day and night and I was utterly exhausted and terribly concerned about her. My mother became obsessed with Ethné, wanting to hold her constantly and do everything for her, which brought about ill feeling between her and Cecil. I would sit in the lounge, sensing the tension between them.

One afternoon Cecil and I started to argue after a bad night with Ethné and my dad walked into the room, saying, "Cecil, is she giving you a hard time? Well, my wife is moaning too. Let's you and I go to the club for a game of snooker and leave these two to grumble between themselves." With that, Cecil got up and the men left in the truck, leaving mom and I feeling even more miserable. Every Saturday night the club held a film show (brought all the way from Lusaka) and mom and I decided to attend instead of sitting grumbling at home. I was terrified, as we had to cross the golf course

54

and, if I'd ever prayed, I prayed hard that night. Ethné, now a couple of months old, was in her pram. As we walked, I waited to hear the cough of a leopard or the snarl of an approaching lion, but we finally arrived safely at the club and went inside. We ignored the two men completely and I saw Cecil grin with amusement, but also watched friends commenting on how we sat apart from our husbands. After the show mom and I started the long walk home, when my dad stopped the truck next to us and Cecil asked sweetly "Would you two ladies like a lift?" Before my mom could sit on her high horse, I accepted and Cecil lifted the pram onto the back and told us to get in front, he would watch the baby on the back. I was only too grateful to thank him and get into the front of the truck.

It rained almost every day, but not all day long. Mom bought flour for the bread our cook would bake, but decided to bake a cake herself. On opening the packet, she found it was full of worms, so stormed off to Mandala Stores to complain. The sales assistant laughed and said, "All the flour has worms during the rainy season, just sift them out and use it anyway."
This is how we coped with the flour from then on and we eventually became quite accustomed to it. One truck bringing flour from Lusaka also carried tins of paraffin, which leaked into the flour, so we were left with no option but to have paraffin-flavoured bread until the new batch arrived.

Ethné was now four months old and had only put on one pound, weighing nine and a half pounds. Every time I suggested to Doctor Taube that it was my milk, he stressed how important it was to breast feed and to introduce nothing else, because she was so delicate. She lay in her pram looking like a little wax doll and my concern was growing. That Sunday I bathed her, dressed her nicely and wheeled her pram into the garden under the trees. Pulling the mosquito net over the pram, I went inside and left her to sleep in the lovely fresh morning air. Some time later her Godparents arrived and naturally their first words were "Where's Ethné?"
Smiling back at them, I answered, "She's sleeping in the garden."
"But it's pouring with rain!"

I ran outside, my heart in my throat and there she was, lying in two inches of water, the mosquito net flat on her face and her little hands waving around under the net, cooing and gurgling happily. Thankfully, even during the rains, it is never cold at that time of year, so no damage was done.

A few nights later, after I had received a lecture from my mother about the baby in the rain, Cecil decided to go to bed. Ethné was screaming as usual and Cecil leaned over her cot and quietly said "If I didn't love you so much I would give you this." With that, he clapped his hands. My mother flew into the bedroom, completely hysterical, shouting, "I'll call the police if you touch her again. How dare you smack such a tiny baby?"
Cecil took one look at me and said, "I'm out of here." And I couldn't blame him, as he had put up with so much from my folks.

The next day Cecil went to see Mister Gush and said, "If you can't find me somewhere to live, I'm going back to South Africa."
That afternoon Mister Gush called Cecil to say he had arranged for a small house in the Polish Camp, a derelict little village where Polish prisoners of war had been placed. The little house we got faced the road to Lusaka and it had a couple of peep holes in the door. I sometimes wondered whether any spying went on there during the war. We moved as soon as we could, despite the fact that we had nothing of our own and so resorted to making our own furniture from wooden paraffin boxes. A paraffin box was designed to hold two tins of paraffin. They were strong and were about sixty centimetres long by thirty centimetres wide, at a rough guess. Four paraffin boxes, placed about a metre from four more, with a broom handle nailed between them, made excellent hanging space for our clothes, with cupboard space on either side. A curtain on the front made it look more presentable. A cushion on each of the paraffin box chairs with a little wrap-skirt made the lounge look quite cosy, with a tablecloth over the home-made table. Mom let us take the bed we had been sleeping on, so we were quite comfortable.

It seems that spiders were to be my Moses and this time it was Tarantulas. Big, hairy ones, with black and white legs, they were truly frightening to look at. The first episode took place just a few days after we moved in. I was cooking Cecil's breakfast, as I did not have a servant at that stage. We were chatting about someone who was leaving for South Africa and wanted to sell their furniture. We discussed whether we could afford to buy a decent table and I was looking at Cecil as I reached back to get an egg out of the basket. I broke the first egg into the pan and reached for another. As I picked it up, it wriggled in my hand and I screamed, dropping the 'egg' like a hot potato. It was a huge tarantula and it started to run across the room. Cecil grabbed the broom and went towards it, as it suddenly reared up on its hind-legs and I watched two little red fangs moving up and down in its mouth, as it attacked the broom. I was horrified to see how vicious this little blighter was, but at least I had learned to respect them and wherever possible, to leave them well alone, but it didn't stop the waves of revulsion that rippled through my body, knowing that I had held it in my hand.

On another occasion, I went to put Ethné in her cot and found one lying on her pillow. This cot was bought from an African and made from reeds and bamboo and being very low, I was afraid of spiders and snakes. A few days later we came home at dusk and Cecil busied himself lighting the pressure lamps. I leaned over the cot to put her down and I thought I saw a shadow moving. Cecil brought the lamp over, but we could find nothing, so I put her down to sleep. As I pulled the blanket over her, I saw the Tarantula. It had been hiding between the cot and the wall, just out of sight. Once the commotion was over to get it away from Ethné, I stood looking down at her frail, sleeping body and I realised that I was going to lose her if we didn't do something soon.

Cecil went hunting that weekend and mom came to visit. She took one look at Ethné and said, "Don't tell Cecil, but I've brought oats and condensed milk with me. Now for heaven's sake, feed that child. Your milk obviously isn't sufficient!"
In those days we had no access to fresh milk and used condensed milk as an alternative. Mom made the oats, pushed it through a sieve and stirred in a couple of teaspoons of condensed milk. She sat Ethné on her lap and lifted a spoonful to her mouth. As the food went into

her tiny little mouth, Ethné went mad and couldn't get enough. She guzzled down every mouthful we offered her and then drifted off, sleeping for a solid eight hours. From that day, Ethné blossomed and my gratitude to my mother for her help was immense, as I realised that my child had been literally starving to death.

We began to buy pieces of furniture until we had quite a nice home and then Cecil decided once again to return to South Africa. We sold all the lovely things we had bought and all that was left were his tools. A very good looking man in his early forties, muscular and bronzed by the sun, knocked at our door and introduced himself as Jock Drotsky. He said he would like to see Cecil's tools, and I made tea while Cecil took him through to see them. A little later we were sitting having our tea (on borrowed chairs) and Jock asked, "Cecil, why are you leaving God's own country?"
Cecil used me as an excuse, saying, "It isn't much of a life for a woman and mine deserves better than this" as he waved his arms, gesturing towards the Polish camp. I might mention at this stage, that ours was the only house that was inhabited.
Jock replied, "Well, it's not my place to change your mind, but I think you're crazy. Why don't you come and have lunch with us on the farm on Sunday?"
We explained that we had no transport, barring dad's truck as he hadn't bought a bakkie yet, and Jock extended the invitation to mom and dad as well. Now that we no longer shared a home, Mom and Cecil were getting along far better, for which I was very grateful.

Our lunch date with Jock and Netta, his wife, was most enjoyable and Netta and I just seemed to bond that day. She was a lot younger than Jock. Although plump, she was pretty and her welcoming smile was a genuine one. We stayed until ten in the evening, the men talking hunting, as usual. Jock was a buffalo hunter, captivating dad and Cecil as he related his stories. Travelling home on the back of the truck, Cecil was quiet for a while and then asked me if I really wanted to return to South Africa. I simply replied, "It was your idea in the first place, but all we have is one hundred and fifty pounds in the bank and your tools".

"No, sweetheart, we don't have a hundred and fifty pounds, I've just bought Jock's Rigby Rifle with it."

Laughing, I replied, "I don't think it's going to be very comfortable sleeping on a gun, but I'm willing to try."

He grabbed me and gave me such a big kiss, saying, "How lucky I am to have someone like you. I'll take you back to South Africa in a couple of years, but in the meanwhile I'm going buffalo hunting with Jock."

So, we started all over again to buy household goods to make a home and once again, in the meanwhile, it was furniture made from paraffin boxes. Then the hunting started in earnest, the bug not only having bitten Cecil, but my father as well. Whenever Jock had time, he took them down to the Luangwa which, many years later, became President Kenneth Kaunda's hunting ground. However in the 1940's, it was wild, rugged and teeming with wildlife. We learned how to make biltong in a forty five gallon drum and absolutely nothing was wasted, as whatever we discarded, the labourers were only too glad to accept. Jock taught Cecil and Dad to always be sure to give the gun-bearers and skinners their fair share of meat. They would leave the meat in very large chunks, lay green branches on the fire and place the meat on the branches, so as to cure the meat by means of heat and smoke.

He also said never to refuse meat to any of the villagers who visited the camp. Many times in the future I watched villagers arrive laughing and chatting and then start clapping their hands. Some would bring a couple of eggs or a tiny basket of maize for us, but mainly they arrived empty-handed and would leave with an armful of fresh meat, simply bowing or clapping their thanks.

Jock had friends from Namibia and arranged a buffalo hunt in the Luangwa Valley. The men would be accompanied by Netta and her two children, as well as Mr and Mrs Smith. Mr Smith was a photographer and was keen to get some good shots of buffalo. Two skinners and two gun-bearers were hired, plus a driver for the truck. A gun bearer accompanies the hunters and looks for spoor of the animal wanted, then follows it until the quarry is found. He also

59

carries the extra rifle if one of the hunters decides to take one. Netta was quite worried about her baby, as while they were travelling a few days earlier, a bridge had collapsed over a dry river bed as they traversed it and the baby was thrown against the dashboard, before hitting the floor of the cab. He did not seem hurt at the time and the doctor who checked him said that he appeared to be fine, but he became very listless and fractious. They were to be away for two weeks and I was advised not to go with, as I was recovering from malaria.

They had been away for about a week when I popped into Mandala Store to buy some groceries. An old madala approached me and said "Dona, the tom toms told me that the bwana has run out of condensed milk and if you give me a tin, I will take it to my village, then it will be sent on from village to village, until it reaches the bwana." I laughed, not knowing whether he was telling the truth, but I bought a couple of tins and handed them to him.

Next morning, the madala came to my home and said "Oh, so sorry, Dona, but the tom toms told me this morning that there has been a terrible accident with a buffalo and one of the bwanas. He has been badly hurt and they are bringing him to the hospital."
My heart felt as if it stood still. Was Cecil hurt? He was such a keen hunter, had he been careless? Or Dad? He was older and slower than the other men. Then I considered Mr Smith and Jock himself. I sat all day, sick with worry. Late that night the truck pulled into the yard and out climbed Cecil, my dad, gun-bearers and skinners. At last I was to hear what happened that fateful day.

It seems that Jock had been persuading Cecil to shoot an elephant and he eventually got quite enthusiastic. Early the next morning, Cecil, Jock and Mr Smith took off with the gun-bearers and skinners to look for elephant. When they eventually came across the spoor of elephant, by the time they started to follow them, the herd had crossed the river into the game reserve. On their way back, they saw a large herd of buffalo. Between them, they shot three and waited for the skinners to clean the carcasses and cut them up, by taking off the hind-quarters, shoulders and the fillet. The innards were always prized by the skinners and with really no meat left on the rib cage, it was left for predators. They climbed back into the truck and Jock said, "If we see another herd, I would like to get just one more." They were about fifteen miles from camp when they came across another small herd and Jock and Cecil slipped off the back of the truck and headed across the dambo, which are wetlands, although they are dry during the winter season.

Jock fired at a large bull and wounded him and the rest of the herd stampeded, making a thick cloud of black dust. Cecil and Jock ran after the herd, but Cecil, being a younger man, was soon way ahead of Jock. The one rule, as far as a good hunter is concerned, is that you never leave a wounded animal to die painfully; you follow it and finish it off. On the very few occasions that I saw our men folk unable to find a wounded animal, it left them fretting for days.

Cecil then heard a shot and a loud cry from behind him and ran back. It seems that the bull had stood still in the black clouds of dust and Cecil must have run past it, but Jock had run straight into it. As Cecil approached, he found Jock impaled through the groin, perched on one of the buffalo's horns, trying desperately to hold onto the other with both hands. His leg was gashed open terribly from the ankle to the knee. Cecil fired a shot into the hind quarters of the buffalo and then another in the enraged animal's shoulder. He was afraid to fire anywhere else in case he hit Jock. With the second shot, the bull threw Jock to the ground and Cecil jumped between the bull and his friend, firing a third shot through one eye and another in the head. The buffalo finally dropped, ploughing into the dusty earth.

Having heard the shooting, the driver had brought the truck across the dambo, ready to load. Mr Smith was horrified at what he saw. The men tore up their shirts to bandage Jock's wounds and slowly Jock regained consciousness. By now it was late afternoon and they lay Jock in the back of the truck. When the driver tried to start the truck, they realised that it had run out of petrol. He had apparently forgotten to fill the vehicle, which was his sole responsibility and no-one had checked to see whether this had been done or not. Jock was in immense pain and also in a very bad state of shock. Cecil offered to take the gun-bearers and skinners back to camp on foot to fetch medical supplies and fuel, but Mr Smith said he would rather go, as there was so much blood around the truck and he was not one of the best shots if predators approached. Cecil gave the gun-bearers the rifles and the water bottle and they set off for camp, leaving Cecil alone with Jock. When the wounded man cried out for water, all Cecil could do was dip a piece of cloth in the truck's radiator and squeeze it into Jock's mouth.

Mr Smith and the gun-bearers arrived back in the early hours of the morning and after doing whatever they could to make Jock more comfortable with blankets and medical supplies, they headed back to camp. Cecil, Dad and the skinners were left to pack up the camp and the truck would return for them later. A couple of villagers passing by asked what had happened and they were the ones who sent the bush telegraph message on the tom-toms, which I received.

Jock seemed to be recovering well, but sadly within a week, he deteriorated and died. The hospital had no such things as X-rays or scans and we believe he had internal injuries, which had not been detected. Cecil made Jock a coffin out of raw timber, bought from the villagers. We then bought white material and lined the raw wood. Cecil laid Jock in the coffin and closed the lid, but from that day onwards, Cecil was a dedicated buffalo hunter and each time he shot one, he would say "That's for you, Jock."
The raw timber used for Jock's coffin was bought from the villagers, who used to cut down trees, dig a deep hole in the ground and one villager would stand in the hole and the other on the bank, using a saw with a handle on either side, held between them. They lay the trunk of the tree across the hole and sawed planks out of it. They then sold the planks to other villagers, who would turn them into furniture. These villagers had lathes which ran on a riempie, (a strip of antelope hide, resembling rope), with a piekanien (a young child) pulling it backwards and forwards to work the same as our 'belts' work.

My mother started begging my father to get Joyce and Charlie up to Fort Jimmy, so he approached Mr Gush, who decided to expand the business and even suggested that my father give up African Housing and the whole family could work for him. He bought a piece of ground called 'Escape Estate' and decided to build three houses and he asked Cecil to do the building. This was wonderful news to me, as we were still in the Polish camp.

Before Cecil started the houses, Mr Gush told him that he had booked us into the Grand Beach Hotel in Nyasaland, now called Malawi, as a gift for Christmas. We would leave on the twenty-third of December and return on the twenty-eighth, with all expenses paid, including our petrol. What a wonderful week we had. The scenery in Nyasaland is every bit as beautiful as Rhodesia, but the lake was absolutely magnificent. It was so large; it looked as if you were standing at the sea at low tide, as little waves splashed onto the shore at your feet.

The chalets were built right next to the water, so that if you lay in bed at night, you could hear the soft lapping of the waves on the shore. The only unpleasant aspect was the mosquitoes. There were millions of them and we had to really drench ourselves in insect repellent to prevent being eaten alive. There were all sorts of facilities for the public in the hotel, such as snooker, billiards, table tennis, badminton and tennis courts. There was also a very small golf course not too far away, but at that stage Cecil wasn't a golfer, so we didn't actually visit it.

We soon made friends with the other guests and the women decided we were going for a swim in the lake. Cecil tried to talk us out of it, saying that the crocodiles would have us for lunch. We all cried him down and someone said, "If a croc approaches you, just clap your hands and the sound will chase him away." We all got into the water and Cecil began strolling along the shoreline. He had only gone a little way, when he returned and said "Joan, come and have a look at this."
I jumped out and followed him. There, on the sand in shallow water, lay the leg of an antelope, half eaten. I decided there and then that I had done all the swimming I was going to do at the lake.

The dining area of the hotel was superb. The tables were covered with snow-white cloths and shining, silver cutlery. There were four waiters, dressed in white, with red sashes around their waists and the head waiter had a red fez on his head. They were running a competition to see how many different designs they could make with serviettes. Our waiter arranged our serviettes in glasses, in the shape of a swan, complete with beak, tail and wings. I never could get this right in later years, when I entertained, although I tried many times.

The day before we were due to leave, I washed Ethne's vest and hung it over the rail of the mosquito net to dry. All the nets had wooden frames around the bed so the net didn't' fall onto you during the night.

After we got home Ethné was very unhappy and seemed to cry for absolutely nothing at all. The next day was her birthday and I had arranged a little party for her. She cried throughout the party and when I bathed her later that day, I noticed her back had little red bumps on. By next morning these bumps had tiny black heads. I took her to see the doctor and he told me they were commonly known as 'poetsies'. The Tumbu Fly lays its eggs on washing hung out to dry and if the garment is not properly ironed before wearing it, the eggs penetrate the skin. On animals, where the fly burrows into the skin under the fur, the maggots get as big as one inch long and as thick as one's little finger before they turn into flies. Ethné had seventeen on her back from the vest I had washed at the hotel. I must mention our irons here. They were huge and made from cast iron. The top lifted off on a hinge so that you could place red-hot coals inside and then replace the lid, swinging the iron to and fro until the coals actually glowed. You could then iron for about half an hour before replacing the coals.

I was told to apply plasters to each one for two days, which I did. A few came out with the plaster, but others had to be squeezed out with the fingers. As I squeezed each one, I watched little maggots with black heads wriggle about. It is quite dangerous to squeeze them, because if you kill the maggot in the flesh and cannot squeeze it all out, the wound turns septic. Both Cecil and I have had many nasty sores from doing just that. They are revolting little worms, similar in appearance to those found in guavas.

Once the rains were over, Cecil started building the three pole and daga (wattle and daub) houses next to each other, concentrating on our home first. I sat under a tree waiting to move in, wet walls and all. It was a simple place of three rooms, side by side. The middle was used as a lounge and dining area, the one side as a bedroom and the other side as a bathroom. There was also an outside kitchen and toilet, and all buildings were thatched. These houses were to be used temporarily, until Cecil could build proper brick homes, but ultimately, the brick homes were never even started. We went along to one of the Indian shops and managed to buy a fair- sized tin bath. In the Polish camp we had managed with a very large bowl, as there were no baths available. Naturally, we suddenly felt as though we were living in luxury and Cecil bought an Axminster carpet for our lounge from someone leaving the town.

At last Joyce and Charlie arrived with their two children, Patrick and Cynthia and we began going out as one large family. After visiting Joyce one day, imagine my horror when I walked in and found Cecil and a friend dismantling a motor bike on my new carpet. Granted, he had put paper down, but the sump was on the carpet, full of filthy, black oil. He just laughed at my reaction and said, "It's raining outside and anyway, we're being careful not to spill a drop. How about a cup of coffee?"

I could never stay angry with Cecil when he laughed like that, with the lock of hair falling across his forehead; he looked like a naughty little boy. I must admit, they never spilled a drop of oil, but perhaps it was occasions like this that made me what I am today. I do not crave fancy furniture, or expensive goods, as long as the article is functional and comfortable, I am happy with it.

CHAPTER FIVE

My baby leopard…..

When I say the folks went hunting at weekends, it makes it sound as if they just slaughtered animals for the fun of it, but it was usually something for the pot or to make biltong. Hunting is like fishing. Everyday is not a hunting day and there are many times that they came home with nothing at all, apart from which there was no form of refrigeration at that time. All we had was a muslin-sided box with a wooden floor, hung under a tree for shade. We would pour water over it three or four times a day to keep it cool. When the story of Jock's death went around Fort Jimmy, Cecil became quite a hero among the townsfolk and many men wanted him to take them hunting. Cecil preferred hunting alone, even when he went out with Charlie and Dad. They usually split up and went their own ways once they were in the bush, as Cecil wanted buffalo and they were out looking for the smaller antelopes.

I must admit there were times I did not enjoy Cecil's sense of humour. When he went hunting, he often came across snakes and occasionally shot one to bring home. He would place it in some strategic spot where we would come across it, much to our utter horror. I've often wondered since if it was his sense of humour, or an attempt at teaching us some valuable lessons regarding the dangers that lurked in the African bush. It did, however, cost him a full dinner service once.

We had guests to dinner one Sunday night and I gathered the four plates, side plates and dessert bowls on a tray and carried them to the kitchen. I was about to put the tray on the table, when the head of a large snake fell onto the top of my shoe from around the table leg. I gave one long, hard yell and the tray dropped from my hands onto the floor, shattering every single plate and bowl. I turned to Cecil, who had followed me. Furious beyond belief, I muttered, "That little joke will cost you a new dinner service."

Cecil, unable to contain his joyous laughter, replied, "Oh, Joan, it was so worth every cent just to see your face."

The next morning I heard Cecil calling to me from the outside toilet. I went outside and he told me that there was a snake on top of the door looking into the toilet. I offered to knock it down with a broom, but he answered "No. You'll knock it into my lap."

I heard him throw a tin of dip at the door and the snake slithered into the thatch. Cecil made a quick exit from the toilet and set fire to it with a box of matches. It got rid of the snake, but it was embarrassing to say the least to keep asking the family if we could use their toilet until Cecil built us another one.

Life went on quietly for a few months and then one day Cecil saw a villager carrying a baby leopard. Guessing its fate, Cecil bought the leopard from him and brought it home. It was no bigger than a small puppy and was literally a little bundle of fluff. I had to feed it with a baby bottle, using powdered milk, which was new on the market. He cost me a small fortune in teats, as after each feed he would rip the top of the teat off the bottle. We made a point of never giving him meat of any kind and I worried about the day he had to be weaned from milk, as I had no idea what I would feed him. There was no possibility of returning him to the wilds, as he was unable to care for or defend himself, having been taken from his mother as a newborn. If we sat down to a meal before he had his bottle, he would sit under the table, extend his claws and drag them down the front of my legs, often drawing blood.

My father never liked him and I think the leopard instinctively sensed this. If we visited Dad's house, he would run across to wherever Dad was seated and scramble onto his lap, then climb onto his shoulder, making the strangest growling sounds. My poor father would freeze and shout, "Get this damned thing off me!"

I taught him to walk on a leash and the villagers would move as far away as possible with looks of sheer amazement on their faces. Like all wild animals, they are never truly tamed and we knew the time was coming for a decision to be made about his future. He was

67

eating porridge and even some cooked vegetables, but it wasn't his natural food. We offered him to the Bloemfontein Zoo, saying that we would arrange for all the necessary documentation and would pay all expenses for his transportation to the zoo, but they were not at all interested. They felt that one leopard would become too vicious, so unless we could offer them a pair, they did not want him. Ethné was sitting in her pram one morning when I heard a snarl and Ethné screamed. I ran in to find her little face covered in blood. She had leaned over the side of the pram and the leopard had struck her in the face with his claws, tearing a small piece of flesh from her nose and cut her cheek open. Cecil made a cage for him, but he was so unhappy that he walked up and down with his nose against the wire until it was just a bleeding mass. Once again, we gave him his freedom and he seemed content living with us, never attempting to run away.

One evening a gentleman called on us and said that he was starting a private zoo. He already had several species of buck, lots of monkeys, a baboon and a young zebra. He asked us to please sell him the leopard. Cecil sat in thought for a while and then said, "I want nothing for the leopard, only your assurance that you will take great care of him".
Sadly I watched my baby, as I always called him, taken away to his new life.

A couple of weeks later I was told that he had been shot by the police. I went to the police station to find out what had happened and they told me that my baby had been chained to a tree, while they erected a cage for him. A woman who was doing the washing was walking over to the wash line when she slipped and hit her head. She had fallen within the leopard's reach and he had licked the blood on her face and then promptly savaged her. Someone witnessed the incident and dragged her to safety, then called the police to destroy him. The woman was hospitalised and was recovering well. My heart was so heavy that this beautiful creature had to die in such an undignified manner, because people had not left him in his own environment.

It was getting time for us to take annual leave and we decided this time to head for South Africa. We had not been out of Fort Jimmy for nearly two years, except for the trip to Nyasaland. We had bought a second-hand bakkie and decided to travel to Lusaka in the bakkie, leaving it at the police station, to continue our journey by train. We bought a duck and fattened it up for 'padkos', but it got so tame that we decided not to slaughter it. My cook unfortunately never understood me when I told him not to kill the duck and when I got home one morning, my tame duck was in the oven, cooking. He packed the duck, some meat pies, sandwiches and biscuits and we said our goodbyes. We had also packed a huge box of biltong for the family and two bottles of honey, taken from a tree in the Luangwa Valley.

The trip over the escarpment was beyond description. It was just after the rains and the land was lush and green. The grass was nearly two metres high and resembled a carpet. As it waved gently in the breeze, it made one think of the movement of the ocean. In the shade of the trees were dozens of flame lilies, red and yellow hues in all their brilliance against the deep green of the grass. It has been a favourite flower of mine ever since I saw that scene. It grows wild in Rhodesia and at Christmas I would pick armfuls to decorate the house. Even the trees were adorned with different coloured blooms and the entire landscape was as pretty as a painting.

When we reached the Luangwa Rest Camp we decided to spend a couple of days there. There was no need to book a seat on the train in advance in those days; you just bought a ticket for whenever you wished to travel. At about eleven that night, the cook in charge (we nicknamed him Cookie) woke us up to tell us that a bus full of passengers had gone over the side of the escarpment about half a mile from us. Cecil grabbed a torch and said, "Bring what you can to use as bandages".
I quickly filled a bottle with water, but I had no disinfectant and no real medication of any sort. This taught me a valuable lesson and I never travelled without a first-aid kit after that. I told Cookie to make a few jugs of tea and took our sandwiches along. There was

boiling water on the Dover stove in his kitchen and he quickly made the tea.

I have felt fear many times in my life, but never as I felt that night. I left Ethné asleep in the room and prayed she wouldn't wake up to find herself alone.   As I walked behind Cecil, I knew the lions, leopards, hyenas and many more dangerous animals were abundant in this region and as Cecil said later, he got his 'toes trod on by the person walking behind him'.

What a sad sight greeted us that night.   Those that were able, had climbed up the embankment and were sitting on the side of the road. Most of them had blood on them, but there were no tears or cries, in fact they were almost statue-like, obviously suffering from shock. The batteries in the torch were low, so we didn't have a lot of light. Cecil asked me to see what I could do for them while he went over the side to search for more survivors.   Each person had some form of injury and a couple of them had broken arms.   Cookie went to find a few strong twigs and I tore Ethne's panties into strips.   I had recently made them for her out of her nappies.   I bound twigs to the fractures as best I could and washed away whatever blood there was, to see the injury underneath.   One old man was sitting with blood from head to toe.   I asked "Where?" and he held his head.   I gently washed the blood from his head, expecting to find a gaping wound, but all I found was a hole, the size of a pea.   It had obviously severed a vein or artery and was bleeding profusely.

Cecil returned to report that the driver was dead, there was a silver rod through the side of his head and there was one other dead man down there.   We told Cookie to stay there and keep going down to the bodies to stop the hyenas from taking them.   We instructed the survivors not to go to sleep, as the smell of blood would attract all kinds of predators.   We promised we would leave immediately for Lusaka to get help.

On our arrival, we reported the accident to the police, who promised to see to it right away.   We left our bakkie at the police station and proceeded to the station.   We got on the train quite early and were surprised at how the steward treated us. We had always found them to be pleasant and smiling, but this chap was surly and we hardly saw him. At last he came back to see if we wanted anything and Cecil had taken out three large pieces of biltong. He passed one to the chap and said, "Look after us and these other two pieces are yours on our arrival in Salisbury".

Needless to say, we were treated like royalty from then on.

Approximately ten miles out of Lusaka the train hit a lot of sheep, killing about twenty of them, so we had to wait while they cleared the line. All Cecil kept muttering was "What a waste of braaivleis".

I took out our padkos and out came the duck. I opened the wrapping, but there was no ways I could bring myself to even touch it. I saw Cecil look very sheepish as he looked at me and whispered, "Enjoy it, sweetheart, but forgive me, I cannot eat him, he was my pet".

I admitted that I felt the same way and we passed it to some children when we stopped at a small station further on.

We arrived in Port Elizabeth and my brother-in-law, Eddie, met us and took us home to his wife, Florrie. Eddie was a fine looking man, tall like Cecil, but with lighter hair. He had studied entomology and met us dressed in a suit, collar and tie. He proudly announced that he had passed his final exams.

Florrie, or Flo, as we sometimes called her, was still the same. A smiling person, quite pretty, but somewhat like me in build, short and cuddly. They made us so welcome and for the first time in two years I saw the shops and the type of fashions women now wore. Boy! Was I a hick from the sticks! Florrie's hair was immaculate; she had been to a salon earlier that day. My hair had been permed and cut by me for the past two years. My clothes had been shabby when we went to Rhodesia and after all that time in the bush, I looked terrible.

Cecil smiled at me and asked, "What would you like most of all today?" I think he was waiting for me to answer "Clothes", or "A

Haircut" and appeared stunned when I answered "Fish and chips, like we used to buy during the war."

Eddie said, "Fine, we'll go to Oelof's and get fish and chips for supper".

I retorted, "No, Eddie, you don't understand. I want fish and chips in newspaper. I want enough for just one and I want to eat it while I look at the shops".

"You can't eat fish and chips on the street."

"Why not?" I asked with indignation.

Well, Oelof's had two entrances. Eddie went in through door one with Cecil. Florrie was talking to her children outside and I slipped in through the other door and asked for one helping of fish and chips in newspaper. As I came out, Eddie and Cecil spotted me and said, "We're not walking with you if you eat in the street".

Without hesitation, I replied "Fine". I crossed the road and they walked up one side of the street while I walked up the other, eating my food with utter enjoyment.

The next day, Cecil took me into a tea room and ordered tea and cakes. Those days the cakes were very small, about two inches square, and were served by the dozen on a platter. They were placed in the middle of your table, but one only paid for the cakes that you ate. Cecil got chatting to a gentleman at the next table and I sat quietly, enjoying the tea and cake. When the bloke left, Cecil turned to me and asked, "What do I pay for?"

My simple reply followed. "Two teas and twelve cream cakes."

Cecil's face was a picture. "No ways, Joan. You can go and pay for them. I only ate two and Ethné wasn't old enough to help you."

While we were on holiday, I bought some new clothes, had my hair cut and we attended the theatre a couple of times. In fact, we had a wonderful month, but like all good things, it came to an end and we left the house to board the train. As we passed through customs, I had the comforting feeling of returning home. I realised I loved the Rhodesias as much as Cecil and also realised I had done a lot of growing up in the past two and a half years. I looked across at Cecil. He had put on a little weight since the last bout of malaria had eased off and I also realised how he had matured as well. I felt the love for

72

him flow through my veins, almost a physical pain. I was so proud to walk with this tall, handsome man, bronzed by the African sun, his muscles rippling under his shirt as he moved. His legs were hard and slim from all the miles he walked when hunting. His strength of character reflected in his face very evidently as we walked onto the station.

On our return to Fort Jimmy, I walked into Mandala Stores one day to get some supplies. The fashions I had found in South Africa included a grey plaid coat, cut on military lines and even though our Rhodesian winters rarely called for a coat, I had decided to buy one, simply because I liked it so much. There was a cool breeze that morning and I had decided to put my coat on for the walk. As I opened the door of the shop, I almost bumped into a woman in a coat which was an exact replica of mine. I laughed and said, "Snap".
She laughingly told me that they had just been on holiday and she had fallen in love with this coat. We became friends because of this incident and for many years we kept in touch.

It was on this holiday that I learned just how much integrity Cecil had. I bought some biscuits in a shop and as I walked away I checked my change. To my surprise, I realised that the assistant had given me change for ten pounds, instead of the five pounds I had handed to her. I laughingly turned to Cecil and said "I'm in luck" as I explained. Without any change in his facial expression, he replied "Take it back".
I looked at him and said "You're crazy. This shop can well afford to lose a couple of pounds."
Looking me straight in the eye, he retorted "Yes the shop can, but they won't lose. The poor young lady who served you will have it deducted from her salary. Now take it back!"
I was ashamed that Cecil had found me greedy and untruthful and quietly went back to the woman and handed her the balance of the money. Her appreciation of my gesture was enough to show me that Cecil had been correct in his thinking and never again was I even slightly tempted to keep anything given to me by mistake.

To Cecil there was never a 'grey area'. It was either right or wrong and slowly I realised that he was making me a much better person, through his strict morals. Thanks to Bwana Kakuli, this selfish young woman was becoming far more mature.

CHAPTER SIX

The sounds of the African bush....

It was not long before Cecil started getting malaria again. Every time he went hunting, he got bitten by mosquitoes and within ten days or so, he had malaria. Doctor Taube used to walk in and say, "Hi Joan, where is he?"
I would reply "In the bedroom."
Doctor Taube would walk into the room and say "Hi, Cecil, turn over." Despite the fact that we took Paludrine weekly to ward off the dreaded illness, Cecil was being given such large doses of Mepacrine that he turned yellow. It would result in either an injection in the behind or another stay in hospital. On one occasion, Dr Taube told Cecil that he had to stop getting malaria. "I have buried five people from the village this month with blackwater fever and you are a prime candidate."

Blackwater fever affects the kidneys so badly, the urine looks almost black with blood and the doctor told us that the kidneys go so brittle that they break up if you move the patient. People used to say that if you see someone with blackwater fever, put a tent over him if he's in the rain, but do not move him.

Jacob, our cook, once told me that the finest medicine for it was to boil the beard of the mealie and give the water to the person to drink. Cecil went into hospital many times while we were in Fort Jimmy, but slowly the attacks became less. Nevertheless he had it at least once a year all the years we were in Zambia and suffered mild attacks in South Africa for about three years.

Soon after Jock's death, the African people had started calling Cecil 'Kakuli'. When I asked one of them what it meant, they said when a buffalo bull who is the leader of a herd is challenged by a younger male and is forced out; he walks alone unless he meets another bull chased from another herd in the same manner. Should they meet, they would team up, but mainly they walk alone. They are fearless and are always in command of any situation, just like the Bwana when he is on a hunt. They named my father 'Kalulu'. Again, when I enquired why, they explained that he doesn't like to make decisions when hunting; he always waits, just as a rabbit would, for Kakuli to tell him what to do and when to do it. I never heard them give my brother a name, but if they had, it would have been to explain his cheery attitude to life, because nothing ever got him down. I never saw him get angry during the twenty five years that we lived practically next door to each other. Cecil became renowned as a hunter and, as a result, calls started coming in for him to help various villagers with animals that had become a problem to them.

Mister Gush came to Cecil one day and asked him if he would be prepared to take a great friend of his on a buffalo hunt. He would give Cecil a full week's paid leave to do so, but also warned him that the man lived in a big city and didn't know one end of the gun from the other. Cecil would do all the shooting, but this man wanted to come on holiday to visit Mr Gush and his family and also wanted to be able to tell his friends that he had been on a buffalo hunt.

When they arrived in Fort Jimmy, Mr Gush brought him to the house for a chat. Cecil warned him that there would be no luxuries whatsoever. He would sleep in the bush with a blanket, there were no sleeping bags in those days (if there were, we had never heard of them) and at night he would wear a poncho made from a blanket with a circle cut in the middle to pull over his head, with a draw-cord. He would sleep with mosquito repellent all over him and there were no bathing facilities. He would have to wash in the river, keeping his eyes peeled for crocodiles at the same time. He would eat only from the hunter's pot. This pot was put on an open fire on the day that you arrived and would stay there until the end of the hunt. Meat and liquid was added as required, but the pot never left the boil. I must admit there is no hotel or restaurant that would produce the flavour that comes from that pot after it has been on the fire for a few days. The meat was soft and melted in your mouth. We used to buy tins of dehydrated vegetables, as there was no weight in these tins, only bulk. A tin was added to the meat every day. Coffee was made over the fire and always had a slightly burnt taste.

I often smile when I see some of these game lodges with their fancy bedrooms and vast varieties of food on spotless tablecloths. Those visitors have no idea what a real bush camp is all about. Most of them wouldn't do a day in the camps to which I had become accustomed. The most irritating little flies, called Mopani flies, buzzing around your face all day, sticking to the sweaty skin and crawling into your eyes and nose. Mosquito bites itching incessantly, the heat so bad that you feel light-headed. Make no mistake, after a wash in the icy cold water of the nearest river, you felt so alive and invigorated, you just knew that you were the luckiest person alive. Between the innate beauty of your surroundings, the excitement of what may happen next, the laughter and stories told around the evening campfire and the compelling aroma of the hunter's pot, life in Africa was wonderful. Nestling down in your blanket at night and looking up at the stars, so bright and twinkling, as the moon cast shadows around you, it was a comforting feeling to move just a little closer to Cecil, knowing that he would take care of any situation that arose.

Cecil's new hunting partner eagerly agreed to accompany him on the buffalo hunt and they left for the week. Cecil got a buffalo for him and was ultimately impressed by the fact that he never displayed any fear and did exactly as he was told during the hunt. By the time the hunt was over, he badly needed a shave and a bath, but had followed Cecil's advice to allow his stubble to grow, as it helped to keep the Mopani flies at bay and also protected them to a certain extent from the harsh African sun. When the hunt was over, Cecil dropped him off at Mr Gush's house and then returned home. As he stood in the open doorway, Cecil threw a pile of ten pound notes over his head as I ran to pick them all up with sheer surprise. Cecil said, "There's our next holiday, sweetheart!"

Mr Gush's friend turned out to be a very wealthy man and had insisted on giving Cecil one hundred pounds for his trouble and 'for the best holiday he had experienced in his whole life'.

A new chap arrived in Fort Jimmy to work on some installation and asked Cecil to take him on a buffalo hunt. There would be no money on this trip, all expenses would be shared and as Cecil was due to go on a trip anyway, he agreed to take Tom (not his real name) along with him. When Cecil returned he told me that he had never been as disgusted with a man as he was with Tom. They left camp early one morning with two gun bearers and after walking for quite a while, came across a herd of buffalo which were too far away to get a shot at. Cecil decided to follow the herd as they moved, when he saw a lone buffalo standing in the dambo. As the two men came out from between the trees, the buffalo spotted them and began tossing its head about. Both men were carrying their own guns at the time and the gun bearers were just behind them. Tom, on seeing the buffalo, took a wild shot, causing the buffalo to charge. Tom screamed, dropped his rifle and threw his arms around the nearest tree. One of the gun bearers ran and picked up the rifle, aimed and fired. Cecil also fired as the animal rushed towards them and it kept coming. The gun bearer reloaded the rifle then fired, but was inexperienced and again missed. By this time Tom was still standing on the ground with his arms around the tree. He was actually a sitting target as far as the buffalo was concerned. Cecil fired again and the buffalo fell just a few feet from Tom.

Ten years later we met Tom in a store and he was dressed in a game ranger's uniform. He turned to Cecil and said, "You may think that you are big stuff, but let me catch you poaching and I'll throw the book at you."
Cecil grabbed him by the front of his shirt and said, "Never, ever, has anyone ever seen me poaching. I fire straight enough to get all I need for the pot during the day, so don't you dare stand there and insult me."
I touched Cecil's arm and whispered, "Let's go, love".
We left the store, but Cecil was furious. About a year later we heard that Tom was walking with a friend in the bush and had passed

under a tree where a leopard was resting and it had sprung onto Tom, injuring him quite badly before his companion shot it. This was the last time we ever heard of Tom.

We once decided to go on a fishing trip and set off to a location that we had been told about. There were no roads, only a few tracks here and there. The directions we had been given sounded a bit like 'ride due north for about fifteen miles, turn east for 2 miles, pick up the track again for three miles' and so on. The arrangements were for Charlie, Cecil and me to leave at five in the morning; the rest of the family would follow in Dad's new bakkie, which he had collected the week before from Lusaka.

It was a dreadful trip, taking narrow gaps between trees and driving through deep ruts and dongas. A donga is a deep gully, formed through soil erosion. Charlie shot a porcupine for our lunch, as we had been told they were delicious. The cook, who sat on the back of the bakkie, accompanied us to clean fish, collect firewood and to cook our meals. Once he had cleaned the porcupine, I refused to allow him to cook it, for when I looked down at it, I saw its dear little feet which were nothing less than perfect baby feet. I opened half a dozen tins of salmon and made a fish pie.

When the others arrived, I knew at once that there was trouble. My mom was complaining and shouting at my dad. She had apparently acted as backseat driver throughout the trip, cautioning "Mind that tree", or "Careful, Bill, there's a stump". On one occasion she shouted so loud about a stump, that my dad swerved and hit another, denting the mudguard. Poor Joyce had to listen to them, so she wasn't in a good mood either. As we sat down to eat, Joyce remarked that I had not removed the bones from the salmon and the food was gritty. I got uptight and the evening was spent in silence.

The men fished through half the night, but no fish were caught and early the next morning Cecil and Charlie decided to break up camp and go home, as they were sick to death of the sulking. We packed up and left shortly afterwards. About five miles from camp, a twig got caught under our bakkie and I asked innocently whether it could do any harm. Both men simultaneously retorted "Don't you start!"

After a while the twig loosened itself and fell to the road, but further down the road was a large donga. Cecil applied brakes and, as you can imagine, there were no brakes. The twig had severed the brake pipe and we had lost all our brake fluid. We hit the donga at full steam and everyone collided with the roof of the bakkie. Fortunately no-one was hurt and even if I had been, I wouldn't have told either of those two horrid men. We took most of what was left of our drinking water to replace the water in the radiator, as the cap had come off and we had lost a lot. Cecil also took a chance and put paraffin into the brake cylinder after getting the pipe together again. I don't remember all the details, but the paraffin destroyed all the rubbers in the brake system, which had to be replaced when we got home.

We had one very large hill to descend before getting home and decided to keep our eyes open for a tree with bark that could be stripped into long sections. At the top of the hill we put Cecil's bakkie in front of my dad's and tied them together with bark rope, so that my dad could hold us back by using a low gear and his brakes. Cecil asked us all to leave the vehicles and he and my father slowly began to descend the hill. We agreed to walk down and meet them at the bottom. Ethné began screaming for her father and I realised that she was afraid, seeing her daddy leave us behind. As they reached the half-way mark, the rope snapped and Cecil was on his own. The vehicle picked up speed swiftly, careening down the hill at a frightening speed. I felt I was about to have a nervous breakdown, but Cecil managed to slide the bakkie sideways against a tree. By now, I'd had all I could take and I took Ethné, who was still screaming, and gave her a good spanking. My mother turned to Joyce and said, "It's a pity that the best behaved child always gets the hiding."

"Oh!" Joyce cried out indignantly. "You mean you want me to give my children a hiding too?" She grabbed each child and smacked them hard.

Eventually there we stood; three fuming women and three little mites, bawling their eyes out.

When we reached the bottom of the hill, we found that a small stump next to the tree had punctured our tyre. Joyce, trying to heal the rift, said, "We'll go on home and get supper ready, as you'll be quite late after getting this mess sorted out."

"No ways!" shouted my mom. "Why should you cook for everyone?"

My dad, not saying a word, got into the bakkie and they drove off. Expecting to see the men fix the puncture, you can imagine my surprise when they took a blanket and pillows from the bakkie and lay down under a tree. I dared to ask what they were doing and their reply was "Don't start again, we're sick of all this and are going to just lie here for the rest of the afternoon and enjoy the peace and quiet."

Much later, they fixed the tyre and we limped home. I suppose, looking back after all these years, a good time was had by all!

It was through these fishing and hunting trips that I learnt to appreciate the sounds of the bush. During the day one heard birds and the odd animal, but usually due to the intense heat, most animals were silent and resting. However at dusk one would hear many species of bird calls as they settled down for the night, or the snort of the hippopotamus from the river. As dusk turned to night, one would hear the roar of a lion in the distance. This sound could take up to a couple of minutes, as it sounded with a full blast and gradually faded to a loud grunting sound. Later, when the camp was quiet, the hyenas would approach and stand under the elevated, dripping biltong and they would whoop and laugh as the blood fell onto their noses. One would hear baboons barking far away and then an owl would hoot from above as it waited patiently for an unsuspecting rodent. On a few very lucky occasions we heard the cough of a leopard as he walked past our camp and even the short little barks of various antelope from a nearby herd. There would be a flurry of wings as a Nightjar flew overhead and occasionally we would hear the soft peep-peep, a sound we could never identify, until one of our gun-bearers said that it was the call of the python. Whether this was accurate or not, I do not know. The incessant buzzing of insects and croaking of bullfrogs filled the night air.

With the dry weather and the heat at its fiercest, we started getting electrical storms. They were the most frightening phenomena I have ever seen or heard. I know very little about them because I was usually under the bed or on top of the bed with my head buried under a pillow. Cecil used to try and get me to watch them, especially at night, saying that they were so beautiful, but the sight of the lightning flashes and the deafening thunder would send me diving for cover.

There were many times that we would get together as a family and we had so much fun. Joyce and I would do all the things that young people do; we tried to diet on Paw-Paw until we couldn't even look at one anymore. Not that we were terribly overweight; we both carried about three kilograms above our normal weight. Ethné was going on two years old, Cynthia almost the same age and Patrick about four. Like all other children, they would play together and then fight. Joyce and I got on so well and I really learned to love her like a sister. I think this time was the happiest for us as a family.

One Sunday morning Cecil and Ethné were sitting on the veranda, when I heard Cecil say in a very stern voice "Ethné, come here at once!"
I heard her ask why and he replied, "Do you want a hiding? Come here." I ran out to see what the problem was and Cecil told me to 'stay out of it'. My heart froze when I looked up and saw Ethné standing near the wall of the veranda, which reached just above her head. On the wall directly above her was a horrible, enormous snake, reared up and weaving its head from side to side, preparing to strike. She slowly walked towards Cecil and what took only a few seconds, seemed an eternity until she had reached a safe distance. Her eyes filled with tears, she went to Cecil and asked, "What did I do, daddy?"
Cecil pulled her to him, hugging her tightly and answered, "Nothing, sweetheart, I'm sorry I shouted at you, I just wanted to give you a big bear hug".
Passing her to me, Cecil immediately killed the snake to avoid any further danger to Ethné.

Joyce came over one morning and said to Cecil "One in the morning is not the time to come over to our home and play games."
Cecil looked puzzled and said, "I have no idea what you are talking about."
Joyce, looking quite angry, replied "Oh yes, you do, you came around the house whooping like a hyena and woke us up."
Cecil denied any involvement and offered to go and investigate. As he walked around their house, he found the spoor of a large hyena, which once again reminded us that we were living with dangerous animals all around us, particularly where the children were concerned.

We were watching the children play at the back of the house one day and Joyce noticed a huge baboon sitting on a rock a little way up the hill behind the houses. As she pointed it out to me, Patrick commented "Oh yes, mummy, he always sits and watches us play."
From then on we kept the children at the front, as we were afraid it might come down and attack them.

On another occasion, Cynthia was standing next to a big tree and noticed a hole in the trunk, so stuck her finger in it. She suddenly screamed and when she pulled her finger out, she had two little puncture wounds on the end of it. Joyce and I pulled the bark away to investigate and found a spider. A few minutes later she was playing again and no harm came to her from that bite.

It was getting close to November and the Indian shops got in a stock of fireworks. Cecil and Charlie were like a pair of kids, choosing a selection, including rockets. The womenfolk, being more practical, started baking as we decided to have tea and eats after the fireworks display. The men had an absolute ball as they started a war with the fireworks and the children's' peals of laughter filled the air. There were fortunately no neighbours to worry about, so everyone thoroughly enjoyed themselves and made as much noise as they liked. After the display, we all went into the lounge to have our tea. On the wall was a black beetle; with a horny back and it had two pincers on the front of its face. Mom and dad were there and mom had brought Micky with her. He ran up to the beetle, attempting to sniff it. The pincers suddenly shot out and Micky yelped loudly. He was bleeding profusely and a small piece of flesh was gone off his nose. Enraged by this incident, Micky jumped up and grabbed the beetle, tossing it among us. There were six adults and three children, all standing around and the ensuing stampede, with all of us trying to get out of the doorway, must have been a picture. Eventually Cecil picked up the beetle, using a piece of cardboard and threw it out the front door. We were all shouting at him to kill it, but he said "What for? It won't bother you if you leave it alone."

Mr Gush had a very dear friend; I will call her Sally, because if her relatives read this book and recognise her identity, they may be shocked at this story, so a pseudonym is essential here. Sally asked Mr Gush to allow someone from the firm to do some repairs to her buildings and he asked Cecil to oblige. Cecil took along two labourers to do the manual work and it was during this period that I met Sally. We became friends, but after the repairs were completed, she found every excuse to get Cecil out to the farm. She would phone Mr Gush, saying, "I need a few groceries and Cecil lives on the road to the farm, won't you let him bring them for me after work?"
She appeared to be quite wealthy. She was a beautiful woman for her age and her manners and speech were impeccable. She exuded confidence and was very persuasive with her requests. I would estimate her age at about thirty five to forty at that time.

Cecil would often get back home late at night and say "I've already had dinner; Sally cooked a steak and kidney pie especially for me, so how could I refuse?"
Another ruse was to ask Cecil to join her for a sun-downer and then announce that her cook had already dished up dinner. Cecil always argued that it placed him in an awkward position, as she was a close friend of Mr Gush. Deep down, however, I knew that she was attracted to Cecil, but had no idea how to handle the situation.

Christmas was coming and Cecil suggested that we invite Sally and her mom to join us for Christmas lunch. I went to a lot of trouble to impress her with whatever I could buy locally. As a starter I used tinned asparagus and naturally, the main course was venison, cooked until it was so tender that it fell from the bone. Dehydrated vegetables had to do, but I did my utmost to ensure that the meal was enjoyable. I had jellies, home-made tarts and a lovely bunch of grapes, which Cecil had brought home. I might mention here that these grapes later cost us a whole twelve pounds, as they were imported from South Africa. When Cecil had selected them at the shop, the shopkeeper warned us that they weren't going to be cheap, he did not have the prices yet, but we could settle with him later. I was eternally grateful for my Dover stove, because it cooked like a dream and I was truly proud of my efforts.

I still had no servant and worked really hard that day. There was all the washing up to be done after the baking and food preparation, but I planned well ahead and managed just fine. I set the table with a bowl of flame lilies in the centre and serviettes I had made in Christmas colours. Sally and her mom arrived at eleven thirty and we sat down with a drink to chat awhile before lunch, when disaster struck. We had only had a couple of showers until then, but the first real downpour started and the thatch roof began to leak. I watched dirty water dripping onto all the crockery on the table and then, much to my horror, all over my guests. I was so embarrassed, but give them their due; they took it in good part. All the food was spoiled and the only place not leaking was a part of the bedroom, so we dragged the bed under the dry thatch. We all sat there, laughing and joking, making the best of a bad situation. This, however, was a perfect opening for Sally, who commented, "You cannot live like this. There is a cottage on my farm and you must move in there as soon as possible."
The arrangements were made that we would move in the early January.

It then became easy for Sally to keep phoning Mr Gush to send this or that with Cecil and she always found something for him to do over weekends, particularly to help her pay the wages to her staff. She always told me not to come, but to rather look after my two year old. She got into the habit of popping in to the cottage to see me and would often lift the lids off my cooking pots, saying, "You really must learn to cook. I've got this or that for dinner tonight; so when

Cecil brings my supplies, I will feed him, because he loves the way Cook does my dinners." Never once did she invite me to join them. It was raining one morning and I suggested to Ethné "Let's go and play in the mud puddles". Ethné really loved every minute of it and we were both wet, full of mud and giggling together happily when Sally appeared. "You know, you are far too young to be married to Cecil."

"I'm nearly twenty three" I retorted indignantly.

"You may be that in years, but you're only ten in your ways".

That was an instant goodbye to my confidence yet once again.

One morning I woke up feeling ill and the heat was affecting me terribly. Sally popped in, took one look at me and declared "You have malaria. Your temperature is very high. I'll get my spare bedroom ready for you, no-one will bother you there and Cecil can come up for all his meals."

Very sweetly, I replied, "No thank you, I am going to hospital."

Sally phoned Mr Gush and asked him to send Cecil home and he tried very hard to get me to agree to move into Sally's house. Eventually I lost my temper and said, "You're always up there anyway. If you are so keen to go to the big house, you move in. I am going to hospital."

He told me not to be so stupid, but did agree to take me to hospital.

The doctor pumped me full of Mepacrine and I developed Mepacrine poisoning. Cecil sat at the hospital until I was out of danger, then the staff put me on Quinine, which was the old-fashioned remedy. This medication left me stone-deaf for a full week. I don't understand why I had such a nasty reaction to the Mepacrine, because I'd had Malaria before and that same drug had done the trick.

When I was well enough to leave the hospital, Cecil drove into Escape Estate's entrance and I thought we were going to visit my mom or Joyce. As he stopped the car in front of our home, he announced, "I have brought all our stuff back from Sally's farm." Then, very gently, he added, "When will you realise that I'm not interested in anyone else? I love you and you alone."

While living on Sally's farm, two incidents remain in my mind. The first one is when she gave Cecil a pig to slaughter and cut up and told him to take half. After slaughtering the animal, Cecil realised that it had measles and one dare not eat this meat, as it is actually tapeworm egg, so we were always told. When Cecil told Sally, she retorted, "Nonsense, of course you can eat it."
Needless to say, we gave our half away and Cecil said, "I'm not eating at Sally's for at least three months".

On pay day for the farm workers, Cecil went to help her and it was getting quite late. I went to the shed where they were busy and I could see that Sally was really tired. I offered to prepare food for them both, but she said "Don't worry, Cook will have done something. Go up to the house and tell him to bring it down to the cottage."
To my horror, when I reached the kitchen, there stood a serving dish of the measled pork, with a salad he had made with vegetables from the garden and buttered slices of bread. Cook took the food to the cottage, but at the table, Cecil buried his pork under his salad and announced politely that he wasn't very hungry. That left me to eat with a smile and a silent prayer that it was well cooked!

The other incident that comes to mind happened just after the Christmas fiasco. We were getting ready to move into the cottage and I was invited with Cecil to dinner at Sally's. I believe this is the one and only time I was ever included in the invitations. When we arrived, Sally was shouting at Cook. He had dropped the glass lid of her casserole and broken it. He was truly afraid, with the way she was carrying on and eventually she asked, "How in blazes did you do it?"
Cook was terrified by now! He took the tea towel in his hand and said "Like this, Dona" and he promptly knocked the casserole off the table as he gestured with his hands. What a mess!

A few months later Sally decided to sell the farm and take her mother and child, who had been in boarding school, over to Australia. She phoned Cecil at work and asked him to pop over to see her. On his arrival, she offered him half the proceeds from the sale of the farm if he would go with her to Australia. When he came home and told me, I knew that all my suspicions had been correct and she had always had her eye on him. I said to Cecil "You'll be rich if you go with her. Don't let me keep you!"

"Do you think that money could take the place of you and my daughter?" he asked, although this did little to restore my confidence in myself.

CHAPTER SEVEN

Braving Muchacha....

Charlie was, by this time, as keen on hunting as dad and Cecil were. I noticed around this time how Cecil was changing. His walk displayed self-assurance and even after more bouts of malaria, his physique was still strong and muscled. His face was the same firm face of a man accustomed to making decisions. Everyone, man and woman alike, looked up at Cecil with respect and always asked his advice on decisions to be made. Even my father relied heavily on him in this regard.

The Government brought out a new law. 'One may not shoot in the Luangwa, unless you own a farm there'. So, we put feelers out and one day Dad came over and said, "I have heard of a farm called 'Muchacha', which is available for leasing for two years. Why don't we go and have a look at it this weekend?"
It was right in the middle of the Luangwa and on the farm was a derelict double-story house. Sections of the building were not safe to go into, but as we only wanted the farm as a 'shooting box' for weekends, the conditions didn't bother us at all.

We had taken two tents with us and moving about two miles away from the existing house, we pitched the tents in the late afternoon. The three men decided to try and shoot something for the pot, because the first thing we always did was prepare the hunter's pot. How does one describe the firelight providing light to the tents, the utter blackness of the night, with hundreds of silvery stars twinkling overhead and every so often a pair of eyes shining back at you from the dark bush? It is also difficult to explain the feeling of excitement that runs through you in the bush and the exhilaration of being alive when you stand up in the early morning and the cool breeze blows on your face. The sun has not yet risen to bring the intense heat of the day. Oh Rhodesia, I loved you and I do miss you so.

It was getting dark and the womenfolk decided to go into the tents. Joyce occupied one with her two children and mom, Ethné and I went into the other. The men were to sleep around the fire in the open air. We had only been inside for about half an hour when the most dreadful smell permeated the canvas of our tents and Joyce called to me "Joan, do you smell it too?"

I acknowledged her question with a simple "Yes, we will have to get the men to move our tents tomorrow; there must be something dead and decaying around here."

With that, we heard the men approaching and Cecil shouted "What the hell?"

A strong rustling sound ensued and we all flew out of the tents to see what was happening. Cecil reached us and explained that as they came into the firelight, he saw a huge male lion standing between the tents and, on seeing the men, it had fled into the bush. This is obviously what we had smelled from the tents, as the lions have a dreadful stench about them.

Every weekend thereafter we set off to Muchacha on hunting expeditions. By this time Cecil had four rifles; his Point Two-Two, a Rigby, a Nine-millimetre Mouser and a shotgun, but he loved his Rigby and wouldn't have changed it for a bigger or smaller calibre. He swore that there was nothing to touch it for buffalo. Considering the amount of buffalo he shot, it certainly met his requirements. We decided to lease the farm for two years and spent all our spare time there. They were happy times and a lot of laughter and contentment was shared. Charlie and Joyce had by this time become true Rhodesians with the kind of attitude towards life that Rhodesians typically have.

Jock had once said to Cecil "If you are in the Luangwa, watch out for 'buffalo bean'. When it gets you, you will itch so much you'll think you're losing your mind. The only thing that helps a little is mud, so plaster yourself with it if you possibly can."

So, needless to say, we eventually found ourselves among the buffalo bean. It is a glorious creeper with brilliant red flowers, but when the flowers dry, they turn into pods covered with fine hairs, which blow about in the wind. If you sit on the ground and the wind has carried the hairs in that direction, your legs and buttocks start itching terribly wherever the hairs have touched your skin. Unfortunately, if you scratch, the hairs go under your nails and in turn onto whichever part of your body you touch thereafter. Poor Ethné was nearly three when she sat on one of the pods and although we rubbed her from head to toe with mud, she cried for ages and seemed to itch all over. Cecil said that one of his life's ambitions was to get a bag of buffalo bean hairs and throw them into the ceiling fan at a New Year's party. He thought it might be fun to watch people's reactions as they were dancing!

Dad and Cecil went out one afternoon to hunt and after walking for about an hour without sighting any game, my dad said he would head back to camp, so they parted company. Cecil arrived back in camp at about four-thirty with a warthog, which is the nicest tasting venison of all, in my opinion. Dad was still not back and by five thirty, Cecil and Charlie were getting ready to go and search for him, when he walked into camp, looking tired, sore and very shaken. It seems he came across two lions and instead of giving them a wide berth, he decided to photograph them. He put his rifle down and got out his camera. The one lion spotted him and jumped up. Dad dropped his camera, but before he could pick up the rifle, the lion charged at him. He climbed into the tree that he was standing near and thankfully, the lion never followed. I suspect the pair were ready for mating, as the female came over and they both lay down under the tree next to dad's rifle and camera. They lay there for nearly two hours, before wandering off into the bush. For a long time, dad was too afraid to get down, in case they were still close by, but eventually he summoned the courage and was quite relieved when he had his rifle in his hand again and was able to head back to camp.

I have always been sorry that we never owned a decent camera during those years. The only one we had was a little old-fashioned box camera that Charlie had given me for my sixteenth birthday. We could have had some fantastic photographs documenting our experiences, as we were seeing nature in every form, from the exquisite scenery to close-ups of all the animals.

The roads in Fort Jimmy were bad enough, but when you left the little town the roads were terrible and during the rains, they were almost impassable. After one hunting trip to Muchacha we were returning home when dad's bakkie skidded and slid into a bank. The three men were in the cab and the womenfolk and children were on the back. I was perched right at the rear end of the bakkie with Ethné on my lap. It was just going dark and the engine had stalled, so Cecil was trying to start it. On the top of the bank where we were stuck appeared what looked like shiny headlights. It turned out to be four lions, their eyes shining in the reflection of the headlights. They walked a little way along the top of the bank and then dropped onto the road, walking straight towards us. The one male was enormous and bearing in mind that we had no canopy on the bakkie, I was too afraid to even turn around to do or to say anything to the men in the front. In fact, I was in a state of shock, as was my mother and Joyce. I now realise the meaning of the phrase 'paralysed with fear'. The perspiration trickles off your body, but you shiver with cold as you look into those enormous yellow eyes. The lion lifted his head to peer into the back and as he did so, the engine roared to life and Cecil pulled away. We were all very preoccupied and hardly spoke on the way home. Believe it or not, the men were angry with us for not telling them about the lions, but I assured them that if I had the urge to use my mouth at that moment, it would have been to scream my head off.

We often got stuck in the mud and a lot of the roads, especially where there was any form of bridge, were laid with a type of bamboo mat. This bamboo often rolled up under the vehicle and you had to get out in the pouring rain to remove it. One always travelled with food and water, just in case of delays and I usually had a spare set of clothes for everyone. Our water was carried in canvas water bags on the side of the vehicle and what nectar it was to drink; usually ice cold, just when you needed it. Sometimes one could sit all night stuck in the mud and when daylight came either a villager saw you needed assistance, or you went to look for them. Somehow this was all fun, because I always knew that Cecil would get the vehicle running again, even when it was engine trouble. I believe it was my trust and faith in him that helped me overcome the difficulties and dangers we encountered.

On one of our weekends in the valley, Cecil and I took one of these leisurely walks from our camp and returned to find my dad in an absolute state of frustration and anger. We had been in camp for four days with not one sighting of a buffalo and while we were away, dad saw a buffalo herd grazing not far from the camp. Needless to say, all my father could think was 'where the hell is Cecil now?' as he paced up and down the campsite.

While out walking the monkeys flit playfully from branch to branch in the trees overhead, chattering incessantly. The baboons watch from a distance, but I didn't trust them and always kept as far as possible away from them. Occasionally a huge stick insect, which is only visible in the bush when he moves, would draw your attention. They resemble whatever branch or stick they are resting on and always fascinated me. It was the dung beetle, however, that got my vote as being the funniest creature of all, rolling their ball of dung all the way to the top of the little hill, only to have it roll all the way back down, the beetle following most inelegantly behind it.

For a few months we enjoyed just hunting at Muchacha, until once again, the government passed another law, this time forbidding shooting in Luangwa unless you owned a 'working' farm there. So, we decided that each family would do six months on the farm working and the others would drive there for weekends. This was not a venture to make money; it was purely for the men's pleasure. My dad could not go down at that time and both Charlie and Cecil were extremely busy at Fort Jimmy Milling Company, so my mother offered to go alone. I looked at my mother with renewed respect. I had no idea she had so much courage. She had never learned to shoot; in fact not one of the three of us women ever handled rifles with the purpose of learning. Now she was going on a venture to start and run something she had never done before, she was going to start the seed beds for tobacco and apart from weekends, she would be entirely alone.

The nearest neighbour was seventeen miles away and we didn't even know their name. In the rainy season one couldn't travel on the track that was the only link between the two farms anyway. Mom insisted on taking Micky with her for company. He had been lucky enough to survive three years in Fort Jimmy, but that was mainly because he never left my mom's side, so was indoors most of the time. We tried to persuade her not to take him along, but our pleas fell on deaf ears. The following weekend we arrived at Muchacha and everyone got stuck in, making the house more habitable. Downstairs was kept as a grading shed for when the tobacco was ready. Upstairs, we fixed up one bedroom and another room to use as a living and dining area. Lastly, one small room was made into a bathroom. Right along the front of the house was a long, narrow stretch of veranda. Once again a tin bath was bought and a Rhodesian Boiler was built outside for hot water. This was a forty-five gallon drum, lying on its side, with a tap in it, built on a ramp. A fire was lit underneath the boiler and you had hot water all day. I often sympathised with the poor labourer who had to carry buckets of hot water upstairs to fill the bath every day.

The thatch on the roof was so thin that you could lie in bed at night and count the stars. They brought down a bed and items such as pots, pans, etcetera and, naturally, the paraffin boxes for furniture. At last it was time to leave and mom stood there, a proud, determined woman. No sign of fear on her face, she bade us farewell, waved and walked back over the dry river bed to the derelict house. She seemed so tiny and vulnerable and I have often wondered just how afraid she really was. It was about three weeks after she began seeding the beds that I decided to do down and spend a week with her.

We left the following Friday evening after work and all headed for Muchacha. My mom had everything running quite smoothly and I have often wondered why she never had the staff problems that I encountered later on. I somehow think that her age and strength of character made her something special with the staff. She never joked with them or smiled at them and while I was there, she actually went at the cook with fists flying when she caught him having a wash in our washing up bowl, using the tea towel to dry himself.

On the Monday Mom was in tears. We had walked to one of the fields she was having cleared to plant more tobacco, when Micky ran into the bush and never came out. We called to him for ages and walked a short distance looking for him, but to no avail. That night, she said to cook "Please go and fetch six labourers to help us look for Micky".
Looking at me, she said "Ethné is asleep, she'll be alright, please come with me."

Well, all the staff had the mutters, they were not happy about being out of their huts after dark. We lit three pressure lamps and set off into the darkness. All I could think of was the wild animals around us. The labourers lit a fire and left it burning not far from the house and we began to walk in the direction where Micky had disappeared. Not too far along was the dry river bed and as I looked down, I saw so many animal spoors that they gave me the shivers. Most of them were padded spoor and I said, "I'm not looking for trouble, I'm going back. We don't have a rifle with us and if we had, neither of us could shoot accurately anyway."
The labourers were having a field day. Dozens of rats were running around in the lamp light and they were catching them, holding them by their tails. I watched a little later, as they held them over the fire to burn all the fur off and then eat them, not even half cooked. We never saw Micky again and I'm certain he became dinner for a hungry leopard.

A couple of weeks later we were given a big dog by a local farmer and we took him down to mom. The following week she related how she had opened the back door in the late afternoon to call him inside, when a leopard jumped out of the bush and took him off the step, dragging him back into the bush. My mother was furious to say the least. She took one of the rifles the men had left at Muchacha ready for the following weekend and went in search of the leopard. As our cook said later, "The dona is penga!" meaning 'the madam is mad'.

95

She had only returned to the house at eight that night, because the batteries in her torch had failed. I realised that mom had a lot faults, but she certainly wasn't short on courage. At that time she must have been about sixty two years old.

At last her six months were up and it was time for Cecil and me to do our stint and Mr Gush was quite agreeable for us to be away for six months. All the tobacco was well established and some was even ready for picking and placing into covered shelters to dry out. One of Cecil's first jobs was to erect the shelters with thatched roofs and slowly the tobacco was picked and stored. To assist the labourers, Cecil built a cart on which the tobacco could be loaded and pulled along. We also started clearing the downstairs rooms of the house for grading purposes. In the one room was a lino square floor and it was in this room that Cecil put his favourite buffalo head. He had shot it some time before and Norman Carr had said that he considered it a record as far as the horns were concerned. I cannot remember today what the actual measurements were, but the length was only one inch under the record and the width of the bosch was nearly double the size of the record head. Cecil tried desperately hard to bring his trophy to South Africa when we left Zambia, but it was confiscated at the border post. Nevertheless, it was his pride and joy for many years.

One night we woke up to the most fearful noise and rushed downstairs to see what was happening. A hyena had come through an opening that had once been a window and was slipping and sliding all over the smooth lino floor, making a terrible commotion in the process. He had the buffalo head in his mouth and was attempting to drag it away, but had no control over his feet. Eventually his fear got the better of him and he dropped the head and scrambled back through the opening, disappearing into the night. Cecil ran over to his trophy to check it, leaving me shaking with shock and surprise.

Sometimes at night the lions would sit outside the front of the house, roaring and often fighting and it was at these times that I would snuggle up to Cecil, thanking the Lord for the strength I felt next to me, even though he was fast asleep. They obviously didn't bother him in the least. We were in the mid dry season and, because of the thatch roof over the bedroom being so thin; all the beams became a hanging space for bats. They were big and had faces similar to bull terriers, but I was terrified of them and really hated going into the room. I usually did this at a full run and dived under the mosquito net for safety. I would sit there, working on my embroidery, while Ethné sat on the bed and played with her toys. I noticed that one bat in particular seemed strangely fascinated by me. Although the remaining bats would only fly in the day if we disturbed them, this bat only had to see me and he would dive straight at me. I would either run back out of the room or head for my mosquito net, whichever was closest at the time and it would flutter against the net, trying to get under it. I used to get the shudders just looking at it, so after a while I asked Cecil to bring some of the staff from the drying shed to kill it. He asked me how they could pick one out of dozens hanging on the beam, but I laughingly assured him that if I walked into the room, it would identify itself quite happily.

One of the staff got a lucky shot in and the bat lay on the floor. He called me over and said "Dona, why are you so afraid of them; come and see, they cannot harm you."
I leaned over the bat and thought 'you have such a pretty face, but I am still terrified of you'. Suddenly the bat opened its eyes and as I jumped back, it fluttered its wings and lifted from the ground in my direction. No-one was close enough to hit it, so I turned and ran as fast as I could along the narrow veranda, the bat following in close proximity. I reached the end of the veranda and stood, facing the wall, screaming as the horrid creature clung to my skirt. One of the labourers ran up, knocked it to the floor and killed it. This encounter has left me with the most dreadful fear of them and I cannot begin to describe the terror I felt as it hung on my skirt. Even the picture of a bat today makes me shudder.

In the first few weeks at Muchacha I spent many hours walking with Cecil in the bush, with Ethné safely at home with the wife of Jacob, our cook. I must say it is a very unique experience to walk in the Luangwa valley. You never know what animal may be behind the next bush or tree. The sky is the most exquisite blue, the white billowy clouds scuttling past, creating such a sense of peace and tranquillity. The birds seem to be calling everywhere and one of the strangest calls I ever heard was from what is referred to as the Litany bird. The Africans say it is mourning its parents and the call says, "My mother is dead, my father is dead and I am alone."

The sound is so mournful and quite eerie. Along the banks of the river there were hundreds of nesting holes with birds flying in and out, their shrill calls filling the air. A Bromvoël, (a turkey buzzard) with his large beak, black-feathered body and bright red head, would call out now and then as he strutted along the dry ground, showing off. They have the longest eye lashes I have ever seen and seem to flutter them flirtingly as they look at you.

We were amazed at how much hard work my mother had done during her six months. Cecil made a few tables from raw timber for the grading of the tobacco and the labourers busied themselves with this arduous task. One morning a labourer shouted "Bwana, nyoka!" Cecil, knowing that this meant that there was a snake in the room, ran in to assist the labourer, who by that time was so excited and attempting to kill the serpent with a spade. In his frantic efforts, he accidentally scooped the snake up with the spade and threw it, the ugly creature going head first down Cecil's gumboot! Without any hesitation, Cecil grabbed the snake's tail and yanked it out, flinging it a good distance from them. It was a cobra and I shudder to think how close he came to being bitten, I even think Cecil was shocked. He was fortunate in the fact that he was so good at hiding his emotions, so I never knew whether he had been afraid or not.

Whilst repairing one of the roofs on the drying shed the next day, Cecil saw five snakes slither past him and warned me to keep my eyes open at all times. The heat was so appalling and it was bringing the snakes out into the open. A few days later Cecil took about six labourers and his cart to fetch firewood for the house and labourers quarters. He returned from the first trip, saying, "I have just seen the biggest snake I've ever laid eyes on. It disappeared down a hole, but if I see it on the next trip I'm going to kill it, as it is close to where the workers' wives walk daily."

On the next trip he kept an eye out for the snake and sure enough, it came slithering out of its hole and Cecil shot it. One of the madalas approached him and said "Oh, bwana, this is very bad. This snake is an evil snake and bad things are going to happen now because, when you kill it, it leaves a curse on you and all those who allowed you to kill it."

Cecil laughed at the superstitious ramblings of this old man, but soon after, one of our labourers, who had been with them that day, hanged himself from a tree not far from the house. One weekend, while the family were there, another was bitten by a snake, but thankfully survived, because Cecil rushed him to Fort Jimmy for medical attention. One of the wives of a labourer lost her baby through a nasty fall and Cecil received news that his father had been badly injured in an accident. It makes one wonder if the African people's beliefs are just simple superstition after all.

The man who was bitten by the snake lay in the back of the bakkie while a couple of extra folk had climbed on to care for him on the journey to Fort Jimmy hospital. Half way to Fort Jimmy the one man called to Cecil and said "It's alright, bwana, this man will live now. We have managed to get the snake's teeth out of the wound."

Heedless of this remark, Cecil still took him to the hospital, to ensure that he would be alright. To this day, we never managed to get the man to explain clearly what he had meant by his description of snake's teeth in the wound. We lost another labourer to a Black Mamba and when Jacob described the size of the snake, I said "Mabodza", meaning 'liar'. He went off into the bush and returned with a dead snake that was the size of a python, at least ten feet long and as thick as my arm.

My dad arrived the following weekend and brought the telegram advising us of my father in law's accident. He was the Senior Carriage and Wagon Examiner on the South African Railways and was found unconscious next to the train with head injuries, but no-one knew how he had been hurt. The telegram asked that Cecil go to him immediately, but my father objected, saying, "Cecil, neither Charlie nor I can take time off at the moment to run the farm, you can't go."

Knowing how badly Cecil needed to see his dad, I quietly said "It's okay, I can manage on my own."

My mom turned on me and declared, "You'll never do it."

I looked straight at her and answered firmly "You did. Why wouldn't I?"

I must admit my heart was beating madly in my chest with trepidation, but my pride would never have allowed me to show it. It was agreed that I would run Muchacha while Cecil went to South Africa. Cecil summoned our kapito, Abason Banda, to the house. When he arrived, Cecil took his hunting knife from his belt and threw it, pegging it into the door and said, "If anything happens to the Dona or the little one while I am away, I will come back and cut your heart out with that knife".

These dramatics were more symbolic than a threat to the kapito's life, and he knew it. I quickly packed Cecil's clothes and within a couple of hours, I stood alone as the family got into the bakkie and drove off. As I watched the lights disappear into the distant bush, I have never been so afraid in my entire life. I knew my nearest neighbour was seventeen miles away and didn't even know their names. I had no vehicle, no telephone or even radio contact in case of an emergency. I was alone in the wildest of the African bush and it felt like the entire world was perched on my shoulders. I stood thinking for a moment and then dismissed the kapito, telling him to return to his family.

"But the Bwana said I must sleep here."

I cut him short with as much authority as I could muster. "Never mind what the bwana said, I am telling you to go."

I felt it was safer to be alone behind locked doors than have someone there who could open the doors to others if he wished, while I slept. He reluctantly left the house and I locked the door. I looked up at Cecil's knife in the door and thought, "Dear Lord, I hope he never needs it for that purpose."

At that, I felt ashamed. How on earth had my mother felt when she stayed here alone and she did a full six months, against a possible couple of weeks that lay ahead of me. I went upstairs and crept into bed next to my precious, little Ethné.

Early next morning I went downstairs and saw Abason standing with all the labourers on the front lawn. I pointed to five or six of them and instructed them to go to number nine field to gather tobacco for grading and then to another couple to fetch twine and bind the bundles ready for drying. I told the remainder to go to the drying sheds and rack the bundles. A bundle had to be tied at each end of a piece of string and then slung over a rod to dry. We were not experienced tobacco farmers and there were probably far more effective way of doing things, but we tried hard without any advice. All the staff just stood and looked at me, unmoving. I asked Abason what the problem was and he said, "In our culture a woman does not tell a man what to do, they will not listen to you".

I ordered him to tell them what to do and he replied, "I also do not take orders from a woman."

I realised I had a major dilemma. Turning on my heels, I marched upstairs and quickly devised a plan. I put on Cecil's clothing, including his hat and picked up the hippo hide sjambok. This is a short whip and Cecil often carried it as a form of protection against the odd snake.

Returning to the staff downstairs, I treated them like a group of children. Gesturing to the pants I wore, I asked them "Whose pants are these?"

"The Bwana's."

"Whose shirt is this?"

"The Bwana's."

And so I went on, down to the boots and up to the hat. Finally I reached the sjambok and to each question, they acknowledged the fact that I was in the Bwana's clothing, my bravado increasing with each acknowledgement.

"Yes, this is the bwana's sjambok and if I have to use it, I will. When I wear the bwana's clothes, I am the bwana."

Amazingly, I had no further trouble. Each man nodded his acceptance in the matter, turned and walked in the direction of wherever he had been instructed to go and work and I silently breathed the biggest sigh of relief.

Needless to say, it was just one of many tests I endured in Cecil's absence. I had another idea, which I felt was a very wise one at the time. I wanted to build a bridge across the dry river bed so that we didn't always have to leave our vehicles on the opposite side. I was so proud of the completed bridge, but when the rains came, my bridge floated down the newly filled river, leaving only a memory of all the hard work we had put into it.

I was awoken a couple of days after Cecil left with Abason calling to me at about four in the morning. He shouted up "There are elephants in the tobacco at field number nine. The bwana would come and shoot them."
My only excuse not to go myself was that I could not leave Ethné, but to be honest, I didn't even know how to load Cecil's rifle, let alone shoot it. I told Abason I had seen the labourers hitting paraffin tins to scare the elephants away and they should do the same. When Cecil returned, I tried to learn to shoot and I aimed at a large bird on a branch, squeezing the trigger gently as he had shown me. The shot went off and my target flew away minus one leg, much to my absolute horror and shame. After that incident, I never looked at a rifle again and had no intention of ever using one.

One of our labourers' wives was such a sweet person and never passed our house without chatting to Ethné, who always sat on the big step at the back door. The woman was always accompanied by a young girl of about seventeen, who was tall and slim, with the most beautiful soulful brown eyes, the kind that smile at you warmly. I was very fond of them both and got to know them well. I wanted to go to field number six to check how far the labourers were with picking and Jacob perched Ethné on his shoulders and walked with me. We had no form of protection whatsoever, but did the journey without incident. The very next day, the young seventeen year old girl walked that same route and came face to face with a lion. No-one knows exactly what happened, but she did not survive the savage attack, which was just another reminder of the dangers that lurked around us.

While I acted as the bwana many incidents come to mind all these years later. One night Jacob had an argument with his wife and I heard him beating her. I put my head out of the window and shouted "Jacob, what's going on?"

Jacob, startled, but very quick-thinking, grabbed his wife and pulled her towards him, "Nothing, Dona, we are just dancing."
As he pranced her around the dusty ground, I could not help but laugh at the sight.

One day two policemen approached the house and asked if they could come in. I asked Jacob to make tea and invited them into the living area. They had mistakenly come to our farm, but were actually meant to be at our neighbour's farm, which was seventeen miles away.
"We are investigating a case of cannibalism." The one policeman explained. "It seems that a villager on the farm has murdered another in a drunken brawl and the villagers have eaten him."
They drank their tea, thanked me and left to continue their investigation. I never heard the outcome of this case, but it made me realise just how primitive an area I was alone in at the time.

Just before Cecil returned, one of the labourers came running towards me, gesturing and shouting urgently "Dona, get the little one."
I ran and scooped Ethné up into my arms from where she had been playing on the ground and looked back at the old man as he pointed. Across the clearing around the house stood a male lion under a tree, his tawny eyes fixed on Ethné as I held her in my arms. The reality of this encounter flooded through my veins and I hugged her tightly to my chest as I thanked the labourer, tears filling my eyes with gratitude. I shivered involuntarily as I thought of all the times she had sat in that same spot, playing with her toys, completely oblivious to any danger around her. It was so close to the step of the back door, yet also so close to where she had been surveyed by the lion.

As I looked at the lion's eyes, they made me think of Cecil's eyes. They had the same look of confidence and strength and in the shadows of the tree they glittered as I had often seen Cecil's glitter in excitement. They were also the same tawny yellow-brown in colour.
I make it sound as though wildest Rhodesia was a dreadful place, but the love one feels for this part of earth is so strong and compelling, that the encounters, although some were terrifying, were all part of

that love for excitement and true living. In fact, there is a saying that goes 'if you drink the water of the Zambezi, you will love Rhodesia forever'. Well, we drank it many times and our love, despite the traumas and dramas, grew and grew. The sunsets and sunrises, when the entire world is brilliant red, orange and yellow, almost fire-like, make you feel so alive, yet humble in their magnificence and ever so grateful for all your blessings. Sometimes those same skies would reflect delicate pinks and blues, or a bleak grey as dawn approached, then they would turn into a kaleidoscope of colour, which would slowly fade as the sun stretched higher and the sky turned its normal blue.

We also had a good few encounters with snakes and scorpions, but each time they were seen before they could inflict any harm and were promptly killed. However the couple of weeks that I spent at Muchacha completely alone seemed to stretch on endlessly. Without a doubt, the nights were the worst and I would try and keep Jacob with me until as late as possible, because once he had left, it would be so quiet that every little sound seemed magnified. The lions would grunt and growl as they prowled around the house in the clearing and if one roared at such close proximity, it was the most terrifying sound imaginable.

At last Cecil came home and life fell into a pattern of work on tobacco all week, then have the family for the weekend hunting sprees. We opened a little shop at Muchacha and I spent hours at the sewing machine, making little dresses to sell. We sold the usual soap, sugar, tea and coffee, I made biscuits and rusks and even some sweets, which were normally passed to the little ones while their mothers were purchasing their supplies. Our customers were mainly the labourers that worked for us. If Cecil shot a buck, we would take only what we needed for our family. If it was not of a big enough quantity to share between the families of our staff, we would put the rest into stock for the shop to trade for maize. Villagers from all around the area heard about this and our labourers would bush telegraph the villagers if we had a supply of meat and they would arrive with baskets of maize. It was usually a day of laughter and good will. I could not speak their language and they could not speak

English, so it was a case of sign language in the form of very comical gestures. They were such a lovely people, so simple and vulnerable in their ways. Their maize was issued, together with dried meat, as part of our labourer rations.

The little shop was quite a way from the house and it was the season for the 'Elephant Grass'. This grass grows taller than the average man and in the end I got a labourer to cut a pathway from the house to the shop. One day Cecil came in, looking very excited, and said "Come quickly."

I followed him quite a way, but saw nothing. Cecil's eyes shone avidly with excitement and it was then that I heard it. A very soft purring, almost a gentle growling sound and I looked up at Cecil and asked, "What is it?"

"A lion. It's in the long grass a couple of yards from us."

Well! I took off for the house as fast as my two legs would carry me. Cecil followed, but when he got home, he was furious and he shouted, "You never, ever run away from anything. The lion wasn't aggressive, he's obviously not hungry and as long as we didn't startle or annoy him in any way, we were quite safe. Your running, however, could have altered the situation drastically."

Once again, my wonderful husband spoke such common sense, so easy to understand, yet so hard to follow.

Cecil noticed we had a lot of baboons on Muchacha and passed the remark that they were nearly the size of a human when standing on their hind legs. I laughed and said something about exaggeration and thought no more of it. One day a labourer killed a baboon quite near to the house and he brought it to show me. He laid the baboon at my feet, holding an axe in his other hand. As I bent over to look at it, taking note of its size (quite as accurate as Cecil had said), its eyes opened and it began lifting its head, its enormous teeth bared. The labourer jumped forward and hit the baboon with the axe, killing it instantly as its blood splattered all over me. I turned and screamed at him "What did you do that for?"

Cecil said quietly as he came up behind me "He probably saved your life. If that brute had got his fangs into your face or throat, you wouldn't be standing here now condemning the poor bloke; you'd be on your way to hospital or dead."

Cecil had an incredible sense of humour, but it wasn't always kind. He was so unafraid himself that he battled to understand fear in others. Poor Jacob had to work in an outside kitchen and when the lions roared at the front of our house, I always thought of that poor cook, who was just doing his job. This was Luangwa at its wildest and we all knew it. One day Cecil called me and said, "Just watch Jacob".

He took a small roll of Hessian from the grading room downstairs and brought it upstairs. He then took a paraffin tin and roared, just like a lion, into the tin. His impersonation was brilliant and the tin echoes the sound terrifyingly through the air. Cecil then called to Jacob to come and fetch the dirty dishes, but the poor man shouted back "But bwana, the lions are close".

"Nonsense, man. Now come and fetch the dishes at once."

Cecil had a way with his voice; he knew just how to command absolute authority over someone if he wanted to, just by the tone in his voice. Seeing Jacob reluctantly leave the safety of the kitchen and approach the house, Cecil stood near the window, close to where Jacob would enter and he dropped the bundle of hessian through the open window, next to Jacob as he went to open the door. Naturally the sound of the hessian crashing to the ground next to him and the prior knowledge that the lions had been roaring must have been more than Jacob could take. The poor, startled man let out a blood curdling yell and high-tailed it for the kitchen, closing the door behind him, leaving only a cloud of dust. Cecil was laughing at the sight of Jacob running away and I could only stand and shake my head at him, my sympathy lying with Jacob all the way. Cecil eventually went downstairs and told Jacob he could go home, to which he replied, "No, bwana, tonight I sleep just here. You called the lions with the tin and they will answer you by coming here."

This same trick of roaring into a tin was to become an issue later in our lives in desperate circumstances. Another trick he had played on Jacob was when we returned to Escape Estate. A young boy had been savaged by a leopard and Cecil was asked to go after the animal. He had been out all afternoon and saw nothing, but walking back to the village in the dusk, he spotted two eyes shining from a tree in his torchlight. Suspecting it may be the leopard, Cecil fired a shot. Sadly, it turned out to be a large Cervil cat, so Cecil brought it home and placed it in the outside toilet, with its head on its paws, facing the door. Early next morning he called to Jacob, asking him to fetch his cigarettes from the toilet. You can imagine the poor man's reaction on pushing the door open. I often wondered why Jacob stayed with us, except perhaps that he liked to brag to his family and friends that he worked for the bwana Kakuli.

At weekends all our labourers and their families would relax and get together with the closest villagers. Of course, the home-made beer would be in endless supply and they would dance to the tom-tom drums. Cecil was in bed with a dose of malaria and they started beating their drums early on Friday evening, the monotonous drumming continuing all through the night. Saturday was relatively quiet for the early part of the day, as they slept off the effects of Friday night's drinking, but by mid afternoon the tom- toms started again. At two o'clock on Sunday morning they had reached a crescendo of drumming, singing and shouting and Cecil, being so ill, had truly had enough. He took his rifle, aimed very high at the tops of the trees and shot in that direction. An instant hush ensued and not another sound was heard, so that Cecil, riddled with fever, could once again sleep properly. I commented about the danger of firing in that direction, no matter how high, but he admitted when he was well that the pain in his head was so severe, he didn't really care and he just wanted the drums to stop.

One afternoon he brought home a baby monkey. A troop had run away as they saw Cecil approaching and one mother threw her baby aside as she ran. Cecil hid for hours, hoping that she would return to fetch the baby, but to no avail. He eventually picked it up and brought it home, as it never stood a chance of surviving the night alone. It had no teeth in its tiny mouth and the manner in which it clung with its miniscule arms to my dress made me love it from the first moment I laid eyes on it. One night when he was slightly bigger, he disappeared and never came back. What happened to him I don't know, whether he left us to join a troop or became dinner to a predator, I wasn't sure. All I knew was that I missed him dreadfully and I prayed that he was alive and well.

We had various types of pets over the years. Several young duikers and a baby kudu, to name but a few, but we always allowed them back into the wild whenever we could. One little duiker we found, we named Bokkie. He was the naughtiest of them all and thoroughly spoilt by everyone. He despised going in the bakkie and if he saw us heading towards it, he would run and hide. We were growing pumpkins at that stage. He would get under the enormous pumpkin leaves and it would take ages to find him. We dare not have left him alone there, so we could not leave until Bokkie was found. One day he walked off during mating season and we never saw him again.

One weekend at Muchacha, it started raining very heavily and the family decided to leave early. The river was still running quite smoothly and Cecil went across with them to their bakkie. I must tell you that my father vehemently refused to walk in the river. He always got the labourers to bring the tin bath from the house. He would sit himself down in it and they would push him across to the other side where the bakkie was parked. It was a really funny sight and always brought a grin to my face.

Dad tried to start the vehicle, but there was no spark, so Cecil began tracing the fault in the engine. He must have been busy for about an hour, but at last it started and the family left. As Cecil approached the river, he realised that it was a lot higher than it had been from the heavy rain and was running quite swiftly and beginning to flood its banks. He stood debating what to do, as he had no way of letting me know what had happened and knew I would worry if he was too long. He stripped down to his underpants, leaving his clothing in the fork of a tree and plunged into the raging water behind a large tree floating past. The river was far stronger than he had anticipated and he was making no headway, but he persevered to get to the other side. By the time he reached the far bank, he was miles from the house and he caught onto a bed of reeds, which just buckled as he grabbed them. He felt himself sink into the water and by then he was so exhausted, he thought he was going to drown. Once again he surfaced and dragged himself over the reeds to the bank. He rested for half an hour, then started to walk back home. Fortunately it is not cold during the rainy season, so being almost naked was not a problem. He came across a couple of huts and asked for a drink and the old lady in the hut put a little tin of water on the fire with a spoon of tea leaves. She used mealie meal for milk and then poured it through a piece of cloth to catch the tea leaves. Cecil always maintained it was the best cup of tea he ever had. He arrived home at midnight, threw his bedraggled form onto the bed and was asleep before I could even find out what had happened.

Our time on Muchacha was drawing to a close when Cecil asked me to accompany him to the drying shed to see the largest scorpion he had ever seen. I really couldn't believe my eyes. It must have been at least ten inches long, gun-metal grey in colour and its pincers reminded me of a lobster. I had no idea until then that a scorpion could get so huge, although we had seen plenty of them on the farm. We decided as a family to leave the house for the weekend, leaving Abason Banda in charge, and camped in tents about ten miles from the house. We all loved camping and the women always felt deprived when the men went off to hunt and we had to stay at the house. We pitched the tents and got the hunter's pot going, when the children began to cry. There were hard, nut-like pods in the trees overhead and these were falling onto the children as they played and really hurt. A little later Cecil lay down on a stretcher, but suddenly he started laughing and called us to him. He pointed to the top of the tree and in the very top branches we saw the monkeys. They were picking the pods and literally aiming at the children, then throwing them as hard as they could.

Both Joyce's children and my own grew up with an appreciation of the world of nature and the love of animals, this being evident throughout their lives. I do believe that these children have been better adults because of their upbringing in the wilds and also being raised in Mazabuka, where colour and race was unimportant. Some of their best friends were Africans and in fact Jeni is still trying to trace a black woman who she went to school with and had become good friends with.

109

We returned to Escape Estate and started visiting Ethné's godparents again. Pam and Joe (not their real names) invited us over for dinner one night and Axan, the cook, got the pressure lamps lit and had a storm lantern in the kitchen. He began cooking our meal in the soft light, dressed in a khanza. This is a shirt which reaches the knees, with short sleeves and a number of pockets. During the day a khaki khanza, known as the 'duty khanza' is worn, but when it is time to serve dinner, the cook changes into a snow white khanza, with a soft white hat which is almost the same shape as a fez. Axan had kept his khaki khanza on, but as it was Sunday and he should have been off duty, Pam closed her eyes to the fact that he hadn't changed when he served dinner. He had cooked eggs, bacon, tomato, chips and toast. I noticed Cecil wasn't eating and Pam asked Cecil what was wrong.
"Pam, please forgive me, but there is a cockroach on top of my egg."
Pam, being very embarrassed, shouted "Axan, come here."
When Axan appeared, she pointed to the cockroach and asked, "What the devil is this?"
Axan, with a big smile on his face, took the corner of his duty khanza and said, "Oh, sorry bwana Kakuli" and wiped the cockroach from Cecil's plate, obviously expecting Cecil to resume his meal without further ado. Needless to say, the memory of Cecil's face has remained in my mind ever since.

One of the insects that became the greatest nuisance was the 'stink bug'. It is a small green bug, almost triangular in shape and slightly bigger than a pea. They would come in swarms, the buzzing being heard from a long way off. One night we went to visit a farmer who had a lighting generator and they were going to show us an eight millimetre cine that they had taken on their holiday. The screen was covered with stink bugs within the first five minutes and we kept pushing them into a paraffin tin. By the time we left, that tin was over three quarters full. The smell they give off is terrible. If you accidentally squash one, or it falls into a pot on the stove, the food is inedible, being tainted with that smell. The farmers said that they fed them to the chickens, but could not slaughter those chickens for at least a fortnight, as even the flesh would smell like a stink bug. They seemed to get in everywhere and it you were at a dance or in a crowd and squashed one on yourself, you may as well go home, as the dreadful smell lingered for hours. It was, however, quite funny to watch the faces of people who did not know them and accidentally squashed one.

We were at a party once, when one of the men took a slice of fruit cake and unknowingly bit a stink bug in half as he bit the cake. He tried extremely hard not to embarrass the hostess by spitting it out, but kept swallowing and then asked for a strong whisky to help with the taste. Cecil and I sat down to eat one night and as Cecil opened his mouth to take a mouthful of food from his fork, a stink bug flew in and Cecil swallowed. That was one night that Cecil never ate a thing and he just kept cursing the damn bugs. Much to my amusement, when we eventually left Zambia and settled in South Africa many years later, I took my sewing machine in for a service, the technician found eight stink bugs in the motor. He wasn't impressed by this woman who obviously stored her machine in a place where bugs could crawl into such small places.

Mr Gush asked Cecil to put up another little house, as he was taking on another mechanic. Cecil erected the building and the new family moved in. They had a very pretty daughter and I went to introduce myself, taking over a tray of eats to do so while they unpacked. The daughter said, "Yesterday I was at the mill and saw the most gorgeous man".
"What does he look like?" I asked curiously.
"He is dark haired and has a lock of hair that falls on his forehead. You must introduce us some time."
"Not on your life", I answered coolly, "he's my husband."
Cecil and his good looks!

Around this time I noticed that Ethné kept pushing her finger against her stomach and rolling it around. When I asked her what was wrong, she said, "I'm itchy inside."
I took her to the doctor and he asked for a stool sample, as he suspected she had worms. When the results came back, he told me she had hookworm. He explained that the worm attaches itself to the intestines and sucks blood, causing the itchy discomfort to the victim.

The treatment was to starve Ethné for forty eight hours to give the bowels a chance to clean out and then the medication had to be given, with another six hours of starvation while the medicine did its trick. My heart bled for her and I couldn't let her out of the bedroom in case she drank water. Every time I looked at her, she complained of being thirsty or hungry and all the cuddling in the world didn't explain why mummy was being so nasty to her. Eventually, some time after the medicine, she passed a mass of hookworm and I was able to give her food again.

A few months later she developed sores all over her legs and arms. There were so many of them, some of them just starting as a small blister and others full of pus and bleeding. Those that were healing were drying up and had scabs. The doctor seemed to be baffled as to what they were and even tried taking Ethné off certain foods in case she had developed an allergy, but nothing helped. We were due to go on holiday to South Africa and on our arrival someone remarked on how my child's arms and legs were bandaged. When I told them about the sores, they recommended that I take her to a certain Mr Smith, who owned a chemist, which I see is still in existence today, fifty years later. Mr Smith looked at the sores and said, "If you had come a month earlier, I could not have helped you, but all the soldiers in tropical areas got the same sores and we now have the medication to treat them. They are known as Tropical Ulcers."
He gave us two bottles of Anthisan and two tubes of the same medication in ointment form. It was the first antihistamine available and worked like a charm, but the sores left nasty scars which took years to fade. It was while on this holiday that one of our most embarrassing moments occurred.

Cecil and I took Ethné to a restaurant and she asked to go to the toilet. I asked the waitress for directions and she pointed to the opposite side of the room. I took Ethné's hand and guided her to the ladies, waiting for her. When she was finished, I pulled the chain to flush the toilet and noticed how fascinated Ethné was, as she looked up at me and asked if she could also flush. I let her pull the chain again and we proceeded to head back to our table. As I opened the toilet door, Ethné shouted across the room to Cecil. "Daddy, these

112

lavatories have water in them and it comes out when you pull the chain."

Ethné had never seen anything but a pit toilet in her entire life. Cecil disappeared so quickly that I hardly saw him move. I went to the counter, paid for the untouched meal and followed Cecil out, never once looking back.

When we returned to Rhodesia, Joyce showed me a red lump on the side of her daughter's face and said, "She has such lovely fair skin; I do hope she doesn't end up looking like Ethné, full of scars".

I don't think Joyce knew just how much her remark hurt me at the time. The lump kept increasing in size and eventually developed a black head. Why the poetsie didn't show a head from the start, we don't know, but once we realised what it was, we smothered it and got the poetsie out.

A few weeks later Cecil went on a hunt and when he returned, he told us the strangest story. He had been walking through the bush with one gun bearer and as he stepped into a clearing, he heard what sounded like a chain rattling behind him. No matter where he turned to face, the sound kept occurring behind him and he looked at the gun bearer and asked, "What the hell is that?"

The gun bearer appeared to be terrified, as he whispered in reply "Bwana, we better go. This thing is someone who died before before."

What 'before before' meant exactly, I don't know, but they moved on and the sound ceased.

On the following hunt we had a really frightening experience in a different area. The three families travelled in the big truck and we took tents with to sleep in. The tents were pitched and the men left camp almost immediately. While they were away, we saw smoke from a long way off, but it slowly got nearer and appeared to be getting wider. At one stage I looked at it and said to Joyce "It seems to be slowly circling us."

Cecil suddenly came running into camp and shouted "Pack up; we have to get out of here, if the wind changes that fire will surround us completely."

113

We quickly packed up camp and loaded everything onto the truck. By that time, Dad and Charlie had also returned and they told us that the fire was approaching at a very fast pace. We all jumped onto the truck and started off, but suddenly the fire seemed to be all around us. Cecil shouted, "Don't panic, I'll get us out of here."

The grass was burning in patches and we rode through sections of track where the grass in the middle of the two tracks for the tyres, was burning profusely. All I could think of was the petrol tank, but Cecil drove carefully and kept reassuring us as we tried to escape the flames. The heat was frighteningly intense and we felt it on our faces and bodies, our fear increasing with every moment. Thankfully, after about twenty minutes, Cecil managed to find a clear path and we left the circling fire behind us. This was one trip I was glad to see behind me. Looking at Cecil when we climbed off the back of the truck, I was amazed at the coolness he had displayed while driving through the fire, but the strain had left him looking very pale, his eyes shining brightly as they always did when he faced danger.

Cecil came in one day and announced, "We are going to get remarried."

Joyce was a Catholic and had often passed remarks about us having been married in the Anglican faith, when I was actually Catholic. I laughed and replied "So Joyce finally got to you, did she?"

"No", Cecil answered, "I was speaking to one of the Catholic Fathers from Madsamoza Mission and he was telling me what a lot of buffalo they have in that area. I want to get into his good books."

So, we got remarried and had Ethné christened in the Catholic faith so that Cecil could hunt at the mission.

The people living near us with the pretty daughter moved on, as her dad had been offered another position in Lusaka, which offered better prospects for his daughter's education. A new family moved in, I don't remember their names, but they had three of the naughtiest children I had ever seen. Joyce and I walked up to her toilet one day and Joyce went in first. Standing waiting for her outside, I heard her say "Get out of there."

The youngsters were playing hide and seek and this particular young boy had climbed into the pit toilet to hide and was hanging from the

114

seat by his hands. The father was a strange man too. We saw him dunking the one boy in a drum of drinking water and the child stank something terrible. He told us that the lad had thrown his car piston into the pit toilet, so he tied a rope around the child and lowered him into the hole to find the piston. They didn't stay in the house very long and we were only too happy to see them move on.

Quite often on Sunday afternoons, we would take Ethné to a nearby river and she used to pick up small red stones, which were called Pyragamies. I believe they are related to garnets and rubies. While she busied herself looking for the gems, Cecil and I would pan the river for gold. We never removed the gold, but it was a lot of fun to see the tail of gold in the pan. I realise today that if we had taken all the gold that we panned and kept it, we could have made quite a lot of money. One afternoon we went for a drive and in the middle of the road was a hole, approximately the size of a big apple. A greenish-blue liquid, which resembled clay, oozed from the hole onto the road. I have been told since that it is a direct pipe to diamonds underground. I have not done any research on this, as I like to think I was that close to getting an engagement ring after all those years, with a diamond the size of a pea!

Cecil came home from work one evening with the legs and fillets of two buffalo and as I was feeling tired; I suggested we pass the meat on to friends instead of making biltong, so we took one leg to Ethné's godmother. The men sat down to sundowners and by the time we left it was too late to visit other people with meat, so we began cutting it into biltong anyway. We cut until midnight and then Cecil asked me to carry on, as he had to work the next day and I could rest. I cut until six in the morning and then went into the yard to put ropes up to hang the biltong. This had always been Cecil's job and I made one of the biggest blunders possible. Instead of tying the rope to every tree, I tied it to the first and then simply looped it around each tree until I tied the knot on the other end. I then hung approximately nine hundred pieces of fresh meat to dry. Cecil came out, ready for work and hugged me thankfully for having completed the task. As he whispered his thanks in my ear, the knot on one end loosened and the entire rope fell to the ground, the biltong landing in the dusty

115

earth below, much to my disgust. Cecil made a quick exit to work and I slowly began washing every piece of meat, placing it back in the brine. It took me until lunch time to finish my task and I gratefully lay back on the bed to rest. Strangely enough, this was some of the nicest biltong we ever made.

Biltong used to hang in rows under the eaves of the roof and it was so funny to watch people as they were leaving our home, lift their arms and simply grab a piece automatically. Everyone knew where it was hanging and they knew they were welcome to a few pieces when they visited. Ethné did all her teething on biltong, as did all the other babies I came into contact with.

We were saying goodbye to friends one afternoon when I stepped into a column of marching army ants. The 'soldiers' march at the front and rear of the column, with the sentries marching on either side. One can usually hear them approaching, as they make a buzzing sound, similar to that of a swarm of bees. The bite itches the next day and is painful to scratch. When a colony is disturbed, as I had done that day by stepping into it, the soldiers run around enraged, biting viciously to ward off the intruder. I was bitten so many times on my lower legs that they were red and swollen for a couple of days and the itching was dreadful.

One day Pam and I were chatting about embarrassing moments in our lives and I told her about my episode with the bucket on honeymoon. She giggled as she said, "You think that was embarrassing, wait until you hear what happened to me."
It seems that Joe's firm sent him to work in Durban for six months, where he met Pam and they fell in love. By the time he had completed his six month task, they decided to marry. Joe returned to Fort Jimmy to find accommodation and then wrote to Pam, asking her to follow. His letter told her of the place he had found, explaining that he only had a few bare necessities and the niceties to which she was accustomed would have to wait until they could afford them.

Pam decided that she did not want children until they had established their home and as there was no contraception in the form of pills, and condoms were most unreliable, Pam purchased a tube of barrier gel which had just been released on the market. On her arrival, Joe told Pam that the District Commissioner's wife, who was arranging the wedding reception, had invited them to stay over until the wedding the following weekend and that they would then spend their first night as a married couple in her home. The house was pole and daga, with no ceilings, so naturally sound carried from one room to the next.

The wedding had apparently been lovely and at last they went back to the house after the reception ended. Joe was somewhat drunk by this stage and he initially embarrassed Pam by using the chamber pot in front of her before he climbed into bed, just pushing it under the bed when he was finished. He made so much noise and she knew that everyone else in the house had heard it too. Pam had placed all her toiletries on the table next to the bed, but before she could reach out and pick up the barrier cream, Joe blew the candle out, plunging the room into utter darkness. She fumbled on the table until she found a tube and quickly used it. She began to feel a slight burning sensation, but before she could do anything about it, Joe had gathered her into his arms to make love to her.

Pam then told me how Joe had suddenly jumped up, saying, "Hell, I'm on fire!"
He sprang from the bed, grabbed the chamber pot from under it and began to wash himself in its contents. Pam found a box of matches and lit the candle, only to find that she had used peppermint toothpaste instead of barrier gel. With muffled giggles coming from the other room in the house, Pam was painfully aware that the entire scene had been heard by everyone.
Cecil had made a little garden in the front of our house, planting marigolds and zinnias. He tried growing vegetables, as they were unobtainable except in tins, but as fast as the shoots came through the soil, the buck would eat them. For some reason they never ate the flowers and the garden was really pretty. I had just gone back inside after watering the flowers one day and sat down at my sewing

machine to work on a dress that I was making. I suddenly remembered my garden fork was still outside and got up to go and fetch it. As I began to stand up, I heard and felt a soft thud as something fell from the thatch roof and landed in my lap. It was a centipede, about six inches long and if I had still been in a sitting position, it would have gone down the bodice of my dress.

After recovering from this frightful encounter, I continued sewing. Ethné was sitting playing on the floor and I turned to look at her when she called to me. She had found a small torch bulb and as I turned, she put it in her mouth and bit on it. In my panic, I grabbed my handkerchief and wiped her mouth out, naturally cutting it badly with the pieces of glass. I quickly fed her some dry bread, insisting that she eat it and then gave her a small glass of milk. I then put her into her pram and started the three mile walk to the hospital, with no form of protection from wild animals. I was almost half way when a big snake slithered across the road in front of me, making me even more nervous.

At last I reached Fort Jimmy and to get to the hospital, I passed Cecil's work. By this time I was so worried and was crying, so I called in to tell Cecil what had happened. He calmed me down, saying that I had done the best possible thing under the circumstances and that the hospital could do no more than that. He inspected Ethné's mouth, which was full of small lacerations, but said that he didn't think she had actually swallowed any glass, because he could see no lacerations near the throat itself. For a few days thereafter we checked her stools diligently, but thankfully she was fine and the cuts in her mouth healed quickly, with us using salt water to keep them clean.

Joyce announced proudly one morning that she was expecting another baby and two months later, I went round to her house to let her know that I was also expecting.

"If it's a boy, I'm calling him Michael," I told her as we sat discussing our babies.

"You can't; I'm naming my baby Michael." Joyce retaliated.

Well, we argued for quite a while, neither of us willing to back down, as usual. I visited Doctor Taube for a routine check up and he expressed concern about the impending birth.

"Joan, for your own safety, please have this baby in civilisation. You had a rough time with Ethné's birth and Doctor Davidson told me that you had a nasty reaction to chloroform."
I took heed of his words and Cecil and I sold our furniture and moved back to South Africa after Cecil had worked his notice period with Mr Gush. It was 1951 and we had been married for six years. We had sold our bakkie and bought a mini, which was overloaded with the last of our belongings and Ethné sat on my lap for the entire journey. When we kissed the family goodbye, we truly believed that this was a permanent move, but little did we know that, within eighteen months, we would return to Northern Rhodesia for twenty years. With tears in my eyes, we got in the car and headed for Lusaka.

CHAPTER EIGHT

I've just witnessed a miracle...."

By this time I was nearly four months pregnant, suffering terribly with nausea, and we travelled slowly due to the poor state of the roads. Just before dark we came to the top of the escarpment and to our utter dismay, we saw lights approaching. Cecil found a slightly wider section of road and parked the car as close as possible to the rocky mountain side. So close, in fact, that I was unable to open my door. The lights approaching were from four army vehicles, which were travelling during the wrong twelve hours. I often wonder if they were expecting trouble somewhere for them to have broken the rules.

Cecil left the car and spoke to the drivers as they approached, instructing me to stay in the car with Ethné. I watched in fear as he stood at the edge of the road, guiding the drivers as they manoeuvred the huge trucks past our car. I must admit that I made many promises to the Lord in prayer, if he would only keep us safe and it would have taken three lifetimes to have fulfilled all those promises. Nevertheless, after about two hours, the four trucks were past and Cecil got back in the car. I told him how I had prayed and made so many promises that I would probably have to become a nun to fulfil them. Cecil looked at me and burst into laughter. "You! A nun? Never!"
When we arrived in Lusaka I made a comment to Cecil that I prayed I would never have to return to Fort Jimmy. Strangely enough, I never did.

The mini was so overloaded that there were times when it just didn't have enough power. At Wylies Poort we realised that the car was not going to make it and because I don't drive, I had to push the car to the top of the poort. We managed to reach Cecil's mother's house in Bloemfontein, when the last valve gave in and the mini was no longer of any use. Cecil began looking for work, but was unable to find anything suitable, even the firm he had worked for previously had no vacancies. He had been out all day and returned home with no news of a job, but told me that he had swapped our mini for a lathe so that he could make lamps and fruit bowls to sell.

His mother suggested that he travel to Bethlehem to his Aunty Flo and Uncle Burt to see whether there were any jobs available there. He bought an old used car and set off for Bethlehem on his own. I received a letter shortly afterwards advising me that he was staying with Aunty Flo and had found a job at Amfra Meubels Fabriek, a local furniture factory. He said that everything was working out alright and that Aunty Flo's daughter, Olive, was being so kind to him. Naturally my jealousy reared its head and I must admit I was not at all happy about the situation. When the next letter arrived, all Cecil could talk about was the family and Olive in particular. I do realise today that at that stage in his life, he must have felt very alone and almost afraid of the future. To a man who was used to excitement and freedom, the future must have looked very bleak. He was used to working in the open air and now he would spend his days in a factory full of fumes.

Bill and Phyllis came through to Bloemfontein that weekend and took me back to Kloof End with them, where I stayed for a few weeks. Bill brought me another letter he had collected from Bloemfontein when he was passing through. In Cecil's letter, he told me how he and Olive had been to the theatre together and someone had let the air out of the car tyres, so they had only got home at three in the morning. I looked down at my belly, now six months into the pregnancy, and said, "Little baby, I think it's about time your daddy came home or takes us back to Bethlehem with him."

I immediately wrote to Cecil, giving him the option of finding me accommodation in Bethlehem so we could be together, or I would return to my parents in Northern Rhodesia. He arrived the following Saturday, complaining about how difficult it had been to find accommodation, but that we were to board at a guest farm, run by a Mrs White. What a lovely person she was. She had been a nursing

121

sister for many years and made us so welcome, giving us adjoining rooms at no extra cost, so that Ethné and the baby could sleep in their own room. We sold the car and Cecil bought a bicycle.

We visited Aunty Flo and Uncle Burt quite a few times before baby arrived, but it was a long walk to their home and Ethné would get so tired. Normally Olive was there when we visited and I felt so big and frumpy next to her, although she was always nice to me. We made a few friends in the boarding house, but the couple who became our closest friends were Fred and Hilda Hanson. They were wonderful people and in the evenings we would play a card game called 'Black Lulu' (Queen of Spades). If you were handed the queen of spades in a deal, you waited until you could 'drop her' on someone else and if that person happened to be your spouse, there was usually snide remarks amid the laughter of the other players, as she meant one hundred points against you if you were caught with her in your hand.

Fred and Hilda had two children, a daughter of fourteen in boarding school and a four year old called Rosemary. The children were always fed half an hour before the adults and then sent off to play while we enjoyed our meal in peace. Christmas was approaching and Cecil suggested that we use the afternoon to buy gifts. I dressed Ethné in a dress I had made for Christmas, a beautiful white voile dress with tiny red spots and lots of ribbon and lace. Reminding her not to get dirty, she ate her lunch with the other children and then the adults went to the dining room to have theirs. As I left the dining room I noticed that the two girls were very interested in something. They had found a tin of bright green paint and had just managed to pry the lid off, when Hilda's daughter saw us approaching. She threw her hands in the air, shaking the tin as she shouted "Look, Mommy."

The hideous paint splashed all over and Ethné, gasping with horror, quickly wiped her hands all over her white dress as I ran towards her, ruining the dress completely.

Hilda and I bought two of the first 'drink and wet' dolls that came on the market. We made each child a suitcase of clothes for their 'babies' and Cecil and Fred bought each child a doll's pram. My baby was due in the middle of February and I got bigger and bigger, my stomach being no ant heap, but rather a full-size mountain. We received a cable to advise us that Joyce had given birth to a baby girl, who she named Margaret.

I received a letter from my mother to say that they were also leaving Fort Jimmy, as were Joyce and Charlie and in a later letter she told me they were living in a small town called Mazabuka, which was the research station for Northern Rhodesia and dealt mainly with cattle diseases and rabies. She was working in a grocery / hardware store for a Mr Fisher, but had asked for three weeks leave to visit us while I had baby.

The end of February came and still no baby, so the women at the boarding house began bringing me bottles of castor oil and would sit there while I very unwillingly swallowed the awful contents. During that week I drank three bottles and, believe me, they were not small bottles! My mom was starting to become agitated, as it would soon be time for her to go back to Rhodesia and she nagged that I was not playing the game. On the Saturday we arranged to go to see a film with Hilda and Fred, using their car. Mom decided to go to bed early, so we agreed to take Ethné and Rosemary along. I put on a maternity dress and, surveying my image in the mirror, I was quite convinced that I was the ugliest creature that ever existed. I pulled out of the wardrobe a dress that had pleats all round and squeezed my oversized body into it. The zip, which was situated on the side, would not even begin to close, but I knew my mom had an 'edge to edge' coat as they were called. These coats did not fasten, but were worn open, so I borrowed it from my mom. Well, it was far from edge to edge on me, but it covered the gaping zip and I was ready to go out. We all got in the car and headed for town.

After the show it was raining and Cecil said to Hilda "It's alright, I'll take Rosemary to the car" and he picked up the child and ran through the pelting rain.
Fred never offered to take Ethné, which made me angry, so I picked her up against my tummy and ran all the way to the car. Cecil turned and asked "Why didn't you wait, I was coming back for her?"

I never answered, but climbed into the car, making it quite clear that I was unimpressed. I find it hard to believe, now that I am old, how I was so quick to anger or to throw a tantrum over silly things, but I suppose no-one is perfect, there's good and bad in all of us. We were only home long enough to drink a cup of coffee when my son decided he'd had enough of his mother's nonsense and put me into a fast and furious bout of labour. Cecil borrowed Fred's car and rushed me to hospital, where Michael arrived at six in the morning, a nine and a half pounder! He was having difficulty in breathing, so he was taken away to an incubator.

I asked where Cecil was and nurse laughed as she answered me. "I walked over to him and told him that he has a son. He grinned from ear to ear and said 'I'll be back', then ran off. I did call after him that you were okay too."
I was told by everyone at the boarding house later when I returned home, that Cecil had blown the hooter and woke everyone up to tell them he had a son. Again, I was in hospital for fourteen days before being discharged.

The next day Mrs White popped in and said, "I will expect your son for dinner tonight." I laughed, making it clear that I thought she was joking, but she looked at me quite seriously and said "I'm serious, Joan. You start him on solids today."
I was very worried, after all the problems I had experienced with Ethné, but when I got there, she had a teaspoon of sieved oats, mixed with milk and sugar ready to feed Michael. Needless to say, he blossomed from day one and I was ever so grateful to Mrs White for her help.

Naturally we had to take Michael to see Aunty Flo and Uncle Burt, so when he was about three weeks old we set off to pay them a visit. Michael was asleep in the pram and Ethné perched herself on the bottom section of the pram so that she didn't have to walk. The evening went off well until Olive arrived home and it wasn't long before she and Cecil were chatting animatedly. Cecil had always displayed a certain radiance while in Rhodesia, but now he was quieter and his face had become solemn. His eyes no longer twinkled unless we began to speak about Rhodesia, when he would suddenly appear so alive. Aunty Flo asked if she could hold 'little mouse man' and Michael became 'mouse man' to me for many years to come. I went to pick him up to hand him to her, when Olive and Cecil burst into laughter and once again my jealousy was sparked. A little while later, I happened to mention that I never refused a dare. Whether Uncle Burt had noticed my discomfort, I don't know, but he suddenly stood up and poured three quarters of a glass of brandy, filling it with water. "I dare you to drink this," he said, a naughty grin appearing as he looked at me.

I looked at Cecil and Olive, then at the glass, took it from him and downed the lot. At this stage I was not even a social drinker, in fact I never drank at all, so you can imagine the effect this glass of brandy had on me.

I began to feel funny and said to Cecil "I think we should go now."
We left soon afterwards, but I don't remember walking home, going to bed or much else that night. My only recollection the next morning was Cecil saying, "Joan, for goodness sake, please stop talking now, it's four in the morning and I have to go to work at six." That was the one and only time I ever got drunk in my entire life.

The time came for Michael to be christened and I told Cecil I wanted Fred and Hilda as godparents, but he replied that he wanted Olive and her new boyfriend. I went and made arrangements at the Catholic Church the next day. The Father was a foreigner, I have no idea which country he was from, but he could hardly speak English. Thankfully I managed to understand that we should be at the church on the Saturday at seven. I told Hilda about Olive and asked her to make sure that she and Fred stay close to me at the church. I warned Cecil that if he asked Olive, Michael would have two sets of godparents.

When we arrived at the church, Olive and her friend were there and Fred and Hilda stayed by my side at all times. Hilda held Michael as we sat down in the pew. The Father called for the mother and the godfather to approach him, so I grabbed Fred's hand and went to the front. He laid an exquisite baby robe over our hands and then babbled away for about five minutes, before saying, "Thank you, baby is now christened".

As we left the church, I saw the funny side and turned to Fred, saying, "I'm sorry, Fred, but I don't know if he christened Michael or married me to you!"

I invited everyone, including Olive and her boyfriend, back to the room for tea and cake. We spent a lovely evening together and after that I seldom saw Olive, but when I did, the tension had eased. Was it because I had once again got my own way, was that spoilt streak still in me, even then? I often wonder.

Life fell into a routine of cleaning, washing nappies and caring for my children. One morning I took some nappies out to hang them, when I noticed a woman who had just booked into the boarding house hanging nappies that were snow white, but mine looked a dull grey in colour. I took them back inside and found out the number of her room, then walked across and knocked on the door. When she appeared, I introduced myself and asked her how she got her nappies so white.

"It's a new product on the market, called Steri-Nappy. Here, I'll give you a little to try." So, I had made another new friend and each day there were two lines of sparkling white nappies hanging out to dry.

The months went by and soon it was Christmas again. It was the day of Cecil's Christmas party and although Cecil was not a heavy drinker, I passed the remark that he shouldn't drink too much, as I was afraid of what the people in the boarding house would say. My own common sense should have stopped me, because Cecil had never been seen even slightly under the weather before. Later that afternoon one of the boarders knocked at the door and began laughing as he said, "I think your husband needs some help. He's got his bicycle all mixed up in the swinging gate."

Sure enough, Cecil had partied merrily and it took some doing to extricate his bicycle and get him safely home and into bed that day. After Christmas, Cecil's firm bought a house and converted it into two flats. We moved into one section and another family moved into the other. They had two little girls, aged about four and six, so they were good company for Ethné. I never mentioned to Cecil how much

I missed Rhodesia and all the excitement, but my present life was far too tame. Michael was a few weeks off a year old when the police knocked on the door to advise that Cecil's mom had passed away, so we arranged a lift to Bloemfontein for the funeral. That was one time I wished that Cecil could cry. He adored his mother and when I sat beside him and watched his stricken face, but no tears, I think I hurt more than he did; my tears were not only for his mom, but Cecil too.

On arriving home, Michael developed gastro-enteritis and I was up day and night with him crying endlessly. On the Sunday he fell asleep and I nodded off in a chair. Ethné shook me awake and said "Uncle Robbie from next door wants to know if I can go for a ride in the car with them".

I was so exhausted that I shouted at her for waking me and said, "I don't care where you go, as long as you leave me alone."

Careless words from a very tired mother.

At about five, Cecil offered to start a fire so we could have a braai and we were sitting at the fire when Robbie came running and said "For God's sake, come quickly, your daughter's dying".

We flew to his car and rushed to the hospital as Robbie explained what had happened. They went for a drive and had left the three children in the car while they popped in to see someone on the opposite side of a busy road. It seems that the children had sat in the car for a while as they had been told to do, but one child needed the toilet, so my little five year old had offered to take her. She took each child by the hand and they stepped from the front of Robbie's car straight into the path of an approaching MG. The children panicked and both the girls tried to pull Ethné out of the way, so they spread-eagled her in front of the MG. The impact threw her up into the air and she landed some distance away behind the MG, her head taking the full force of her landing. The four year old was unhurt, her sister had rolled along the tar road and had lost quite a bit of skin which caused a lot of discomfort, but she wasn't badly injured.

When I reached the hospital bed, I looked down at Ethné, who was unconscious and resembled a little rag doll. She had suffered severe head injuries, a shattered arm and muscle damage right down her one side. The doctor whispered to Cecil "She has excessive brain damage; don't pray for her to live, because if she does, she will be either mental or paralysed, or both."

I refused to believe this and went to every church in Bethlehem, asking them to pray for my little girl. Her arm was put into traction, but they could not do anything else, due to her head injury.

Hilda took care of Michael, gastro and all, while I stayed at Ethné's side. I rested my head on the bed covers next to her, when she suddenly began to cough. As I looked up, I realised that she was coughing up huge clots of dark red blood. I flew in search of a nurse, who came running at my call. I think I must have woken up every patient in every ward as I screamed for help. The nurse took one look at the blood and smiled. "It's okay" she said, "this is all the blood she swallowed. It seems that a vein or artery under the tongue had been severed in the accident. If fresh blood comes up, call me, but at the moment she's alright."

I began my vigil again and Ethné lay in a coma for six days. I would slip away to get something to eat or drink, then return immediately to be with her.

I had been to the shop and was walking back into the hospital, when the doctor came up to me, smiling as he announced, "I have just witnessed a miracle".

I asked him why and he explained that when one has a brain injury, both eyes fall to the opposite side of the injury and the doctor had been watching this all the time. When he had examined her a few minutes earlier, the eyes appeared to be crossed which, he said, meant that there was no brain damage. Ethné was still in a coma and he had no idea whether she would regain consciousness with a good memory or not; only time would tell.

Early next morning Ethné opened her eyes quite out of the blue and uttered, "Mommy, I want to go home".

How does one describe the joy you feel at a moment like that? My precious little girl was awake, she knew me and she could speak perfectly normally. I remember whispering to her "I'm so sorry that I was nasty to you when you woke me up."

A few weeks later we were able to take Ethné home, but due to the severe muscular injuries, she was unable to walk, so I had two babies to care for. My dear friends had rotated the duty of caring for Michael while I was at the hospital and I will never forget the deep gratitude I felt for each of them. My mom came down once again and arrived a few weeks after Ethné was discharged. She stayed with us for two weeks and during this time, she turned to me one morning and said, "Dress the children, we're going shopping."

I put Michael in the pram and sat Ethné on the bottom. When we arrived in town she headed straight for a toy shop and, turning to Ethné, she asked, "Which doll would you like?"

Ethné pointed to a particular doll and said "That one, Granny."

Mom then told her to choose a pram for her doll, which Ethné gleefully did. My mom placed the doll in the pram and turning to Ethné, she said, "If you want the doll and her pram, you have to push it home."

"But I can't walk!"

"Then you don't get the doll or the pram. It's up to you."

I watched, tears streaming down my face, as my little girl determinedly took one or two steps with her pram, then fell to the ground.

I recall my mother saying firmly behind her, "You can do it, Ethné. Get up and walk."

This continued all the way home, but Ethné's determination to take home her new doll in its pram won, thanks to the ingenuity and love of my dear mother. From then on, Ethné insisted on walking and before we knew it, she was well on her way to recovery. Cecil, however, seemed very unsettled and one night as we sat in the lounge, said, "I don't like city life. My little girl would never have been run over in Fort Jimmy, there's too much politics being spoken at work and, to top it all, I'm the only English speaking person there." At this stage, South Africa was preparing for an election and Cecil was right, everyone was talking politics. I could sense the restlessness within him and he continued to speak about Rhodesia every day.

Winter set in earnestly; so bitterly cold that when it hailed one Sunday, the hail was still visible the following Wednesday. I kept the children indoors as much as possible and arranged for Ethné to start school the following January. Christmas was nearing and we had to attend a Christmas party at Cecil's work. On the day of the party, I made savouries and snacks nearly all day at my flat and they were collected in the afternoon. I got dressed, filled with excitement, and then I received a message from the lady who was to look after the children that evening. She was unable to make it and sadly I realised that Cecil would have to attend the party alone. I went to bed at about ten and was awakened much later by a loud knock at the door. There stood Cecil's two most senior bosses, holding a completely inebriated Cecil up. "We apologise for his condition" the one man giggled, "but the three of us were getting on so well, we didn't realise how much we were drinking."

All three were so drunk that they were holding each other up to walk.

Cecil related the course of events at the party to me the following day. Two tables were laid out, one for the workers and one for management. Only beer and brandy were served to the workers, but the managers were given beer and whisky at their table. Cecil walked over to the managers' table and poured himself a whisky. One manager approached him and said, "Sorry, Slabbert, but this is the managers' table. Your drinks are at your table."

Cecil replied, "I'm a Rhodesian. I drink whisky. There is no whisky at the workers' table and, as a Rhodesian, let me tell you that after hours there are no workers and bosses. We are all just men."

The manager was so taken aback by Cecil's words that he called another manager. He asked Cecil to repeat his statement, which he duly did and then they pulled out a chair and asked Cecil to join them. They kept him there all night and brought him home after the party. Nevertheless, after telling me all about his evening, Cecil said, "I've had South Africa! I'm still a South African citizen and I won't change that, but at heart I'm a Rhodesian and I'm going back as soon as I can."

Early in the new year Cecil wrote to my dad to tell him that we were returning to Rhodesia. My dad was thrilled and wrote to say that he had started a hardware and builders merchants, called Excel Construction Company. He insisted that we be there by March, so Cecil went to his manager to resign. Visibly upset, he said to Cecil "You are the finest French polisher that we have ever hired."

He took out his cheque book and placed it on the table. "Name your price to stay."

This was a wonderful compliment to Cecil, but he shook his head and replied, "You're too late. I'm going back to Rhodesia where I belong."

My father decided to drive to South Africa to fetch us. We moved out of the flat into a tiny boarding house, only to find that all the children living there were ill with measles. A few days later Michael went down with it and was a very sick boy. We had to pay personal tax before we could leave South Africa and I asked Ethné to watch him while I quickly went to pay the tax. I had been writing a letter to my folks and I told my father that the conditions at the boarding house were very low-grade and the food was dreadful. I had exaggerated, hoping that he would come sooner than he had planned. I left the unfinished letter on the dressing table and checked on Michael, who was asleep. There was a long queue at the tax office and it took me quite a bit longer than I had expected. When I returned home, Ethné met me with a huge smile and announced "Mummy, after you left, Micky woke up and messed himself. It came out of his nappy and he painted the walls with it, so I called Mrs Smith, the owner of the boarding house, (not her real name) to help me clean it. She washed Micky and changed him and then she wiped the walls and read your letter."

I was so ashamed and apart from thanking her for helping Ethné, I avoided her like the plague.

At last Dad arrived in his bakkie and he told us that we would have to go to Cape Town first, as he had business there. It turned out that he was looking for someone he knew, but they had moved away, so we left Cape Town immediately and headed for Rhodesia. On our way, we stopped in Hermanus and bought fish and chips. Eating as we drove, we must have already covered about twenty miles, when Cecil looked at my dad. Without a word, my dad nodded, turned the car around and we drove all the way back to Hermanus to buy more of the delicious fish and chips.

It seemed a terribly long journey with a little girl and a fifteen month old baby. I had made a bed in the back of the bakkie for the children to sleep and we locked the canopy door so that Ethné couldn't open it. We stopped over in Germiston to see Bill and Phyllis, who were living there now, and spent one day with them before continuing on our journey. Dad and Cecil took turns to drive and, after what seemed like a lifetime, we finally reached Mazabuka. It was a nice little place; there were a couple of houses on the hill, each side of the main road and at the bottom of the hill was a hotel. There were a few Indian shops in town, a post office, petrol station and further down the road was a small police station and power station. It was mainly a farming community.

CHAPTER NINE

Meeting Japhat....

My dad had booked three plots of ground and we each paid for our own plot. As usual, our plot was in the middle, between my parents and Joyce and Charlie. Joyce worked in the shop and my mom still worked with Mister Fisher. My father had just signed a contract to build a hospital at Chikankata Mission, which he asked Cecil and I to do. We were to live on the mission for nearly two years while the hospital was erected. So, once again, we were back to living with no electricity or running water, as the only available dwelling at Chikankata was not on their supply.

Another problem I encountered at Chikankata was that there was no school, so I wrote to an address in Salisbury and arranged to teach Ethné myself as far as Grade Three. Imagine me, with no education, attempting to be a teacher! However, I was really proud when I sent her work to Salisbury for correction and they wrote back, saying they were so impressed with her colouring in, that her work was to be mounted and hung in the Salisbury school hall. We decided to buy Ethné a really good set of paints for Christmas and mentioned this to everyone. Needless to say, Ethné received paints from us, her grandparents and Joyce and Charlie and, believe it or not, from the Salvation Army Christmas party for the kids!

Our house at Chikankata was once again a pole and daga, but Cecil prepared a lovely garden, built a duck pond and bought a few ducks. We befriended a lot of people there, but there are a few couples in particular that come to mind; Audrey and Don Seiler, from the American Salvation Army; Doctor and Mrs Gauntlett and also Phil Laverty and his wife. Phil used to go fishing with Cecil quite often. Audrey had a little boy, I forget his name, but he was a bully to say the least. Every time he and Mike played together, he would hit Mike and make him cry. I kept telling Mike to hit him back, but for a

long time he endured the bullying without retaliation. One day we were having tea and we heard Audrey's son cry out "No, no".
I ran outside with Audrey to see what the commotion was about, only to find him running across the yard, with Mike running after him, hitting him on the head with a chamber pot.

Mike was the type of child who refused to keep his pants or nappy on. He would tug at them until he got them off and would run around the yard in glee, naked from the waist down. This habit came to an abrupt end one day after he encountered a certain duck in our yard. I heard him scream one morning as I was baking cakes in the kitchen and hurried outside to see what was wrong. The scene before me was utterly hilarious. The duck had grabbed hold of a certain part of Mike's anatomy and was trying to swallow it. I can only think that it thought it was a worm, but naturally Mike was pulling in the opposite direction, yelling at the top of his voice, while the duck tugged at it incessantly. Never again did I have a problem with Mike and his pants!

Mike had the knack of keeping me very busy and giving me my fair share of heart failures! Ethné came running in one day shouting, "Mommy, Mike fell in the duck pond."
I flew to the pond and found Mike floating face down in the water. I grabbed him, threw him over my shoulder and ran for the hospital. I believe that the bouncing brought up any water that he may have taken in, as before I got to the hospital he was breathing normally again. He always seemed to be in trouble of some sort. He was almost two and refused to give up his bottle, but insisted on breaking every bottle I gave him. There were no plastic bottles those days. One afternoon I ran out of bottles and Mike screamed incessantly. I took a beer bottle, placed a teat on that and gave him his milk. He drank the milk and then began swinging the bottle with his mouth as he bit on the teat. Naturally, the teat came off and the bottle flew to the ground, smashing as it landed. Mike went to pick up the broken pieces before I could get to him and this resulted in him having sixteen stitches in his hand.

There was also a funny side to this incident. Cecil picked the child up after using his handkerchief to stem the flow of blood, pushed him into the truck and raced up to the hospital. As the truck disappeared over the hill, I suddenly realised that I was still standing there and took off after them on foot. I ran behind the truck all the way to the hospital and Cecil never looked in the rear-view mirror, so he had not seen me.

During our years in Northern Rhodesia we had always been very lax about the African sun, but when Ethné had a severe case of sunburn and was ill for a few days, we became more aware of the dangers and insisted that the children wear hats. It is a shame that we, as adults, never took the same precautions. The skin on my face suffered permanent damage from the harsh sun and I now suffer with pigmentation problems on my arms and legs.

Cecil developed a condition on his eye called Pterygium, which became terribly inflamed and painful. The doctor told him that it would have to be cut off the eye and booked the procedure. Once it was over, his eye was bandaged and he was instructed to leave the bandage on for three days and then return to the doctor for a check-up. That afternoon the truck broke down. Cecil kept lifting the bandage to see what he was doing while he repaired the truck and a few years later the Pterygium grew back. This is again just another instance where we Rhodesians never allowed our health or well-being to interfere with everyday life in the bush. We would work, suffering with Malaria, until we dropped and wounds that went septic were never treated by the doctor, we simply used poultices to draw out the dirt. The first antibiotic that we ever saw was called '693'. This came in tablet form, but was used as a gargle after being dissolved in water. Someone told me to buy a bottle and keep it in the cupboard in case of the children getting a fever. In this case, it was used as one would use a Dispirin. I have no idea how harmful this was, but it did work well and as they say, "ignorance is bliss!"

We received a message from Doctor Gauntlett that we should all get to the hospital as quickly as possible. On arriving, he informed us that they had just diagnosed a case of Typhoid and it was imperative that we all have inoculations immediately. Ethné began to whimper and I reassured her, saying, "Don't be afraid, darling. Look, I'll have my injection first to show you it doesn't hurt." I very confidently stuck my arm out and the doctor proceeded to inject me. Well! I thought he had injected me with hot lead. It slowly travelled up my arm and the entire arm became numb. Funnily enough, everyone else was fine by the time we got home, but my arm was really painful for two days.

Every Sunday I attended the Salvation Army church service and at Christmas, I helped with their Xmas Tree party. They used to have huge bags of clothing sent to them and before they were handed out to the poor, the staff would select a few items and pay for them. I was often asked if I wanted any clothing, as it was all from America and of a wonderful quality, so I would buy for the children. Some of the lepers at the institute did beautiful embroidery and I was shown a blue dress that one leper had embroidered. The lilies ran up from a bunch at the hem, to a single stem at the waist and there were eight sprays of lilies on the skirt. It was beautiful to say the least and I was asked if I would like to buy the dress for two pounds, which I duly did. On the very first occasion I chose to wear it, the bakkie got stuck in the mud and I had to push it, as I couldn't drive. As I pushed the vehicle, the wheels spun in the mud and my beautiful dress was drenched. It was impossible to get the stains out, so I said goodbye to my beloved frock.

We used to travel back to Mazabuka over weekends to spend time with the family and would often drive the one hundred miles to Lusaka to attend the theatre. Joyce and I would dress up in our fancy clothes, with stockings and high-heeled shoes, our hair curled and styled, and the men wore their khaki shirt and shorts. During rainy season, if we got stuck, Joyce and I would bring out the sandwiches, home-made meat pies and flasks of tea and coffee. We would wait patiently for another car to come along and the men-folk would then push the vehicle out. Everyone that travelled this road would take along their eats and drinks and, in fact, I even carried our little G1 stove wherever we travelled. These stoves were issued to the American soldiers during the war. They were small and compact, but gave off a wonderful heat, so we could always make extra tea and coffee. Each person would also have a clean set of clothing. I recall one trip that we took to Lusaka just after we arrived in Mazabuka, or Maz, as we called it. We went in Charlie's car, leaving early as usual, and Mike was still on the bottle. Margaret had already been weaned onto a cup, but when she saw Mike's bottle, she began to scream for hers. She had worn herself out completely by the time we arrived in Lusaka and thankfully slept right through the film. On the trip home, we had a repeat performance and then the car's engine cut out approximately twenty miles from Maz. Joyce, Cecil and I pushed the car up every little hill until we got home, the children screaming all the way. At some stage I lost my high heeled shoe in the mud, so I took off the other shoe and threw it away, pushing the car in my stockings.

On another trip we had a dreadful storm and the Kafue Bridge lost all the filling between the girders. Cecil told us to all get out of the car and he would drive the car across on the girders. I do not know to this day how he managed, using only the headlights to see, but as I watched the car move slowly across the precarious bridge, it felt as though my heart was in my mouth. We then followed, holding tightly onto the rail as we walked slowly across. Somehow the only one who enjoyed the challenge was Cecil and the rest of us were only too glad to get home that night.

One morning we received a message to say that we were needed in town with the truck to load timber at the station. It was late at night by the time the timber was loaded and fastened down and we set off for the mission, which was forty eight miles away. We were about half way there, when the black sky lit up. Cecil stopped the truck and we got out to look more closely. It appeared as if there was a hole in the sky and it was filled with brilliant orange and white light. This lasted for about ten minutes, then it slowly closed and the sky once again became black, with a few stars twinkling here and there. I have never been able to find out what it was.

Phil Lavety showed Cecil a new camera and explained that it took slides. Not knowing what slides were, Cecil asked if he could see one and Phil invited us to visit him that night. What an experience! Phil put on a slide show of Hawaii and various islands in the area. He had taken them when he was stationed there a few years previously. They were in colour and the quality of the pictures was excellent. Cecil was so impressed and badly wanted to buy himself a camera and slide projector.

Shortly afterwards a letter containing one hundred pounds came from his father; the money was from his mother's estate. Cecil drove to Lusaka and bought his first camera, a Voightlander Tessa and later on, he bought an Exacta, which cost him a small fortune. Photography became one of Cecil's great loves and he spent the next twenty years taking excellent photographs and slides. Sadly, many of our slides were stolen when we returned to South Africa twenty years later. Some of them were wonderful close-ups of wildlife, African landscapes and sunsets. I sometimes look at professionally-taken photos of wildlife today and smile, knowing that Cecil's photos were every bit as good.

Once my dad had seen the camera, he and Charlie bought themselves one each and suddenly hunting was not quite as important as it had been. Weekends were still spent in the bush and of course, rifles went along to provide meat for the pot, but the men spent most of the weekend shooting with cameras. I think that Cecil and I were at our happiest during this period. He enjoyed work and the company of the men, who were mostly Americans. Our love for each other seemed to deepen even more and we settled into a warm, comfortable relationship.

We bought Mike a tricycle and taught him to ride it, but he had strict instructions not to move from the pathway. One day he came running inside, screaming "Bite. Bite."
Looking down, I saw two small puncture wounds on his leg and I froze with fear, as I thought of all the poisonous snakes I had seen. I kept asking him "What bit you?" However once I had calmed him down, he told me that he had fallen off his bike and the pedal had caused the wound. It was then that I realised that he had been saying 'bike' not 'bite'.

I was terribly hurt one morning when one of the ladies at the mission popped in to see me. "I would appreciate it," she said quite frankly, "if Ethné did not play with my children anymore. I am terrified that they get that awful South African accent."

I have always been proud to be South African, although I was born in Britain. Even though we referred to ourselves as Rhodesians, Cecil was horrified when we were told at one stage to get British or Rhodesian passports. He told the official that if he was not allowed to be there as a South African, he would pack up and go home. Fortunately we were never forced to make that decision.

Needless to say I never allowed Ethné near the woman again and her children never visited us, which was such a shame, because they all got on so well. Christmas came once again and I offered to help with the Christmas tree party. Mike was nearly three and was in absolute awe of the huge tree. Cecil acted as Santa and was handing out gifts when Mike shouted loudly across the room "That's my daddy."

I jumped up and explained to the children that it was true, but only because Santa's one reindeer was ill and he couldn't get to us in time. "His name is Rudolf." I said, "He has a very bad cold and his nose has turned red and Santa has told him to stay in bed".

This caused such a stir among the children and I spent the next half an hour answering questions until my imagination had literally dried up.

When every present had been handed out, I turned to see one little boy standing there, very obviously without a present. We had no spare gifts (another lesson learnt), so I ran to Mike and said "I promise you I will take you tomorrow morning to buy whatever present you want, but right now, you have to give me this one."

I took the tractor from his hands and walked over to the little boy, putting my arms around him as I knelt beside him. "Because Santa isn't here to do his job, Uncle Cecil made a mistake and gave your present to that little boy over there. He says he is sorry and he will tell Santa what happened. Here is your present."

I handed the tractor over to the overjoyed youngster and then turned back to my own son. Taking him in my arms, I said, "I'm the luckiest mom alive to have a son like you, because other boys would have thrown a tantrum and refused to part with his toy."

All Mike kept uttering was, "You won't forget your promise, mommy, will you?"

The next morning my son chose three dinky cars instead of his tractor and my promise was kept.

Eventually the hospital was completed and it was time to move to town. While we were at Chikankata the family got on quite well and arguments were few and far between. We received word that there was to a shareholder's meeting and we drove down to my father's house. My dad came outside and said, "Come in, Joan".

Cecil was about to get out the car, when my father turned to him and said, "Not you, Cecil, shareholders only and I've given Joan five hundred shares."

Cecil asked whether Joyce was inside and my dad replied, "Of course, she works in the shop, although not a shareholder."

Cecil looked terribly hurt and I felt so sorry for my husband as he sat and waited for me, but I didn't have the courage to make an issue out of it with the family. Many years later we spoke about it and Cecil admitted that he had felt pushed aside and truly injured at the time and I realised that I had failed him on that occasion.

The episode passed and we began to build on the plots. Cecil took a bond for two thousand pounds to build our house. It was nearing completion when my dad asked Cecil whose name the house was registered in, to which Cecil replied "In my name."

"That's not good enough," retorted my father, "You will go and register it in Joan's name tomorrow".

Cecil turned to my dad and replied, "I'm quite capable of taking care of my wife and children and this house will remain in my name. If I die, Joan will automatically inherit the house and as far as I can see, it has absolutely nothing to do with you anyway."

There was a heated argument over this, but Cecil remained adamant and I felt tremendously proud of the way he stood up to my father. He was in a rather difficult position, though. He was employed by my father, not a shareholder and therefore had to tread softly. I realise now that all these things are there to mould you in life, but because they humiliated him, there were constant arguments. Ironically, it was always Cecil that the family turned to when something went wrong. He was always expected to either 'fix it' or 'heal it'.

Mom and dad would not go on holiday unless we went along with them. My dad kept Cecil at his side wherever possible and I sometimes think it was because he felt inadequate. Cecil's strength of character shone in all situations and he bowed to no man. Proud, strong, courageous and a born leader, Cecil stood his ground in every way, just as the lone buffalo after which he was named. Life settled into a comfortable pattern. We befriended the owners of the new petrol station called Hillier's motors. John and Nelly Hillier became very close friends for many years. Nelly was plump and quite pretty, very efficient and ran the administrative section of the business. Originally from Switzerland, she had worked for John's father in Britain. It was there that she and John fell in love. John was a tall, skinny guy; nice looking in his own way, but always seemed to be nothing but arms and legs.

Stoffie and Koen Pretorius came into our lives at this stage, as well as George and Miempie Luden. Koen, George and Cecil were nicknamed 'the three musketeers', as they were always together. Koen was a short, stout man, as hard as nails. Also a buffalo hunter, he was quite a bit older than Cecil. Stoffie, bless her heart, was plump and full of fun. She remained a dear friend until she died just a few years ago. George was the complete opposite of Cecil and Koen. He was Martin Luden's son and, like Martin, he was gentle, softly spoken and although he loved going hunting with them, he was inclined to keep the camp tidy and watch the hunter's pot rather than do any hunting itself. I have never met another man to touch his gentle ways, nor his innate kindness. Miempie, his wife, was wonderful with a rifle and actually accompanied a group of men to Britain to partake in the Bisley Competition. George became like a brother to me and was always there when I needed him, in all the years we lived in Maz.

To reach Lusaka from Maz, you had to go over the Manali Pass. At one stage a lion from the area became such a nuisance, that he was commonly known as the 'Terror of Manali". The pass was quite steep, with a narrow road and cars would negotiate the turns at very slow speed. The lion would stand on the high banks above the road and jump down onto the cars as they drove past. Several people went out hunting him and one day we received news that he had been shot. Cecil grabbed the camera and off we went to see the lion's carcass. The hunter had brought it home to Maz and I still have the slide of the Terror of Manali to this day. There was nothing exceptional about him; he didn't have a nice mane and wasn't even a very big lion. I soon lost interest in looking at him, but Cecil and the hunter were discussing the hunt and I wandered over to a cage in the yard. In this cage sat a group of what looked like puppies, bundles of fluff and absolutely adorable. I asked if I could hold one and he obliged, handing me this little mite with beautiful big eyes. I asked him what they were and he answered "Hyenas."

Who would have thought that these adorable little creatures could become so ugly and ungainly as they grew up?

It was time for a trip to South Africa and my father bought himself a new Jaguar. We had a Zodiac at that stage and we all set off on our holiday. Dad told Cecil to drive in front, because he was afraid of leaving us behind, his car being so fast. We got to Livingstone and waited, but no Jaguar appeared. We turned back to look for them and found them half way back to Mazabuka, sitting on the side of the road with a puncture. Dad was not strong enough to loosen the wheel nuts, so Cecil busied himself changing the wheel. On arriving at Livingstone we stopped for a mixed grill and coffee, having decided to travel through the night. We arranged to meet in Salisbury, but once again the folks didn't turn up and we had to retrace our tracks to find them. They were seventy five miles back, parked on the side of the road with engine trouble. Cecil opened the bonnet and within ten minutes we set off again, only this time dad was told to drive in front and we would meet at the Beit Bridge border post.

We turned a corner in the very early morning en-route to Beit Bridge and found a car lying on its hood with the wheels still spinning. Cecil stopped the car, jumped out and began to help a woman out of the vehicle. She had a nasty gash on the top of her head and I grabbed my first aid kit, treating the wound as best I could. I bandaged her head and we took her belongings from the car and headed back to the hospital in Salisbury. I put her in the front with Cecil and sat in the back with the two youngsters. She had a cream-coloured coat on and blood was dripping from her head onto the coat. I tried to apply pressure with my hand, but the bleeding continued and Cecil increased his speed as much as possible. The sight of the blood made Ethné queasy and before we knew it, she was vomiting all over the back seat. This naturally set Mike off and he, too, began throwing up. Needless to say, the stench in that heat was unbearable and I was glad to reach the hospital for more than one reason. Once we had got the woman admitted, we cleaned up the car before continuing our journey. On our return trip, we stopped and enquired about her and the hospital staff told us that she had been discharged after a few days.

We had lost about four hours travelling time and Cecil rode as fast as possible until we reached Beit Bridge. As we got out of the car, my father shouted, "I told you to stay in front and let the better car keep an eye on you. Look at the time you've wasted."
Realising that a row was about to develop, I started laughing and said "Oh stop it, dad, I was busy acting as Florence Nightingale and lost my lamp on the way."
This diffused the situation somewhat and we set off for Durban. On two more occasions dad's car gave engine trouble and I was ever so grateful that he could not hear Cecil's remarks about the 'piece of junk dad had bought' as we drove along.

At last we reached Durban and we stayed with Eddie and Florrie, who had been transferred there from Port Elizabeth. On the first morning we went to the beach and my mom told Cecil that their car had developed a squeak and she wanted him to look at it. This must have been the final straw and Cecil retorted angrily "Look, mom, do me a favour, will you? Take that piece of junk, drive it into a tank of oil and please leave it there. Find something else to drive home in."

There was awkward silence for the rest of the day, but on the whole it turned out to be a lovely holiday. We rode in a rickshaw, the children swam at the beach every day and we thoroughly enjoyed the lovely weather in Durban.

Our trip home was uneventful, apart from me opening my big mouth at customs. As usual, we were asked if we had anything to declare. I had bought quite a lot of items for my home and when Cecil answered in the negative, I was afraid that we might get into trouble, so I bravely said, "I did buy a tea set."

Cecil looked at me as though I had just arrived from outer space and I quickly added "But it's only a cheap Japanese one".

The customs official looked at me and said, "Japanese goods are not allowed in this country. We will have to confiscate it."

My mind flew to all the other items we had bought and I think my face must have been a picture. Suddenly the serious look on the official's face turned to a completely bemused one, he smiled and said "Enjoy your tea set, I'm only joking."

When we got to the car, Cecil muttered, "Do me a favour. Next time we get to customs, show yourself, then get back in the car and stay there."

When we arrived home, we found that our servant had left and taken all his belongings with him, so I was on the look-out for another. A couple of days later an African man walked into my yard and said, "I'm looking for work, Dona".

He appeared to be respectable and I was trying to decide on the spur of the moment, when he announced, "Dona, I'm not a pinch boy."

This somehow tickled my fancy and I hired him. He was married with one child, from a Catholic background and he worked very well. So well, in fact, that he stayed in my employ for seventeen years and when we left Zambia, he begged me to take him and his family with us. His name was Japhat and he fathered another three children over the years, all of them born in the little house we had provided for them in our back yard.

One of the prettiest sights I ever saw was early on one Sunday morning, when they were dressed up to attend the local church. Japhat was attired in his best trousers and jacket, looking quite the distinguished gentleman. His wife, a petite woman who was always smiling, was wearing one of my dresses (I always gave her clothes) and the little ones were in black shorts and white shirts with bow ties immaculately positioned by their mother. I have always regretted not having taken a photograph of them that morning; it would have been a very special one to keep.

I don't think we ever realised during those days, just how hard Japhat worked. He would enter the house at five thirty in the morning and clean the kitchen first. We entertained regularly, so there were always a lot of dirty dishes to be washed. At six he would knock on my door and quietly announce that tea and coffee was served. On a little table outside the bedroom door would be a tray with two pots, one containing coffee and the other tea. Cecil's clothes were always washed, ironed and placed on a chair for him. When we were dressed and came out of the bedroom, the table was set and he would serve a hearty breakfast, usually bacon, eggs, tomato and toast. Occasionally he would cook sausages and chips for breakfast as well.

I was very involved with MOTHWA at that stage and was doing Brown Owl for the Brownies as well. I would leave Japhat with instructions regarding the lunch menu and confidently attend my meetings in the knowledge that lunch would be served promptly at one. Japhat would change from his working khanza into his crisp, white khanza and serve us our lunch. He did all washing and ironing, cleaned the house and was a very capable baker. He would go off from two to four, heading straight for his khaya (home) and then return to bake either cakes or biscuits, which he would serve with coffee at five thirty.

He was terribly efficient and I was able to just give him a menu if we were entertaining and inform him of how many guests would be attending and at what time. Japhat would enter the room as our guests arrived and announce that drinks were served on the veranda.

Alcoholic beverages were served for the guests and soft drinks for the children and the women who preferred this to alcohol. He would serve dinner at eight sharp, usually a beautifully prepared roast, with all the trimmings. Many a compliment was made by guests on the meals prepared and served by Japhat. I would often tell him to leave the dishes and go home a little early, knowing how hard he had worked to deliver such perfect meals.

Japhat never grumbled; he was always a smiling, happy man. He was off duty on Sundays and every couple of months we would give him a week to take his family to the village where they were from. He was a Chinyanja and visiting his village was important to him. About a month after he started working for us, Japhat became ill and I sent him to the doctor. Our doctor's name was Smith and near him lived a family by the name of DeSmidt. One of these farms had belonged to Wilbur Smith, the famous author, but that was before we lived in Maz. The doctor gave him a letter addressed to me, informing me that Japhat was to return every day for the next three days for injections. I phoned the doctor to find out what was actually wrong with him and he casually stated that Japhat had Syphilis. I was utterly horrified and said "I must fire him right away."
The doctor laughed and said "Joan, you could hire another ninety nine and ninety five of them will have it."

I asked why it was so rife and he explained that when a young village girl got married, her wedding night was spent with the Headman of the village, who would then confirm the following day that she was virgin. As the headman usually had syphilis, he passed it on to the woman, who in turn passed it on to her husband. "Don't worry, the injections keep it under control and you won't have any problems."

It wasn't long before Japhat had become my right hand man (and my left!). The business was flourishing and each year a percentage of our dividends was put back into shares. By this time Cecil had also bought shares and during one meeting, my father told us that each person's shares were worth three hundred and fifty thousand rand.

However this was on paper and we were not allowed one penny of it as my father felt that no money should be drawn for ten years.

I bought Cecil an African Grey parrot for his birthday. It cost me twelve pounds and its name was Polly Sonderbroek. Translated, this means 'Polly without pants', as the parrot always pulled its tail feathers out, leaving nothing but a bare behind. Cecil put his hand into the cage, trying to coax the parrot onto his finger, but Polly simply bent his head and gave Cecil a nasty bite. Cecil shouted "Ouch!" and tapped the parrot on its head to chastise it. From that day on, every time Cecil put his hand into the cage, Polly would shout "Ouch" and then duck, shaking his head from side to side, but he never bit Cecil again.

Polly would sit in his cage and rock his body from side to side, saying "Clackety-clack" and we realised that he was imitating the train that brought him down from the Congo. He was a beauty when it came to talking; he picked up new words so quickly and was like a naughty child. I would take him out of his cage on my finger, lay him on his back and say "Polly, die."
Polly would lie completely inert with his little feet sticking up into the air. Every time a woman entered the room, Polly would wolf-whistle at her and males were politely told to "Push off, you bloody fool!"

When Don Seiler called in on one of his trips from the mission, Polly swore at him and Don admonished him by saying, "Polly, you are disgusting. You have diarrhoea of the mouth."
One morning an elderly man from the Jehovah's Witness group came to ask if he could spend a few minutes discussing the bible. He looked old and tired and I felt so sorry for him, so I invited him in for tea, but told him that I would prefer not to discuss religion, as I had my own beliefs. He gratefully accepted and, of course, Polly was determined to join the conversation. "Push off, you bloody fool."
I wouldn't have felt so bad, if the old man hadn't turned to me and said "I hear your parrot talks."
"Yes, he does. Please excuse him, he has absolutely no manners." I replied with as much grace as I could muster.

147

The old man gently pointed out that 'someone had taught him everything he said' and of course I knew that the three musketeers were fully responsible. Nevertheless, I was truly embarrassed and was relieved when he stood up to leave. At that moment, Cecil drove into the driveway. Polly was shouting "Daddy, daddy. Where's my cheque book?"

The old man said goodbye, thanked me for the tea and walked out. As Cecil came into the room, I turned on him. "Cecil, you guys haven't played the game, teaching Polly to swear. He has been calling that poor old gentleman a bloody fool."

Naturally Cecil roared with laughter and said "Well, perhaps he was!"

As he said those words, I turned to see the old man walk back into the lounge, gesturing to his hat, which he had left on the table. My face must have been a picture as I saw him and I could have died with shame.

Polly loved tomato, but he wouldn't eat it when you gave it to him. He would wait until someone stood near the cage, then he would bite a piece off and fling it at them and it usually landed on their clothes. He loved music and would spread his wings and rock and roll in his cage when he heard it. I laughed one day when the gardener came and asked me for newspaper. I asked him what he wanted it for and he answered "For the bloody fool bird."

At this time Ethné started begging for a puppy and we bought her a little Daschund, which she named Shorty. He brought Ethné a lot of joy and we all became very fond of him. Some time later, I visited someone who was trying to get rid of a young daschund-cross and I decided to take it. Cecil complained, but I determinedly announced that it was my puppy and I was keeping it. I called him Chappie and he followed me everywhere from then on. These were the first pets we had allowed ourselves to get in the Rhodesias, because of the fear of rabies.

I received a phone call from Cecil's cousin, Ronnie Slabbert. He and his wife, Sue, were in Salisbury and wanted to visit us for a weekend. Ronnie wasn't as big a man as Cecil, but he was extremely fit, being a skydiver and avid sportsman. Sue was a small woman with dark hair, very vivacious and she loved pretty clothes and jewellery, particularly diamond rings. They had a son named Valmore, who was about twelve at the time. Ethné was twelve and Mike was seven. Ronnie brought his rifle along to go hunting with Cecil, who had befriended a farmer on the Kafue Flats, by the name of Mr Seaman. He had over one thousand lechwe on the farm and the men went off hoping to shoot one, while Sue and I stayed at home. They returned a few hours later with a lechwe that Cecil had shot. Ronnie never got his rifle up fast enough and the lechwe were on the run, so Cecil had shot it. I must mention that our men never used telescopic sights. Cecil carved himself a small sight out of warthog tusk so that there would be no reflecting glare from metal when he was shooting. Cecil always said "I don't need a telescopic sight; I like my animals to have a sporting chance."

Despite this, he was an amazing shot when it came to long distances. After their first visit, Ron and Sue visited us regularly every six months or so for a weekend. On one such weekend we all went to Cyril Seaman's farm with our Landrover. We all enjoyed the ride and admired the animals as we went along. I had given one of my little duikers, named Bokkie Two, to Cyril Seaman and I went to say hello to it. Bokkie Two had been with him for nearly a year and during that time he had been placed with Cyril's pet kudu and after all that time, Bokkie had run under the kudu and stuck his horns into its belly. Cecil had to shoot the animal, as it was too badly injured.

We drove down to the Kafue River to show our guests how beautiful it was on the flats. You could see for miles and at certain times of the year the river would flood and the flats had markers in the grass to show how high the river had been, turning the flats into swampland. Ethné had beautiful long hair, reaching her waist and when I plaited it, the plait was as thick as my arm. The plait had loosened with the wind as we travelled. She never tied her hair up again that day and when I said that she should, she told me not to pamper her. At the time, she was laughing at Valmore as Sue wiped the dust from his face. "He's twelve, mom, but he's a real mommy's boy."

149

When we got home, her hair was so tangled that we were forced to cut it short and she cried bitterly.

Ronnie had bought a Desota Firesweep motor car and on their next trip up, they came to visit us in it. It was a luxury car and there were only four in Rhodesia at that stage, I believe. He kept eyeing Cecil's new Zodiac and asked him if he wanted to swap. Cecil, who was madly in love with Ronnie's Firesweep, jumped at the opportunity and the exchange was made. Later that weekend Sue traded her bike for Ethné's typewriter, so we all felt that a profitable weekend had been had. We arranged to collect the bike on our next trip to Salisbury, as it was again time to go on holiday to South Africa. We got our new triptique (insurance and third party cover for South Africa), updated our passports and arranged a letter of credit for five hundred pounds and proudly set off in our new Firesweep.

We hadn't even reached Beit Bridge when a tyre burst and a garage owner from Messina told us that the Firesweep needed special tyres, available only from Firestone in Port Elizabeth and he had none in stock. We slept in the car that night and next day the owner contacted a friend who owned a garage and fortunately he was able to help us. As we travelled, we quickly learned that the car's petrol consumption was horrendous. Another tyre blew near Bloemfontein and another in Cradock. Every time we stopped somewhere, it would take ages before we could leave again, as every man in sight was admiring the car and wanting to look at the engine.

We spent Christmas with Bill and Phyllis. Bill had his own business and gave us a Christmas to remember. The tree was piled high with gifts for us, especially for me. Cecil knew I had a passion for soft toys and he had bought me a fluffy white cat. When the tail was wound up, the cat would roll over and over to the gentle tune of Braham's Lullaby. After Christmas, we travelled down to Port Elizabeth for a couple of weeks.

Needless to say, the tyres from Firestone were specialized ones and cost us a fortune. We had to cut our holiday short by more than a week, as we had certainly not budgeted for this expense. On our return journey, we had only travelled as far as Bloemfontein, when one of the 'special' tyres burst and we lost another just before Pretoria, as it threw rubber from the tread. To our utmost dismay we blew another tyre just outside of Messina on the way home. We managed to get a replacement, completely different in size, but it was all they could offer us. The delay caused us to reach the border post after closing time, so we had no option but to settle down in the car for the night. Cecil took out the G1 stove and we started making coffee (thank the Lord for powdered milk, also a new product on the market). By now another five cars had pulled up behind us. I made a bed for the children next to the car with blankets and put them down to sleep. The tantalizing aroma of the coffee began to waft through the warm night air and the men from the other cars began to chat to Cecil about his car! Slowly their wives followed and we offered coffee to them all, their grateful smiles being payment enough. We all sat drinking our coffee and chatting until the early hours of the morning. This was really a case of ships that pass in the night and left a lovely memory for all.

At six the next morning we passed through customs and we arrived in Salisbury on a Sunday, with more tyre trouble. After spending hours looking for a garage that was open, we found one that obliged and took the rest of the little money we had left. We were down to just a few shillings. The children were hungry and Ceil bought three meat pies. Handing one to each child, he broke the other in half, which we shared. At Chirundu we got another puncture. A man there was kind enough to trust us by giving us a tyre and we promised to send the money to him when we got home. He went so far as to make sandwiches for the children while Cecil fitted the new tyre. Most Rhodesians are like that. They always go that extra mile to help someone in need, as if they were all one big family.

Twenty miles from home, we blew another tyre, but the Lord looks after His own. A car came along and the driver promised to phone George about our problem. About two hours later George arrived with hot coffee, sandwiches and another tyre. He was always a man in a million.

Cecil said he suspected that the strips were responsible for all the tyres bursting. They are two cement strips, laid for miles along the roads for your car to travel on, but if there is an oncoming car, you have to get off the strip in order to pass it. Sometimes the ground has eroded next to the strip, making it three or four inches higher than the actual road. Being so rough, this would wear the tyre on that particular spot.

When we got home we sold the Firesweep, bought another Zodiac, brand new and green and white in colour. Three weeks later when we went to Lusaka again, Cecil saw a red and white one in the showroom and went in to have a look. An hour later we left Lusaka in a red and white Zodiac, having traded in the green one. When one has plenty of money, one spends it foolishly, thinking that life will always be like that. However, when the day of reckoning arrives, you realize that you haven't saved enough and life becomes hard and cruel.

On our trips to South Africa we would have to pass through the Tsetse Fly building. It was a long brick building, just off the main road and you had to drive through the building before reaching customs. As you drove inside, the doors were closed and the vehicle was sprayed underneath with insecticide. Before the door in front of you was opened a guard on duty would come with a little net and check your car inside for tsetse fly. When he was satisfied that there were none, he would open the doors and let you through.

These holidays never seemed to start for Cecil until he reached his destination, so we would travel straight through to Port Elizabeth, with just the odd stop for fuel and food. Apart from putting his head back for half an hour during our short stops, Cecil would drive the entire distance without decent sleep. I would take the children out into the open and show them where the fairies lived, keeping them occupied while Cecil snatched a little sleep behind the wheel. We would seek out various shaped leaves and branches, which we guessed the fairies used as tables and chairs. Tiny flowers and bits of leaves were their cups and plates and my children truly loved Cecil's rest periods en-route to our holiday destinations so they could seek out the fairies.

While driving, we would play games in the car to keep the children occupied, such as spotting certain cars or colours first. I would also give them an old camera, without a spool in, and they would happily snap away. The hours were long and without these diversions, the children would have been so utterly bored that they would fight endlessly. One memory of a trip to SA was when I told Mike, who was three at the time, we were going on holiday. Not knowing what a holiday was, he kept asking me all the time we were away, and even when we returned home, "Where is the holiday?"

Kariba was in the early stages of being constructed and we keenly followed the progress through each stage. The African people said that people would never tame the Zambezi God and the people building Kariba certainly had a few nasty setbacks, especially the time some poor chaps fell of the scaffolding into quick-drying cement. We often drove down to Kariba to watch the water slowly flooding the land. We sadly watched some of our old hunting grounds disappear underwater forever, with the odd island forming in the middle of the lake. This was when Operation Noah came into being. How fascinating it was to watch these dedicated men in boats, rescuing animals, both large and small, even snakes and creepy crawlies. They did a fantastic job and we truly admired their courage and determination.

Cecil had become tired of our home being a run-through for the other families. There was no malice intended, but no matter what we were doing, Mom would pop in and say "I'm just on my way to Joyce" and vice versa. Cecil put up a fence and bought some geese and my mom said he had done it on purpose, making Cecil simply smile and reply "No, mom, I've always wanted geese." Some time later we were made an offer for the house and we decided to accept it. We bought a plot on the top of the hill, quickly erected half a house and moved in.

Soon after moving, my dad decided that the three men would go on a hunting trip to the Mulobezi area. We had a bookkeeper by this time, whom my dad thought radiated sunshine, and he accompanied them on the trip. They had to travel by truck to Livingstone and then put it on the train and travel to Mulobezi. This train belonged to the Mulobezi sawmills and was designed to carry timber. It consisted of flat-beds instead of coaches. Once the truck was loaded, the men put their blankets around the vehicle to rest. The train was fed by wood from the sawmills and each time wood was placed in the furnace, sparks would fly out of the chimney. During the evening one of these sparks set Cecil's blanket alight. However, soon after leaving Mulobezi, the train suddenly stopped and the driver got out. When asked what was wrong, he replied "Nothing, I need some meat for the pot at home, so I am going to shoot something quickly." With that, he disappeared into the bush and the passengers sat and waited for nearly two hours for him to return with an antelope.

They continued the journey until the train stopped again and the driver advised the men that they had reached the best area for hunting. There was no siding of any kind, so how they got the truck off, I do not know. Then it was a case of drive through solid bush with no tracks of any kind in sight. I have a short film taken with an eight millimetre cine camera of this particular hunting trip. As usual, Cecil did the driving and took charge of the whole procedure of setting up camp once they reached their destination. Cecil then left camp and shot a zebra for the gun bearers. He then left a second time to get an antelope for the pot. He set off on his own onto a form of plain and found a herd of buffalo grazing. Before he could do anything, they stampeded towards him and the closest tree to him was full of thorns. Having no other choice, Cecil heaved himself into the branches just in time, as the herd passed beneath him. The branches were thin and he was afraid that he would fall into the stampeding herd at any moment. Despite the thorns that were piercing his skin and embedding themselves in his body, he hung onto the branches for dear life until the herd had passed.

The most difficult obstacle was extricating himself from the tree without further injury, which was humanly impossible. He limped back to camp, where the gun bearers tried to dig the thorns out of his wrist, but they never touched his knee. By the next morning, Cecil was unable to walk. A thorn had penetrated his leg under the knee cap and would have to be surgically removed. He also had thorns in other parts of his body, but the men in camp had removed them and although these wounds were red and painful, they would heal in a few days. His wrist was also very swollen and Cecil reluctantly broke the news to the other men in camp. Having no option, the men packed up camp and followed the train tracks to Mulobezi.

The local doctor operated on his knee and told Cecil that he had taken out what he could see, but he wasn't sure whether every bit of thorn had been removed. "They will work themselves out in time" he said.
He then worked on Cecil's wrist and the verdict was the same. The men put the truck back on the train and instead of being away a few weeks, they returned home after only four days. The last thorn came out of Cecil's wrist over a year later, but his knee healed without further trouble.

Hunting trips were few and far between since the men had become so obsessed with photography. Cecil already had three thirty five millimetre cameras and between the men, they had spent thousands at the Indian shop in Lusaka. They each had an eight millimetre cine-camera and we began visiting game reserves to take photos. Our favourite reserve was Wankie. I marvel at some of the experiences that we had there and I often wonder if we drew drama to us in our lifetime together.

A chap had come to Maz to work at the power station and Cecil had invited him to join us on one trip, as he had never been in the 'bush'. He was new in the country from overseas. On our first evening in the bungalow, Cecil offered him a whisky. He shook his head, saying that he did not drink alcohol at all and opted for one of my soft drinks. We set off early next morning and came across a kill. Two big lions had killed a buffalo, so we parked the car and waited for the sun to rise to take some photos. Another car arrived and instead of parking near us, they went in front of us and blocked our view of the

155

furiously feeding animals. Cecil was upset to say the least. It's not often you are lucky enough to get that close to a kill, so we backed up and tried to get past the car in order to get a better view. In doing so, the wheel caught the leg of the buffalo and pulled it slightly away from the lions. The one male leapt up and jumped onto the bonnet of our car, his bloodied face snarling at us through the windscreen. Well, this poor guy nearly had a heart attack! After a few minutes, the lion went back to his meal and we got our photographs.

We returned to camp for lunch and then set out on a different route. In front of us was a large hill and the road was cut half way up the side of it. Just ahead of us, standing in the middle of the road, were two magnificent elephants. Cecil, realising that this chap was nervous, said "It's alright; we will wait here until they are gone."

They began to climb the hill and Cecil started the car and moved slowly forward. As we reached the corner and proceeded to go around it, we saw a herd of elephants on the road. Cecil decided to back up a little and turned to look behind us. The two elephants that we had seen first, had come back onto the road and were directly behind us. Cecil edged the car forward, hoping the herd would move, but one of the cows charged. Cecil's face was dead white, the children were screaming and I pushed them onto the floor of the car. Cecil revved the engine as hard as he could, then drove the car towards the cow and she turned and ran back down the hill at the very last moment. Slowly we edged our way through the herd and heaved sighs of relief as we looked back at them once we were past.

You are not allowed to leave your vehicle while travelling in the reserve, but Cecil stopped the car and went to the boot. He came back with a whisky and water and held it out to the chap in the front seat, who silently grabbed the glass and downed the contents. "That's the closest I've ever come to climbing into a car's pistons." He muttered as he handed the glass back to Cecil.

"You wouldn't have to climb, mate, you would have been pushed!" Cecil retorted.

As usual, after danger had passed, Cecil and I would start laughing. This guy could not understand what we found so amusing and became quite upset with us. "This life is not for me." He stated flatly with a disillusioned tone of voice.

We offered to leave him in camp while we went out the next morning, but he chose to go with us rather than be alone in camp. "Anyway" he said "We've had our excitement for this trip. I can't imagine anything else happening."

Having tempted fate, we accidentally came across a herd of rather agitated buffalo that promptly stampeded. I sat with my heart in my mouth as they thundered past us on either side of the car. I was not surprised that the poor guy never accompanied us on a trip again.

On another occasion, when it was just my family, we passed an elephant on the side of the road and the children suddenly shouted "Ride, Daddy! It's chasing us."

Sure enough, when we looked back, the elephant was running after the car and gaining on us. The road was very narrow and we were approaching a horseshoe bend. The elephant, very cleverly cut across the veld and before we knew it, it was in front of us. Cecil managed to back up and turn the car around, heading back in the direction from which we had just come and once again we escaped what could have been a nasty experience. And so life went on, with one adventure after another. The next adventure was the following Sunday.

We were out on the Kafue in a friend's boat and we were teasing the owner about his boat being made of metal and terribly heavy. "It's a miracle that the damn thing floats." Cecil joked. "We'll land up being lunch for the crocodiles."

No sooner were the words out of his mouth, when the boat lurched as we hit something solid under the water. As we passed over it, a hippo broke the surface behind us, looking quite indignant. We waited a while to check whether the propeller had injured it, but it seemed to be fine. As quite a few more were entering the water, we decided it was safer to move on. We were all pretty silent after Cecil asked "How would we have fared in a light wooden boat?"

We all knew that if the boat had overturned, some of us would never have seen dry land again.

Around this time Mrs Morton came to see us. Her little girl was of school age, but there was still no school at Chikankata Mission, where they were working for the Salvation Army. She asked whether her daughter, Dorelle, could board with us and we agreed. Ethné and Dorelle became best friends and we would find them giggling into the late hours of the night in their bedroom. One morning Ethné announced that she was feeling ill, so I left her in bed and Dorelle went to school. By eight thirty she was back home, saying that she also felt ill. I put her to bed and went on with my sewing. A short while later I heard them laughing and when I walked into the room, they were playing merrily. Naturally after that episode I was more careful when one of them cried illness!

Dorelle boarded with us until she and Ethné were ready for high school in Lusaka and I came to love her dearly. She called us 'mom and dad two'.
Mike had reached school-going age and he started in the January. His teacher was a friend, a farmer's wife, by the name of Mrs Barrett. She met me one day and asked "Where did you get that child from?"
I laughed and asked her why.
"When it's time to learn or do anything in the line of work, he has a headache, but if I leave the classroom for a moment and peep through the window, he's the first one up with his ruler, looking for someone to challenge in a sword-fight. The other day I asked the class what a warrior is and Michael shouted out 'It's a person what worries a lot."

Mike was now seven years old and he was very skinny and tall for his age. A few weeks after I had spoken to his teacher, I found Mike in the garden one morning playing with two beautiful dinky toys and I asked him where he got them from. He replied that he had found them.
"Impossible!" I retorted. "They're brand new."
After some coaxing, Mike admitted that he had stolen them from one of the Indian shops. I picked them up and took Mike by the scruff of the neck, marching him to the shop concerned. After all those years, the owner knew me well; I even had an account at his shop. I left Mike outside and approached the owner to explain. "Please

remember that he's just a little boy." I pleaded. "Put the two cars onto my account, but I am sending him in to you now, do whatever you think is best, but please don't involve the police."

He laughed and said "Typical little boy, Mrs Slabbert, send him in to me."

Mike was in the shop about ten minutes. I have no idea what transpired, but his face was snow white when he left the shop and he never stole again.

Mazabuka was slowly increasing in population and so my brother arranged for a film every Saturday from Lusaka, which he showed at the Settler's Club. All the Maz folks would attend and then they started holding dances on Friday nights as well. After all those years of Cecil claiming that he could not dance, we began attending the functions and he proved to be a beautiful dancer. John and Nellie would accompany us and we met up with many other friends there. I spent many hours during the week making myself a new dress for Friday's dance. Cecil could not stand being dressed up in a tuxedo, so by nine his jacket would be taken off. As soon as Cecil had removed his, the other men would do the same. By ten the ties were removed and shirts were open to the waist. Everyone was relaxed and enjoying themselves and it would slowly become evident that the men had been drinking.

I loved Cecil when he'd had a few whiskies. He would laugh, joke and play the fool, but never did he embarrass me through drunkenness. I saw other men do things that would bring tears to their wife's eyes, but Cecil was always the perfect gentleman. I saw him once on the dance floor with Nellie and they were playing a Spanish song. Nellie was waving her handkerchief matador-style and Cecil was playing the bull. The fun was clean and brought many a laugh to the people attending the dances. By midnight the guys would disappear and come back half an hour later, with wet hair and their clothes and shoes damp. They used to jump into the reservoir to cool off and then return to the dance with fresh vigour. On one very hot evening, one of the women suggested that we go for a dip. When we reached the reservoir we heard a male voice shout "Move, guys, here come the women."

All we saw were a number of white bare bottoms fly over the side of the reservoir as they all dived for cover.

The men had become so fanatical about photography that they each had their own dark room and printed their own photos. Cecil was a very creative and capable photographer and even printed his own slides. He did several weddings and was asked to do quite a few portraits of children. Charlie was using his wife as his model and we all seemed to be getting on better as a family. I also think our moving out of the middle house to the top of the hill helped, as we were no longer in each other's pockets, so to speak.

One day Norman Carr came to visit and brought Big Boy and Little Boy with him. They were two lions about which he wrote a book. I still have a photo of the game guard holding Big Boy in his arms as he stood in my back yard. Speaking of Norman, his wife was one of the tiniest women I have ever seen. To have watched her on the dance floor was to have witnessed a fairy dance, she was so light and graceful on her feet. Strangely enough, when I decided to write this book, I initially named it 'Kakuli'. However, after doing some research on internet, we discovered that Norman had written a book of the same name about buffalo.

Time marched on and on one of our visits to friends, we were driving in the car and the children were arguing in the back. I turned and said "I'm tired of you two fighting all the time. I'm going to have another baby who won't fight with anyone."
So the idea was born. I was thirty one years old, my children were growing up and I realised that another baby would be nice. Cecil wasn't keen and said "If you have another baby, it's yours. You change diapers and sit up at night when it's crying. I'm through with babies."

A few weeks later I developed a pain in my side and I went to see the doctor, who by this time was a dear friend of ours. It was just before Rhodes and Founders, two public holidays that fell after the weekend, which meant that we had four days of holidays approaching and planned to visit the game reserve. I explained what we were planning and then told him of the pain in my right side. "I don't feel well enough to go away and the family usually argues when they're on holiday together."

He nodded and said "Stop your trip. I think it's your appendix and we will have to take it out. I'll book you for Friday morning."

I went into hospital, which consisted of six beds for females, six beds for males and very little else. They did have a very small, basic operating theatre and I was soon wheeled in for the op.

When I came around, I said to Cecil "It was terrible. The anaesthetic was so black."

Cecil asked me what I meant, but it was difficult to explain. There had been a terrible blackness and it wasn't nice at all. The family visited and I passed the same remark to them. The doctor called in to see me and said "There was nothing wrong with your appendix, but I removed it anyway."

Somehow the horror of that anaesthetic would not go away and I knew instinctively that something had happened. A little later a friend popped in to see me, announcing "Gosh, Joan, but you gave us all a fright."

I immediately knew that my suspicions were correct. I laughed casually and said "Did I?" as if I knew all about it.

"Yes," she said, "Doc was terribly worried. Your heart stopped on the operating table and he couldn't get it going again. As he was about to inject the heart, you suddenly took a deep breath and began breathing on your own again."

I had been told after Ethné's birth that I was not a good candidate for anaesthetic, so whether it was just a bad reaction or too much anaesthetic, I don't know. However I felt ill even when I went home and returned to the doctor a few days later. He told me that it was completely normal after an op and not to worry. A couple of weeks passed and I realised I may be pregnant, so I consulted him again.

"Could I be pregnant?" I asked.

He examined me and shook his head, intimating that it was all imaginary and once again reminded me that all these symptoms were normal after surgery.

A couple of weeks later I was really feeling ill and returned yet again to the doctor. He suspected that I had a dose of malaria and injected me with Mepacrine. Three days later I was standing in my bedroom when the baby I had wanted so badly miscarried. My mom wrapped it in cotton wool and called Cecil, who took me to hospital. I was heartbroken, but this made me even more determined than ever to fall pregnant again. My grief caused me to lose weight and falling pregnant became almost an obsession. The doctor put me on fertility pills, but it took nearly two years to conceive again. During this time Cecil was so patient with me and remained just as caring as always. He was still the passionate lover that he had always been and made me feel a complete woman.

CHAPTER TEN

The battle to save my life…..

Once again Cecil contracted Malaria quite badly and went into hospital for a few days. He came out looking as yellow as a marigold and he was terribly thin. He couldn't even keep his trousers up with a belt; they just slipped over his lean hips. My dad suggested that he spend a few weeks at home to recover, but within just a few days Cecil was bored to tears. He had washed a petrol tank and filled it with water a few weeks previously and decided that it could now be welded safely. I was inside when I heard a dull thud and looked out of the window to see what the noise had been. I saw Cecil switch off the welder and walk, very unsteadily, towards the house. As he opened the door and I looked up at his face, I felt sick to the stomach. The petrol tank had exploded in his face, burning it quite severely. His one eye was closed and he looked dreadful. I packed a bag as fast as I could and George drove us to the hospital.

At this stage the hospital was being run by Catholic nuns and they admitted him immediately. One nun began unpacking his bag and then casually said "You didn't bring a sundowner for him."
Aghast at her words, particularly from a Catholic nun, I expressed my surprise.
"Nonsense," she replied. "All the men are allowed their sundowners at night."
She led me to a cupboard and, lo and behold, there stood a bottle of whisky with a patient's name on it. Someone else had a six-pack of beer and another had a bottle of rum.

The doctor examined Cecil and dressed his face. As I turned to leave, he walked over to me and said "I cannot say yet whether Cecil has lost the sight in his eye. It's too swollen and it will be at least five days before I can examine it, but I'd like him to stay in hospital."

And so began the most anxious days of my life. However when I visited him that night, I found the four men in the ward sipping sundowners happily. There was one chap with an abscess in his ear and two with Malaria. All four wives sat and sipped their husbands' drinks and we began to chat. Eventually stories and jokes were being told and the poor bloke with the abscess begged us to stop, because it hurt when he laughed; then in the next breath he would personally tell a joke and laugh with us. I was told that even prisoners were allowed to leave their cells between five thirty and seven in the evening to sit under the trees and enjoy a sundowner. It was truly a wonderful way of life and very few countries enjoyed the freedom that we did. At about eleven thirty the sister came in and said "Okay, gang, the party's over. My patients need some beauty sleep now." She threw us all out, but I'm sure that her patients recovered far quicker than in a normal hospital. What a relief a few days later when the doctor announced that Cecil's eye would be fine, but the blast had pushed minute pieces of metal into the skin around the eye, which remained there until the day he died.

While Mike was small I was always afraid of him falling over the Victoria Falls, as he was a typical little boy and always ventured right to the edge to peer over. Cecil finally had a brainwave and whispered to Mike "I'm very worried about mommy. She keeps going to the edge and she may fall over. Would you please look after her for me?"
There was no more trouble after that, Mike would pull me back long before we reached the edge, saying "Not so close, mom, you might fall over the edge. I'm looking after you for daddy." The one and only time I made a fool of myself at the falls was while standing quite close to the edge. I stepped backwards and my foot went into quite a deep culvert, causing me to lose my balance and fall. I truly thought I was going over the edge and I do believe that my screams were heard in Livingstone, quite a few miles away.

There was a little game reserve at Vic Falls and we would spend hours there looking at game. Both Cecil and I loved the wild animals, both big and small. They had a couple of tame rhinos in the park and these were our greatest fascination. So big and queer in

164

build, they would stand at the fence while we scratched their faces. They seemed to enjoy the touch of our hands on their skin. They always made me feel as if they were mentally deficient, or should I say just plain dim, yet they were so trusting that one just had to love them.

The breathtaking panorama of the Victoria Falls has been photographed from so many angles; it needs no introduction, nor vivid description, except for its rainbows and the sound one hears when you are near it. Its African name, Mosi oa Tunya (the smoke that thunders), could not be more accurate. When you stand at the falls, the earth beneath your feet trembles with the speed and volume of the gushing water and you cannot speak to each other above the roar as it cascades to the jagged rocks in the chasm far below.

I found I always got butterflies in my tummy when I looked over the edge. During the rainy season, when the Zambezi is in full spate, the thundering water cascades down the falls, sending a vast, misty spray into the air, reminds one of the magnificence of God's creation as it gently mists your face. The rainbows that form above the falls have a brilliance beyond description. A myriad of colours, that dazzle the eyes in the warm sunshine, leave the spectators in absolute awe of their beauty.

Cecil and I were lucky enough to visit the falls when it was in flood and it was an experience never to be forgotten. Standing above the falls on the bank of the Zambezi, it appeared as if the water was at least six times higher in the middle of the river than the banks it had already covered. It seemed to be in such a hurry, climbing over itself and forming huge waves. At this stage the river was so wide that I could not see the other side and the earth trembled forcibly under your feet. I felt fear spread through my veins like hot lead, as I stood and watched the angry Zambezi. Its volume created such thunderous roaring that it made conversation impossible and left me feeling very small and humble in its magnificent grandeur.

Quite close to the falls was a little tea room on the banks of the river. If you placed anything on the tables outside the tea room; it would be gone in a flash. The monkeys would steal food from your plates as you sat there. We parked at the falls one day and while Cecil was busy taking photographs, he asked me to fetch another spool from the bakkie. As I closed the door, the film clasped in my hand, a huge baboon grabbed the film and took my hat off my head. Taking me by complete surprise and being far too big to argue with, I had no option but to follow him quietly until he tired of carrying them and dropped them to the ground.

Monkeys are somewhat like small children. Our bakkie was parked next to another one that had a sail fastened to the cab and laid across the open back, the fall of canvas forming a slide. When we returned to our bakkie, there were about six monkeys sliding gleefully down the canvas and then clambering back to the top of the cab to slide again. We watched with amusement as they played, oblivious to our presence and chattering happily amongst themselves. There is nothing more wonderful than watching wild creatures, sometimes so human-like, amusing themselves innocently without fear of danger or reprimand. On another occasion, we rounded a bend near the falls and came across a troop of baboons. The huge male barked his warning and the rest of the troop joined hands and crossed the road in a line, while the male stood between them and our vehicle. If this is normal behaviour, I have no idea, but I witnessed it with my own eyes.

The Kafue Plains are situated just a few miles from Mazabuka. For a large part of the year the area is just miles of rolling grassland, with palm trees scattered here and there. They were said to have been planted by the Arab traders of long ago, so as to be used as a guide by the traders as they led the slaves to their ships. When the wind blew gently through the palms and the leaves rustled softly, it reminded me of the shuffling footsteps of the many poor slaves as they were led along the sandy pathway. It was an eerie feeling, trying to imagine their thoughts as they left their families and sweethearts behind forever, with the terrible knowledge that they would never again feel the freedom of the African bush.

To see the sun rise over these plains is magnificent, the world washed in glorious shades of pink, with the heavens above being the pinkest of them all. Once the rains started and the Kafue's flow increased, it would slowly creep up on the plains. It was in this area, just a couple of years before we left Zambia, that a large sugar estate started and became a thriving industry. There was also a research station which specialized in irrigation, fertilizers, drainage, the correct choice of crops as well as weed and pest control. This was known as the Pilot Polder and it was here that Cecil was asked to shoot a hippo that was destroying crops at night. I went along with him to see the animal once it had been shot and only then did I realize what a huge animal the hippo is, and I was fascinated by the whiskers, which are large, black and very stiff to the touch. The African people from a nearby village cut up the meat, giving Cecil grateful nods of appreciation and toothless smiles that warmed my heart.

The reason that the women were toothless is because their front teeth are knocked out when they are young. It seems that long ago various tribes would attack another peaceful tribe, steal all their maize and their young women. To prevent their women from being taken, the elders decided that they would knock out their front teeth to make them unattractive.

A few days later we got a message from the Boma to say that a train-load of refugees from the Congo was passing through Mazabuka. The ladies of the MOTHWA and the Women's Institute gathered food and clothing and we waited at the station for the train to arrive. This was my first encounter with refugees and if ever my heart bled for people, it was that evening. Some of the poor women had fled the country in their night dresses, which were thin and sleeveless and they were shivering in the cool night air. I suspect they shivered, not only from cold, but also the shock of whatever it was that they had witnessed before leaving the Congo. Very few spoke English, so our sympathy was conveyed by means of hand gestures and tears, as we cried with them at their plight. Many of their children had been in boarding school very far away from their homes and were left as the mothers fled. Some had left husbands and parents behind as well and I was overwhelmed with compassion. They only stayed in the station for half an hour, but when the train pulled out, there wasn't a dry eye in sight.

A request was received from the headman of a village just outside Mazabuka; they were having trouble with two buffalo wandering into their fields at night. Our three musketeers went off in Cecil's Landrover to see if they could do anything. On arrival at the village, the headman introduced them to his son, who had just arrived back in the village from Oxford University in England. There were no buffalo to be seen, but the headman assured them that his son would direct them to where they usually grazed during the day. It was a few miles away, so they all got into the Landrover and this was when the amusement started. The son, in the most eloquent English, said "Please drive five degrees to the North East. Okay, now one degree back to North."
This continued, with Cecil literally just following the hand gestures as the son showed him which way to go. Eventually they found the buffalo and shot one. They dropped the son back at the village and told the villagers to collect the meat. The villagers were always grateful if the hunters shot something for them and they would celebrate long into the night as their meat cooked on the fire. All the way home, the men would insist on every turn to tell Cecil how many degrees north or south he should turn!

Cecil and I discussed it and decided that a car was not the answer for our travelling. We agreed that it would be more comfortable for the children if we had a bakkie, so we sold the car and bought a Ford F100. Driving home in our new bakkie, we came across two huge snakes in the road. The one was curled up and inert, but the other was in a terribly agitated state, rearing its hooded head up high, with its mouth wide open. There was a pattern on its hood, but we were too far away to see it clearly. We were later told that they were Egyptian Cobras.

Cecil was absolutely mesmerised by the snakes and curious as to why the one lay so still. He got out of the cab, taking his rifle as protection, and walked closer. The huge male cobra suddenly spat at him and the venom hit Cecil's gun and his arm. He walked back to

168

the bakkie to show us, but the poison had crystallized and blew away in the breeze. He realised that the other snake had been run over and was dead, but the male was protecting its body. We slowly drove the bakkie around the snakes, the male watching us and turning as we passed. This was a story that Cecil loved to tell in later years, it seemed to have made a huge impression on him. The male was certainly one of the largest snakes I had seen, apart from the mamba on Muchacha, but he was beautiful in a scary sort of way.

We started taking a holiday every year, mostly to Port Elizabeth, but also sometimes to Durban. Cecil loved going to the Tugela River, north of Durban, as the fishing was good there. We always camped, rather than stay in hotels or bungalows and this made our holidays even more of an adventure. I would buy pretty clothes in town during our trips, but could only wear them once we had returned to our home in Mazabuka. It was never city life that attracted Cecil, but rather the wide open spaces and the ocean and rivers.

I had finally decided to shelve the idea of having another baby, as I had waited a long time with no luck. Ironically, as soon as I made this decision, I conceived. Little did I know that this pregnancy would leave me with a doubt in my mind forever and would bring me so much heartbreak and tears. I was about four months into the pregnancy and I realised that I wasn't blooming like I did with the other two. I looked drawn and old, my skin had a yellow hue and I felt awful. To make matters worse, I went to Lusaka for a haircut and they cut my hair far too short. I looked like a boy and it was so short that I couldn't even curl it. I do not know to this day how much of what happened was in my imagination, as my self esteem was at an all time low.

Joyce started coming over every night to cheer me up and when I asked her how Charlie felt about it, she said "He's so busy with his stamp collection; he doesn't even know I'm not there."
A couple of weeks later I saw Cecil preparing two glasses with lemon juice and sugar, frosting the rim decoratively. I asked him what he was doing and he said "Joyce and I enjoy a ginger square and these are for us."

I have never been a drinker, except on occasions when protocol demanded it, preferring soft drinks. This became a daily ritual and Joyce and Cecil would sit and drink their ginger squares, while I sat there with very little to say. I could feel jealousy consuming my soul, but had no idea how to handle the situation. If we went to Lusaka, Joyce would join us, saying she had to place orders for the shop. Even when Cecil suggested we go to Salisbury to buy clothes for the baby, Joyce had to go with, as she wanted to visit the wholesalers personally instead of always buying telephonically. Because she suffered with travel sickness, she would sit in front with Cecil and I would be in the back seat.

When Joyce decided she wanted to learn to drive, Cecil offered to teach her. They would be gone for over an hour and when I asked if I could accompany them, Joyce replied "No, I will be too nervous."
So my jealousy mounted and caused me a lot of heartache. Communication would have been the answer, I know that today; I should have asked Cecil outright if there was something going on between them, but I was too proud. I know that as tough as he was and as high as his morals were, he was also a man and Joyce had reached her prime. Although she was never a beautiful woman, she was very attractive and vivacious.

I asked Cecil one day to take me to Lusaka, as I wanted to buy a jersey. He smiled and said "I'll buy it for you."
Of course, Joyce came with us and when I chose the jersey I liked, Cecil turned to Joyce and said "Would you like one too?"
So, we both got jerseys and I withdrew even more, my jealousy increasing by the minute. Cecil bought us each a gift and put them on our laps as he got back in the car. Mine was a little vase, nothing terribly special about it, while Joyce's was a vase with a little rickshaw man pulling it. I don't even know if he was aware which he had given to whom, but I was so hurt that she had to share these things, when a little gift especially for me would have meant so much more.

I started becoming quite aggressive and withdrawn from them both and had no idea how to handle my problem. I remember about six weeks before the baby came, Cecil gave me three hundred pounds for accounts and food for the month. I promptly went to Lusaka with my dad, bought two maternity outfits and a pair shoes, returning with only fifty pounds. I threw it on the table and said "If you want to eat this month, find some more money!" This was my way of trying to hurt Cecil, because of my own pain.

About a week before baby was due, Cecil and Joyce went alone to Lusaka, saying it was too close to my due date for me to be travelling on the rough roads. When he returned, Cecil handed me a beautiful box containing an exquisite, imported petticoat and panty set. It was adorned with the loveliest lace and embroidery and I was so thrilled, I threw my arms around him and kissed him. Some time later Joyce popped in and said "How did you like your present? It took us ages to choose it."

As soon as she left, I took the box and threw it at Cecil's feet, shouting "Take your gift and give it to the girlfriend who chose it. I don't need you and Joyce to choose my underwear for me, thank you, I can do that myself."

Without a word, Cecil picked up the box, looking at me with a really strange look on his face and then he walked out of the room.

I never saw it again and I never asked what he had done with it. On the trip to Salisbury to buy baby clothes before Jeni's birth, Joyce and Cecil began discussing baby names. I realise today that with a silent, brooding woman in the back, they probably found it hard to keep conversation going, so chose a subject that I might take part in. After they had asked me how I felt about a couple of names, I retorted "You two can come up with all the names you like; I have already chosen the name. My baby will be called Jennifer."

Somehow the name just popped into my head, I hadn't even thought about it until then, but I had said it, so I had to stick to it. So much of what happened could have been in my imagination due to my lack of confidence and feeling so low during the pregnancy. It had been an awful one and I never felt well during the whole nine months. It was with a sense of relief that on the Sunday afternoon I felt the first twinges of labour.

On Monday morning the doctor came and ordered a pethidine injection and I managed to sleep for a couple of hours. I awoke at about eleven in full labour and the doctor had gone home. At about twelve thirty, I called the sister on duty and said "Sister, I've had two babies, something is wrong."

The sister looked at me condescendingly and asked "What?"

I couldn't answer her, but my instincts were telling me that there was something terribly wrong inside. I called her back half an hour later and begged her to call the doctor. She examined me and told me that everything was fine. I hit the bed with my fist and shouted "Damn it, phone the doctor now."

I heard her pick up the phone and say "Doctor, I'm sorry to worry you; I know you are recovering from malaria, but Mrs Slabbert is getting hysterical on me."

At about one thirty the doctor arrived. He walked into my room and asked "What's wrong, Joan?"

"I don't know, Doc, but I just know there's something wrong."

He bent down to have a look and uttered "Oh, I'm just in time."

With that, he caught the baby and announced that I had a little girl. He was saying something about ten fingers and toes, when he suddenly looked down and exclaimed "Oh my God."

I watched in horror as his shirt and trousers turned red and his face went snow-white. I remember him trying to stop the bleeding and shouting to the sister "Phone the research station and tell them to find people with O positive blood group and bring them here as quickly as possible!" He then called to Cecil "Get in here quickly. Talk to her and don't let her close her eyes for a moment."

So the battle to save my life had begun. My veins collapsed, so the only place that they could use to transfuse blood was through my ankle. Cecil sat beside me and talked and talked, until I weakly whispered "Oh shut up and leave me alone."

He sat there quietly, holding my hand, his face drawn with worry. The doctor had overheard my remark and looking across at Cecil, he said "It's okay, Cecil, go out for a while."

Cecil quietly left my side and disappeared for about an hour. I heard later by someone who had been in the shop at the time, that Cecil had walked into the shop and said to Joyce "Joan doesn't want to live, she isn't even fighting."

Little did he know just how I was fighting. I had another baby to look after and I had to make it through this ordeal. I received four pints of blood, straight from people who had come rushing from the research station. In fact, when I was well again, I visited the Women's Institute and gave my opinion on something and one woman turned to me and remarked "I can hear you got a pint of blood from Doctor Black from the research station, you sound just like him with that remark."

It was long after seven that night before I saw Jennifer and I was too weak to hold her. By the next morning my cheeks were flushed and I was running a high fever. The doctor sat on my bed and asked me how I felt and I just nodded. He turned to the sister and whispered "Watch her carefully for septicaemia, I don't like that fever."

By evening my fever had abated and my cheeks were a healthy pink. I took out my makeup bag and when I looked in the mirror, the ugliness I had seen during my pregnancy was gone and I was looking really pretty once again. It had been a long time since I had seen such healthy colour in my face.

During my fourteen day stay in the hospital, I walked with Cecil and Joyce to the door after visiting hours one afternoon and Cecil put his arms around me to say goodbye. He held me at arm's length and whispered "I had forgotten just how tiny you are."

I decided not to point out that I was standing on a step lower than him at the time!

A week after I got home, we heard that the queen mother was going to open Kariba and Cecil suggested that we go. On the Friday he went up to Lusaka and came back with a double string necklace of white crystals, with matching earrings. He said a jeweller had placed a white velvet cloth in the window and displayed a white, red and blue set on it. He later bought me the blue one, but the red set was already sold. We left for Kariba very early in the morning to see the opening and arrived just after dawn. There was nothing to be seen at that stage and the children were running around on the causeway. I found a tree and settled down with Jeni in the shade. Slowly people began to arrive and workmen were preparing a dais for the Queen Mother and chairs for VIP guests. Ethné and Mike came to me, crying that people had chased them away and they couldn't see over their heads. I was angry. After all, we had driven a long way to see her, mostly for the sake of the children and we had been the first to arrive. I turned to them and said "Today you don't belong to me. Push your way, in fact elbow your way, through the crowd until you get to the front."

Well, they went one better and elbowed their way right up to the dais and sat on the edge of it. The Queen Mother smiled gently at them and nobody told them to leave, so they sat motionless through all the speeches and had the best view of the opening of Kariba.

Cecil had taken his cameras along to take some photographs, but was turned back by an official, who later disappeared into the crowd. Cecil saw a bloke open his jacket briefly and say "Press."

He then walked past the guards and found a suitable spot from where he could take photographs. No trouble to Cecil, he walked up to the guards, flashed the inside of his jacket and said "Press."

He managed to get some beautiful slides of the grand affair and looked quite smug when he returned to me. It was looks like this, almost that of a naughty little boy, that endeared him to me so much over the years. My love was stronger than ever and I knew I was at my prettiest after the transfusions, but my confidence was still very low.

We were, by now, living the life of the wealthy. We had several servants and I was treasurer to the MOTHWA, secretary for the Women's Institute and brown owl to the Brownies. Cecil was treasurer for the MOTH and on the committees of both the Settlers and the Golf Clubs. Needless to say, weekends were spent playing golf with his friends and colleagues and so our lives were busy and not spending a lot of time together, we slowly began to drift further apart.

Little Jeni became our pride and joy. Cecil, for all his speech about her being 'my baby', just couldn't put her down. At two weeks old, she was on his lap, sipping whisky and tasting whatever he ate. She had no hair, but had a lovely little face and a sturdy body. Someone suggested that we enter her into a baby competition in Lusaka and she came second. The little boy who took first place had a stronger back, but he was two months older than Jeni's four months. She was just over six month's old when the Mazabuka Salvation Army decided to hold a baby competition. On the morning of the competition, Jeni awoke with a nasty nappy rash and Joyce said she had heard that the quickest way to clear it up was to alternate hot and ice cold water on the skin. We sat her in a bowl of iced water and she began to scream. Then we moved her into the warm water, then back to the cold. By now Jeni was highly indignant and screaming at the top of her lungs. Cecil arrived and grabbed her from us, saying "No baby competition is that important. Leave my child alone."

Despite the nappy rash, we took Jeni along and lo and behold, we were asked to leave nappies on. Jeni came second again and we were thrilled.

I was in a sub-committee for a flower show that we held every year and Cecil always claimed first prize for his Barberton Daisies. I wasn't showing anything, as I normally helped with the public who needed advice on where and how to show. During the course of the morning, Neisha, a good friend of mine, asked me to lend her a fairly low vase for her arrangement. I told her to ask Japhat to find her one back at the house. Thinking no more of it, I was shocked rigid when my name was announced as being the overall winner of the show. I looked questioningly at Neisha, who simply smiled and said "I saw it in your kitchen when I was looking for the vase, so I entered it."

It was a really beautiful ruffled Gloxinia, purple and white in colour, but it was planted in a dirty jam tin. Neisha had not even repotted it into something more attractive, but had simply entered it, dirty tin and all, in my name.

Out of the blue, Ron and Sue came to see us and the men began to talk about a hunting trip. Cecil promised to take Ron and let him shoot a lechwe. We all went down in the land rover to Kafue. Cecil threw a can into the river and told Ron to shoot it. Ron fired a few shots, but each one missed and the tin continued to bob up and down in the water. Mike asked if he could have a try. He aimed and fired and the tin disappeared. We got back in the land rover and eventually found a lechwe bull. Cecil stopped the vehicle and Ron took aim. The shot broke the animal's back and Cecil, who didn't have a rifle with him, told Ron to kill it with a second shot immediately. Ron looked at him and said "We used all the other bullets back at the river, I don't have another one."

The rear part of the Lechwe's body was paralysed and had sagged to the ground, but its front legs were still erect and as it looked at us, there were tears running down its face. I could see the anguish on Cecil's face as he cursed, then grabbed a knife and ran to the animal to put it out of its misery. We were all very upset, but nothing in comparison to how Cecil felt. From that day on, he never took anyone hunting unless he had his own rifle on him as well.

We spent four days in the bush with Ron and Sue on a later visit and Joyce, Charlie and their children joined us. Cecil, Charlie and Ron left camp after an early breakfast and headed for the bush. We had cooked breakfast on a plough disc, onto which Cecil had welded three legs. The children were up and full of bounce, chasing each other all over camp. Even Valmore was becoming more of a bush baby by this stage and was thoroughly enjoying the trip. They were all chasing Mike and, looking back to see where they were, he ran straight into the plough disc, which toppled over and fell onto his leg. He screamed and I ran over to him, horror filling me as I looked down at his leg. The one leg of the plough disc had penetrated his shin near the ankle and ripped it as far as the knee cap, right down to the bone. The flesh folded open and the pearly white bone shimmered like mother of pearl in the sunlight. It was bleeding profusely and I shouted for someone to grab the medical kit and after a few seconds, they shouted back "I don't think it was loaded onto the truck."

Joyce ran over to look, then ran back to Sue and they both just stood there staring at me, obviously expecting me to take charge. I pulled the two folds of flesh together, using both hands, and waited for the bleeding to abate a little. Looking at Mike's ashen face, I said "Mike, grit your teeth hard. This is going to hurt."

I took a full bottle of methylated spirits and poured it over the open wound. Poor Mike winced in pain, but because the other children were watching, he never uttered a sound and although his eyes filled with tears, he wouldn't let them fall.

I tore up the tablecloth and bandaged the leg well. Unfortunately I couldn't do any more, because we had no form of analgesics in camp. The men got back at about three in the afternoon and I related the story to Cecil, who said that he had heard that the spirits could cause tissue damage on a wound. Cecil gently removed the bandage and once again Mike was told to grit his teeth. Cecil poured a bottle of whisky over the wound and then pushed the two folds of flesh close together again and bandaged it. Today Mike has such a thin scar that it isn't even noticeable unless pointed out to you. We cut the trip short and packed up camp the next morning. Late the following afternoon, Cecil and Ron went to Cyril Seaman's farm and shot two lechwe, which we used to make biltong for them to take back to Salisbury. This was the last hunt that we ever went on, because we met a chap by the name of Jack Pike, who had an enormous dam on his farm and we became keen on boating.

Cecil bought a red and white boat called a Cobra. What fun we had as a family in this wonderful boat. We went out onto the Kafue River for a while and then Cecil suggested we go to shore and have some coffee and eats. We pulled up near the bank and I was daydreaming, so when Cecil spoke, I thought he said "Jump over so I can get out." I never gave it another thought and jumped overboard, expecting about a foot of water, instead of which, I had jumped out on the wrong side of the boat, into the full depth of the river. What Cecil had said, in fact, was "Move over, so I can get the anchor out."
I sank like a stone and believe me, if you are drowning in the Kafue, it isn't your life that flashes before you. All the way to the muddy bottom, my head screamed 'crocodiles, crocodiles, crocodiles'. I am not a good swimmer, so as my feet touched the bottom, I kicked off and as I floated back to the surface, my mind screamed 'crocodiles, crocodiles'. I broke the surface, red in the face for the want of air and scrambled up the nearby bank, saying a silent prayer of thanks for my safety.

Some time later we sold the Cobra and bought an Impala boat. It was a lovely blue and white boat and we decided to try it out on Jack's dam. Cecil offered to teach me how to drive it, but I refused. He laughed and said "Okay, I'll leave it running and jump overboard and then you'll have to drive it."

He hadn't even finished speaking when I hastily took a dive over the side of the boat, scraping my leg badly in the process. Cecil was furious and told me I could have got caught by the propeller, but I was too busy nursing my leg to care.

Around this time, Ethné was given a bush baby and it was an absolute menace in the home. It slept all day, but kept us awake at night as it scurried around, jumping from furniture, to curtains and pelmets. Its fur was soft to the touch and he was the size of a tiny puppy, although fully grown. Ethné had a little toy dog and its head and tail were about six inches apart. The little bush baby would climb into this space to sleep during the day. One day I picked up the toy dog and it began to fall apart from being urinated on over quite some time. When Ethné went to boarding school, she gave the bush baby to a friend and I breathed a sigh of relief at its departure.

Then it was Mike's turn to bring home unusual pets. First it was three field mice, with bushy little tails. The next pets were three white rats and Mike had used my glass cabinet to make them a nest for breeding. I found five large eggs wrapped in clothes in his drawer and on enquiring, I was told "Don't move them Mom, I'm breeding crocodiles and the eggs must be kept warm and in an upright position."

I found two little squirrel-type creatures in a drum in the yard. I turned the drum on its side and set them free, but Mike was heartbroken when he found out, saying "You let Micky and Minnie Mouse go and I wanted them to have babies." Then we had chameleons walking all over the house, as well as red fluffy insects that resembled ticks, which he called Christmas Beetles and finally, silkworms in a shoe box. I had threatened dire consequences if he brought a snake home, so thankfully I was spared this encounter.

Cecil bought Mike a pellet gun for Christmas and it wasn't long before Joyce came and accused him of shooting the pet rabbit, which they found lying dead in the cage. Mike's eyes filled with tears and he claimed that he hadn't shot the rabbit, but he was ultimately blamed and given a good hiding. Afterwards, Mike looked at me and said "Mom, I never shot the rabbit, but all the other kids use my gun too, it could have been one of them." I had never known Mike to lie, he had his faults, but lying wasn't one of them. I believed him and when I began writing this book, I asked him again and, as a man in his middle fifties, he said "Mom, for the last time, I didn't shoot the damn rabbit."

The end of the pellet gun came shortly afterwards when George Luden's son, Keith was playing with Mike and got a pellet in his back. Mike owned up immediately and said it was an accident, but Cecil decided to confiscate the pellet gun for good. Mike had the utmost respect for a big rifle, but he seemed to regard the pellet gun as a toy. Fortunately the pellet had not penetrated too deeply and once Cecil had removed it, Keith resumed his cowboy and Indian game with vigour, only this time with toy guns purchased from a shop in Lusaka.

Most of our friends had bought boats and with Kariba not too far away and the Kafue's abundant fish life, we all began fishing and the men started a fishing club. Cecil was chairman and I was treasurer. We organized a fishing trip on the Kafue and all the chaps who had boats entered, making a total of about twenty members. As all the folks arrived, they paid their entrance fee to me, so I was pretty busy for a while. I asked Cecil and Jeni to pack our boat when I was nearly finished. I had left my hat in the car, so ran to fetch it, putting my handbag with all the items to be packed in the boat. Cecil was waiting for me on my return, so I jumped in the boat and we took off to find a good spot, travelling about two miles up river. I asked Jeni, who was five years old, to pass me my bag and she said "It's not here, mommy."
Much to Cecil's disgust, we returned to shore to look for the bag, only to find it sitting quite safely where I had left it. Cecil was not amused, for he had lost over an hour's fishing, but we returned to

our spot and threw the anchor out. He told me to fish as well and put a worm on my hook. "Cast it out" he said, as though it was something I did every day of my life. Not wanting to upset him any further, I stood up and casted out, only to hear Cecil shout "Give slack."

What the hell was slack? I had inadvertently caught Cecil's thumb with my hook as I was casting and because the line was tight, I was nearly pulling him overboard. Well! He managed to get the hook out of his thumb, but now he really had the mutters.

Jeni asked for a piece of line with a hook on and I decided to do the same, thinking that it would be safer than more casting. Cecil got no bites on his rod, but I caught a small fish on my hand line. "Ah," Cecil said, "Live bait."

"Oh no," I retorted, "This is my fish and I'm keeping it."

A little later Jeni caught a fish and refused to give to Cecil, saying she wanted to keep it too. Cecil tried with no luck and then a boat pulled up next to us with friends who wanted to know how we were doing. Yvonne turned to me and said "I'm in the dog box. Tony started the motor and I'd forgotten to lift the live bait cage into the boat. The propeller cut the rope and we lost all our live bait and the cage."

I told Yvonne about Cecil's thumb and the fact that we wouldn't give him our fish and assured her that I, too, was in the dog-box. The men finally agreed to drop us on the bank and then continued fishing on their own. By the end of the day they had caught absolutely nothing and we all went up for the weighing in. Trying to bring a smile to their faces, I handed my little fish to the man doing the weighing and said "Don't forget my catch."

Laughing at its size, he replied "It's the first fish handed in."

Naturally Jeni ran forward with her fish too. A little later Cecil was handed the list of prizes and as chairman, he had to announce the winners. "First prize for the largest bream to Mrs Slabbert. The prize is a fishing reel. First prize for the largest pike and overall prize of the contest to Jennifer Slabbert."

This was the last time I ever fished and I gave Cecil the reel.

My dad began to get boils and no matter what the doctor prescribed, they just kept appearing. All together he had over one hundred all over his body. The last one was in the centre of his back near his spine and it got bigger and bigger. Eventually the doctor had to cut it out, leaving a huge hole in his back, which took months to close up and heal.

Charlie then complained that he had a boil on his leg. It looked terrible, but he wouldn't let anyone touch it. Joyce complained because it was weeping onto the sheets at night in bed. One night, when we were all together, he was talking to my dad who was back from hospital and in bed. Joyce, who was sitting next to Charlie, decided to quickly squeeze the boil while he was talking. As she did so, we stared in amazement as the largest poetsie I have ever seen popped from his leg. It was at least half an inch long and as thick as my little finger. It wriggled around on his leg and next to it was a huge, gaping hole. It always left me with a feeling of revulsion to see these live maggots pop out from under the skin.

Our business had been doing well for nine years and my parents decided to take a trip to England by ship. They were to board in Beira, so Cecil and I agreed to take them there and then return on our own. Everything was fine until we reached the border between Northern Rhodesia and Portuguese East Africa at a place, if my memory serves me correctly, called Villa Manika. They asked for our blue book, which is provided with every car sold, and Cecil reached for the cubby hole to take it out. Our gardener had cleaned the car the day before and had taken the book out without telling us. Cecil tried to explain and eventually they agreed to let us through on the condition that we would be out of the country within twenty four hours.

We set off for Beira and within half an hour, our water pump packed up. We sat on the roadside for a while until a car pulled up next to us. It was a Portuguese lady, who had a very dark skin. I could have slapped my son when he turned innocently to me and asked "What does the nanny want?"
She offered to sit in our car while we went to Beira in her car to get another pump, or to take Cecil there and then bring him back with a pump, which they decided was a better plan of action. She refused to

181

allow us to pay for fuel and said it was her pleasure to help a stranded motorist. We got the folks onto the boat just in time to sail and after they had left, Cecil told me that the pump had cost so much, we only had just enough money left for petrol to get home. However, we needed to rest before driving all the way back, so we slept on the beach. Out came our blankets and we made up a bed by pushing the sand into heaps to act as pillows and covered the sand with one blanket. It was a night never to be forgotten. Cecil and I just cuddled up next to each other and fell asleep.

How does one explain in words, the feeling of waking up to an early dawn of a new day, lying on a beach with the sound of the waves lapping close by? We sat in awe as the sun slowly rose over the mountains in the distance, our blankets beginning to dry from the dew that fell during the night. The peace of no other sound, except the gentle slap-slap of the waves and your body warm and cuddled up next to your beloved, as he slowly opens his eyes from a deep sleep. As his arms tightened around me, I realised that no coffee would be made just yet.

Later, we ran into the warm ocean and washed the sand from our faces and bodies. Relaxed and so alive, we realised just how lucky we were to witness the smile of the ocean as the sun's rays danced on its rippling surface. It was a sad moment when we packed the car and said goodbye to Beira beach forever, but at least we had a memory that would never fade. As close as Cecil and I were in Beira, on our return home we got involved in our committees again and within a few weeks, spent very little time together.

Everything seemed so perfect to me at that stage in our lives. We had a lovely home, a smart car, plenty of money every month, our three beautiful children and I felt secure. We were even having a lot of fun at the Women's Institute. Each woman who could do something really well was asked to teach the others the tricks of her trade and we would all pay five pounds to charity. So, I learned to make professional soft toys, to ice cakes and the finer points of dressmaking. At one of our meetings, someone had brought a fortune teller along to read our cups. I listened to a few of the readings, but she really didn't impress me. At last it was my time for reading and she sat next to me and said "You should always wear green; it is your colour in life."

Suddenly her eyes changed and became almost vacant. "You are going to leave Mazabuka for a while, but you will return. Where you are going, you will live with creatures with four legs, creatures with two legs and creatures with no legs at all."

As her eyes seemed to focus again, I silently said to myself 'what an actress' and thought no more about her words for many months to come.

Most WI's in Rhodesia were doing what we did to raise funds for charity and one of the ladies in Southern Rhodesia offered to bring her cook in to teach members how to make cherry cake. It so happened that one of our members was attending this meeting while she was on holiday. At the meeting the cook was brought in and asked to demonstrate how the cake was made. Everyone watched as he mixed the butter and sugar, following his recipe carefully, until the time came to put the box of cherries into the mixture. He opened the box, put every cherry into his mouth to suck off the sugar and then dropped them into the bowl!

At this stage life was really good for the whole family, when absolute disaster struck. Cecil came into the shop one day and asked where Charlie was. Joyce told him that he was at the bank next door and asked why. Without answering her, Cecil turned and left the shop, heading for the bank. A few minutes later they both returned to the shop and Cecil called to us to join them.

"We are millionaires on paper, but I'd like you to take a good look around at our present stocks. According to the books our timber stocks are valued at five thousand pounds, but the stock I see is worth about five hundred. On the books the paint is valued at about four thousand five hundred pounds, but I can only find no more than two dozen tins." So Cecil went on and took us through all the stock discrepancies he had discovered. We decided to send my father a telegram to come home at once, as he and mom were still in England.

Our chief suspect was our bookkeeper, of whom my father thought the world.

As soon as dad arrived, we hired a firm of auditors from Lusaka and they began to investigate in earnest. They found that there were a number of books missing and eventually declared that we should liquidate the firm. They could find no hard evidence against the bookkeeper, because most of the relevant documentation was missing. Due to the fact that the bookkeeper was never charged, due to lack of evidence, I must give him the benefit of the doubt and he left of his own accord. Cecil suggested that he withdraw from the firm immediately to save on salaries in order to try and keep the business going. Unfortunately there was unrest in the country and people weren't building as much, so Cecil knew it would be difficult to earn sufficient money for our use, but the decision was made and Cecil pulled out and tried to find work on his own.

We were struggling to make ends meet, when the bookkeeper approached Cecil and asked him to build a double story building opposite our business. He was planning on opening a hardware shop, with a flat above. Cecil was desperate enough to accept the job and my family called him a traitor. He quietly explained how much we were battling and said "His money is exactly the same as anyone else's and right now I need money to care for my family." We were all very hopeful that the unrest in the country would settle down and that when Cecil finished this job, plenty of other work would come in. Sadly, we were far too optimistic. The family eventually decided to liquidate Excel and remodel the premises into a garage and tea room, where they would sell B.P. petrol. Cecil and I chose not to join them on this venture, as the family had an argument while discussing it.

I can recall only one amusing episode during the difficult time when Cecil was working for the bookkeeper. Cecil had to throw a slab of concrete to separate the two floors. He started work early one Saturday morning and by midday, a couple of labourers began to feel ill and asked to be excused for the remainder of the day. Now short-staffed, Cecil worked right through the night. As they lay the last section of slab on Sunday morning, a Dominee stopped his car below

and got out. Looking up at Cecil and speaking in Afrikaans, he said "To think that one of our own flock would work on a Sunday!"
Cecil, tired and disgruntled, looked down and retorted "Firstly, Dominee, I am not one of your flock and secondly, on what day of the week do you work?"
One highly indignant Dominee got back into his car and drove off without uttering another word. Once the building was complete, Cecil was unemployed once again. Friends found him small jobs to do, but even this stopped after a while.

We were so desperate for money to feed the family, that we would take money paid to us for building materials and buy food, then book the materials on account, planning to pay this at the end of the month. One thing led to another and before we knew it, we were two thousand pounds in debt. Cecil was under extreme pressure; the laughter had gone from his eyes, but thankfully his fighting spirit remained intact. He never gave up looking for odd jobs and we bravely battled our way through the creditors' phone calls. We had almost reached our end when a phone call came for Cecil. It was a Mister Critchley from the Game Preservation Society and he offered Cecil a contract to build a school camp in the Kafue National Park.

He explained to Cecil exactly what the contract would entail. "Children will visit the camp during the school holidays and we will have a wildlife lecturer to take them out on field trips in the mornings and then lectures in the afternoons. The camp will contain small dormitories, a dining area, ablution blocks and a lecture hall. You will have to make your own bricks and it will be twenty miles from the nearest camp in the park. It is very close to the Congo border and there are no roads, so you will have to make them. We are having quite a time trying to find someone who is willing to undertake it, would you be interested?"
Cecil was desperate and said "Yes, I'll do it."
Mister Critchley told him that the job was to commence as soon as possible and he should make arrangements to get on site within a few days.

First, Cecil had to find labourers. Tradesmen were easy to find, he hired a couple of the staff that had worked at Excel. He packed the bakkie and kissed me goodbye, not knowing when we would see each other again. He was a proud man once more and he was doing this for his wife and children. I stayed alone with the children, no money for food or anything else, for that matter. I used to say to Mike "Go and visit Granny at the tea room, perhaps she will give you a pie, but don't ask for one."

Mike was very unhappy at school; his teacher disliked him and always referred to him as the 'ducktail'. Poor Mike went to school each day with only a cup of black coffee in his stomach and he was still expected to concentrate. Only ten years old, he was too young to understand how our lives had turned upside down so quickly, but the little man that he was, he took off with the pellet gun the day after his dad left and returned some hours later with a chicken for dinner. I never asked whose chicken it had been; Japhat roasted it and we managed to make it last for four days. I had paid all the servants off, except Japhat and I then told Japhat that he should leave as I could not pay him, but he replied "No, Dona, one day when you have money again, you will pay me. I will not leave Bwana Kakuli's family alone when he is not here to care for them."

Ethné was in boarding school, so I knew that she was alright. A couple of days later, Japhat came in with two sweet potatoes and said "Feed the little bwana, he is hungry."
I was touched beyond belief to think that a black man, who was struggling himself and now had no income, was prepared to share his little bit of food with us. The following day I found a small box of groceries on my veranda, with no name or message. I phoned the store where they had been purchased, only to be told that they were not allowed to reveal the name of the person who had bought them. I was never able to find out who this kind Samaritan was, but I was eternally grateful nevertheless.

Jeni was fifteen months old and went down with malaria, being hospitalized almost immediately. After a couple of days the doctor called me one side and said "Jeni is gravely ill. Not only does she have malaria, she is also pining for Cecil. I suggest you get him here as quickly as possible, as I can do no more for her."

There was no way to contact Cecil in a hurry if I phoned Chilanga head office and they radioed Johnny Uys, the ranger, later that afternoon. Johnny would then send a runner to Cecil, over twenty miles away, the next morning. What scared me most of all, was that there was a possibility of Cecil not being able to leave right away. After all, he had a labour force to take care of and was busy making bricks. He had been gone about two weeks at that stage.

I sat at home a very worried woman. That afternoon Koen and Stoffie visited me and while telling them about Jeni, I felt the tears welling and, being such a proud person, I ran outside and leaned against the wall, trying to compose myself. Koen followed me outside and, without a word, he took me in his arms and just held me close. What strong, comforting arms they were. I put my head on his shoulder for a few minutes while I got my tears under control and then he said "Stoffie has made the tea, let's go in."

Koen suggested that I phone Chilanga the next morning to explain how urgently Cecil's presence was needed and plead with them to chase things up.

There is a saying that God looks after his own and at about eight thirty that night, Cecil walked through the door. I flew into his arms, sobbing uncontrollably and told him about Jeni.

We went straight to the hospital and when Jeni saw him, she went wild with joy. Gone was the sick, fretful child I had seen that morning. Her little face glowed with happiness as she held onto her daddy. She truly was a 'daddy's girl'. The doctor said Jeni should go home with us, as that was what she needed most. Cecil and I sat at home that night and he put a proposal to me. He wanted me to go back with him to Tree Tops. It would mean living in the bush, no tent, no mattress and no comforts whatsoever. I would have to rough it as I had never done before. Even in Fort Jimmy we had always had some form of shelter, but in the park I would sleep in the back of the bakkie on dried grass and during daylight hours, I would accompany Cecil wherever he had to go. I happily agreed and then asked him what had brought him home.

He told me he had not been to bed for nearly three days, as one of the men who were cutting down tress to clear the area, had buried an axe deep into his leg, right down to the bone. Cecil had put him on a blanket on the back of the bakkie and got a couple of men to sit with him on the back with the block and tackle and they headed through the bush for Lusaka. It was time consuming and three times on the journey the men shouted to Cecil to stop, as the injured man was dying. Cecil took his whisky bottle and poured neat whisky down his throat and this was how he was kept alive on the nightmarish journey. On their arrival at the hospital, the sister in charge gave Cecil a lecture on giving whisky to a gravely injured man, but at least he had kept him alive. Cecil was so tired and had decided to drive the eighty miles back to Maz to rest for the night before returning to the park.

Next morning Cecil phoned Chilanga and requested permission to take Jeni and me into the park. They were reluctant and insisted that he sign an indemnity form, relieving them of all responsibility for us in the park. Cecil told me to 'pack small', as he had to take supplies back with him and pick up the labourers in Lusaka. I sat down and thought about what would be the best items to take with. I took a tiny suitcase for our clothes, plus a few items for Jeni. One small doll, one small box containing paper dolls a scrap book, six crayons, a few scraps of material, cotton, needles and scissors. Jeni spent many hours in the park making doll's dresses out of the paper in the scrap book, drawing in the same book and pressing grasses in it. When she tired of these occupations, I would cut dresses from the scraps of material and show her how to sew them for her doll. She was a good little girl and never cried or moaned about her restricted freedom, as she had to stay at my side all the time. Japhat insisted on accompanying us to the park to care for his bwana and the Dona.

I swallowed my pride and asked my mom to care for Mike so that he didn't lose any schooling. The next day, with a fully loaded bakkie, we set off for the game park. I didn't know it then, but I was entering the most exciting phase of my entire lifetime. Although there were so many dangers in the park, I look back on it now as being the happiest time in my life. I must mention here that this school camp was built in 1961 - 1962, which is about forty three years ago. My memory of all the various camp names in the park is somewhat dimmed by time, but this is a story of adventures, not a travel documentary, so I trust readers will forgive if I am unable to name every camp correctly.

CHAPTER ELEVEN

Tree Tops....

The scenery as far as Mumbwa was pretty, but not any different from that to which I was accustomed. A few miles on, we had to cross the river by pontoon to enter the park. This was a new experience for me. There were eight men waiting on the wooden platform of the pontoon and Cecil slowly drove the bakkie on and some villagers wanting to cross also boarded. The men pulled on steel cables, which were attached to both banks of the river. Slowly the pontoon progressed to the other side. We all climbed off and Cecil drove the bakkie off and we were on our way again.

All at once, the beauty of the Kafue National Park was evident. I have been in many game parks in my life, but Kafue is the only one that makes me feel like I'm in a real park. It was a couple of months after the rains and everything was at its glorious best. Everywhere was so green, the trees were in bloom and some of the grass was still short, so it resembled a lawn. We passed through Chunga Camp and continued on to Kafwala. The road was not too bad, the river was quite narrow and the trees seemed to form umbrellas over the slowly running water. I was happy to sit and look at it forever, but Cecil was anxious to get to camp, so we headed for Lafupa Camp, where Johnny Uys was the ranger. Cecil and Johnny had formed a close bond and I was greeted with a welcoming smile. I always found Johnny to be very knowledgeable about the trees in his area and we became good friends. If Johnny happened to be in our area, he would pop in for tea, as he knew it was always available in Cecil and Joan's camp.

I really don't know how to describe Johnny. He was one of those people who were of average height and looks and one could easily lose him in a crowd, much like me. We didn't stay with him very long and then we left for Tree Tops. That was when I realised just how difficult Cecil's job had been. There was a faint track where Cecil had passed through twice in the bakkie, but now the block and tackle came out to help us through the dongas. Cecil, Japhat and the four labourers worked hard for the next twenty miles to get us 'home'. I found all this very exciting, until a tsetse fly flew under my skirt and stung me five times before I could get it out. After this I had a healthy respect for the little blighters, as the bites burn for ages. The tsetse fly causes sleeping sickness and as I explained earlier, the Rhodesians used large buildings where they would spray the cars to try and eradicate this problem, which not only affects humans, but livestock too.

It was late afternoon when we arrived at Tree Tops and I saw Konda Kamali for the first time. I have seen many baobabs in my travels over the years, but this tree was utterly magnificent. Its African name refers to the 'tree that ate the maidens'. Legend has it that several maidens sat under the tree and disappeared, never to be seen again. Apart from the tree, there was a small area that had been cleared of bush ready for building. I saw the bricks being made in another clearing near to the river. The river was quite close to camp and I could hear the hippo splashing about. We all started unpacking the bakkie and as soon as it was empty, Cecil got a labourer to clean it out and then lay grass on the back. I put a blanket over this grass, which was to be my mattress.

Japhat got a kettle going for tea on the fire that was never allowed to die during the five or six months that we were there. I cut bread and buttered it, too tired to cook supper that night. I gave Jeni a wash and put her to bed in the cab of the bakkie. Cecil went to put a huge log onto the fire and poured himself a whisky. He allowed himself one whisky a night, as finances were not good, even though Mr Critchley had paid out a small sum of money to cover the first month's work. We sat quietly that night in the firelight on the ground. There was no conversation, the silence was only broken now and then by the snort of a hippo or the odd guinea fowl call as they settled to roost for the night.

I sat there, quite frightened of what lay ahead in the months to come and was very conscious of the fact that we had no rifle. The only weapon we had was the knife on Cecil's belt, as no person is allowed any form of firearm in the game park. I sometimes wonder whether Cecil was also afraid, having his wife and child to protect as an added burden. In a way, it wasn't a happy evening and I was glad when Cecil suggested we go to bed. What a night that was! The grass stuck you all over and mosquitoes buzzed incessantly around us. Every sound from the bush made me edge closer to Cecil, but at last dawn broke and after a nice hot cup of coffee, I felt more refreshed.

My first day in camp had begun. As I watched Cecil working I realised how much I loved him and yet we were like strangers. There seemed to be nothing to say to each other, but as time went on we began to grow closer as we had to rely on each other for company and we would sit for hours discussing various subjects. We had no books to read and usually bed time was straight after dinner, as Cecil was often exhausted by all the manual work he was doing during the day, which started at dawn. I noticed Cecil never asked a labourer to do anything he could not do himself and so he was an inspiration to all around him. Japhat worked as a labourer for Cecil so that he could draw a salary and I did all the camp chores.

Living as we were in the bush, one had to use your imagination when it came to cooking. There were no recipe books around and no stove. We did all the cooking on the open fire. We made bread and all meals were literally out of tins. I found that the basic Vetkoek (similar to Popovers) mixture could do wonders. One could add bully beef, fish, sweetcorn or tinned curry and make fritters. They were also lovely, with a little jam and rolled in sugar to make doughnuts and even made koeksusters from the same dough. Not quite the real thing, but a delicious substitute out in the bush. I found a piece of iron and used it to make crumpets on and also scones.

Cecil put up a circular structure made from bamboo and sticks, covered with grass. Within this structure he dug a pit toilet and then erected another structure under a tree, from which he hung a paraffin tin with holes in the bottom for us to shower. Each morning I would stand under the tin and Cecil would pour a bucket of water into it. The first cold water that hit your body literally put you into a state of shock, but once you were dry and dressed, you felt invigorated and were ready to face the challenges that the day would bring. He also planted four poles under the baobab and put a little thatched roof on top, which made a shelter from the midday sun.

Cecil would go over to where the bricks were being made and he would leave the bakkie close to my shelter. I was happy to sit with Jeni and keep her busy, knowing that it would only take a second to climb into the cab if danger threatened. The weather was perfect all the time we were there. Our staff had made a camp a couple of hundred yards from ours and at night we could hear their talk and laughter quite clearly, even though we couldn't see them. They kept their fire burning day and night and slept in blankets close to the fire, with their axes at their sides.

The lack of communication between Cecil and I was the result of me hiding my feelings since Jeni's birth with regard to the 'Joyce' problem. We had both been so busy with our various social commitments. I was still on all of the various committees and Cecil was on the Golf Club committee, as well as the Settler's Club and also chairman of the MOTH. To complicate matters, I had joined two other ladies on a project where we had to furnish a house completely, even to linen and crockery, at the cheapest possible rate for the African Housing. We had spent many days and evenings away from our homes and on evenings when I was at home, Cecil would be out at a committee meeting or vice versa.

Only now, as I sat in the game park, did I realise how far we had grown apart over the past two years and now he was the only person I could hold a conversation with. Cecil was busy on the brick making for quite a few days until his staff was trained and he could trust them to carry on alone. He then started on the foundations of the buildings and began going out for thatching grass every day. Jeni and I would go along in the cab, with three or four labourers on the back with sickles to cut the grass. These trips for grass were always my favourite. There were always animals to be seen, mainly antelope and so many species of birds. Cecil would assist the labourers while Jeni and I remained safely in the cab. I watched this man of mine working as hard, if not harder, than his workers and when he saw one having difficulties with something, he was there in a second to help and show him the correct way. I noticed how the staff adored their bwana Kakuli, who would speak to them in their language, Cecil laughing heartily at their stories. He would tease them incessantly and they just loved it all.

The first load of supplies for the buildings arrived and Mister Critchley had sent us a packet of meat. What joy to savour fresh meat after a couple of weeks of eating tinned foods. Cecil asked the driver to bring him a small fishing rod and reel, a hundred fish hooks and several spools of line on his next trip. I should mention here that Cecil had done as much as was possible on the road between Johnny's camp and Tree Tops to enable these trucks to get through, but it would never be a proper road. The following week Cecil was the proud owner of a rod and reel. He gave hooks and line to every labourer and went down to the river after work, catching two lovely bream. The Lafupa River is well known for both its fish and crocodiles.

I accompanied Cecil to the river bank so that while he was fishing, I could be on the lookout for animals. We took our bream back to camp and braaied them over the open fire. Talk about nectar for the gods! The meal was delicious and so, after that, every other night we would have fish for dinner. We started a new game with the staff. We held fishing competitions for them and would give the winner a prize of a tin of fruit or cigarettes and matches. The prize wasn't always awarded for the biggest fish, sometimes it was for the smallest and it helped to ease the boredom for the men in camp. On another occasion, Cecil arranged for the driver to bring a projector and the film called 'African Lion', which he showed to his staff. They were so appreciative and talked about the film for days afterwards, but this only happened once the generator had been installed and the camp almost completed.

Collecting of thatching brought many adventures over the next few weeks. One day Cecil and his crew left Jeni and I in the bakkie and walked some distance to start cutting, when Cecil came running back and said "Leave Jeni here. Come quickly."

Thinking someone had been hurt, I rushed out of the bakkie to follow him and as I stepped into a clearing, three cheetahs were standing there looking straight at me. In my confusion I thought they were leopards and turned tail, running for the bakkie. Cecil followed and asked "Why did you do that? You will never again see such a pretty sight. They were beautiful specimens and didn't seem afraid in the slightest. You could have looked at them at your leisure, but instead you startled them by running and they disappeared into the bush."

Another time we were rounding a bend, when two elephants were standing at the side of the track. Cecil stopped to look at them for a few minutes, but the men on the back kept saying "Ride, bwana, ride."

His eyes twinkling with laughter, Cecil drove on a little way, then stopped and put the bakkie into reverse. He had no intention of going anywhere near the elephants, but he was teasing the men. The shouts from the back were ear-splitting and when Cecil once again moved forward, they collapsed with relief on the back, laughing as they did so. How they adored and respected this bwana Kakuli, despite all his teasing.

The weeks were slowly passing and once again I was sitting in the bakkie watching Cecil at work. Our relationship had improved beyond all expectations. I could see how this life suited Cecil; he seemed to be in his element. With all the hard work, he was lean and muscular again and he reminded me of a Greek god. The sun had turned his skin to a deep brown. His hair was almost on his shoulders in soft waves. The only thing that marred his perfection that day was his bottom lip, which had cracked open from too much sun. He was using good old Germolene every couple of hours to ease it. Somehow that slight disfigurement only added to his attraction and as I sat in the bakkie, I began to take stock of us both. Apart from being so handsome on the outside, he was what I would call a man who 'walked tall'. He never did anything that went against his conscience and he was compassionate and kind.

I, on the other hand, was not faring so well. My fair skin had burnt badly in the harsh sun. My hair was long and so straight that I had broken a plastic knitting needle, twisted my hair into a makeshift bun and pushed the needle through it. I was walking in sandals all the time, so my heels were cracked and the soles of my feet ingrained with dirt. They reminded me of feet I had seen in African villages where shoes were never worn. I had no sunglasses and the continuous screwing up of my eyes had produced wrinkles in my parched skin. Frankly, I looked a mess.

Our clothes were washed in the river, so Cecil's khaki clothes only went a deeper shade with the muddy water, but my couple of dresses, that had once been pretty florals, were now a soft shade of pale brown. With no iron, they were just a mass of creases. I could see no redeeming features for my life in the bush; my face reminded me of a half-boiled lobster. However, on the inside, I realised I had learned a lot of lessons, some of them being tolerance, trust, honesty and integrity and, the most important one of all, love. I was able to love everyone and understand their needs and to this day I never condemn, no matter what the situation. Living in the bush with Cecil had been a humbling experience and the life we had lived together so far, had been a good teacher.

I suddenly realised one morning that what the fortune teller had said, was true. My creatures with no legs were the fish in the Lafupa, the creatures with four legs were the animals and the creatures with two legs were birds and, of course, we were going back to Maz when the job was completed.

In the top of the baobab was an old look-out post. One of the staff had measured it and said that it was sixty three feet up, but I don't know if this was accurate. A lot of the rungs of the ladder had rotted away, as had quite a few of the floor boards in the look-out post itself. Sometimes a duiker, or even bigger game like kudu, would venture into our camp and one could really sit and admire them close-up. It was moments like this that will remain in my heart forever.

It was a Sunday night and almost dark, when Japhat called to me, saying "Dona, supper's ready". I walked across and dished up our meal of bully beef, tinned peas and some rice. The bully beef had been made into a sort of stew. We walked over to an anthill, just outside of the direct firelight and sat down to eat our supper. There was a rustling in the bush nearby and I saw Cecil tense as his hand went to the hunting knife on his belt. It was a knife I had bought for his birthday the previous year and was called a Puma. Today I believe that the same knife costs over five hundred rand. Out of the bush appeared a hyena and he stealthily crept up towards Cecil's plate, which was on the ground next to him. We sat very still until it was so close that Cecil could have touched it. Suddenly Cecil's foot shot out, kicking the animal on its rump as he shouted "Voertsek; nobody invited you to dinner."

The poor animal got such a fright, let out a shrill cry and almost did a somersault before bolting back into the bush, while Cecil and I doubled up with laughter.

Cecil made himself a catapult and sat one afternoon, hoping to shoot a quali (a type of partridge) for our dinner. Sure enough one popped out of the bush and walked into a clearing within shooting range and Cecil pulled back the rubber and aimed. With a loud twang, the rubber snapped and much to our disappointment, it was bream for supper yet once again. At that time we announced to the labourers that it was time for another fishing competition. On their return, Cecil asked who had caught no fish at all and one labourer stepped forward, looking a little ashamed of himself. Their faces were a picture when Cecil handed him the hamper we had made, containing matches and candle, bully beef and a tin of fruit. The chap who had caught the biggest fish looked rather disbelieving, but they all went back to their camp laughing. Believe me, I never buy bully beef today, although I must also admit that the bully beef available today is nothing like the one we used to buy then. It was solid meat and absolutely delicious.

I think we were all a little crazy at that time. Johnny Uys came through quite often and once complained about trying to count a herd of buck. "They keep moving" he said "which makes it impossible to do an accurate count." Cecil laughed and said "But Johnny it's easy. Count the legs and divide the total by four!" Johnny asked me if I'd like to join him on a trip to the Busanga Plains in the landrover. What an experience! Cecil kept Jeni with him and Johnny took me about three miles onto the plain, riding on the weeds. I don't know the exact depth of the water beneath the weeds, but Johnny said it was between two and three metres. As he drove, he swung the wheels from side to side to prevent us from sinking through the weeds into the water. We came upon a place where the water was shallow and there were several buck standing in the water. As we neared them, they took off, running through the water, which splashed up around their legs. I had never seen them before; they were a golden brown colour and Johnny told me that they were Sitatunga. They spent their entire lives in the swamps, so have soft feet with long toes, which are actually too long for them to walk on hard ground. I have often been sorry I never saw any more of them during my stay in the park. Eventually we turned and headed for camp and although I thoroughly enjoyed the trip, I was glad to get back onto dry land safely.

Strange as it may seem, in all the time we spent in the park, we never saw one snake. We certainly had our share of creepy crawlies, but I was used to them by this time and either ignored them or swatted them. However, the minute it seemed to get quiet in the park, with no adventure for a few days, you could be sure that something was about to happen.

We started off early one morning to fetch thatching grass and having cut most of the grass close to the track, we decided to head further into the bush and eventually came across a derelict fishing village, which was a couple of miles from our camp and not far from the river. We took the bakkie right into the village and our one back wheel went into a hole. The stench was unbelievable and we worked as quickly as possible to get the vehicle away from the hole. It seems at certain times of the year, the African people move into the village and fish every day. They dig a large hole and this is used to discard all the guts after cleaning the fish. The fish are then laid out on racks to dry. After a few months they cover the hole with sand and move on, taking their loads of fish with them.

We headed for the Lafupa River and spent hours washing the wheel, but nothing seemed to help remove the stench. A week later we visited Johnny's camp and, pinching his nose closed; he approached our vehicle with a grimace and asked "Where the hell have you been?" It took weeks before the smell eventually disappeared completely.

The buildings were now half way up and Cecil was afraid a bushfire may come through and burn all the grass in that area before we could collect enough thatching to complete the project, so we worked overtime on gathering grass. We had only gone a few hundred yards when we came across four lions on the track. Suddenly I was afraid. Somehow I had always put an imaginary fence around our camp and until then we hadn't had any dangerous animals near it, or at least I hadn't seen them. Voicing my fears, I said to Cecil "That one male looks really mean."
Cecil gave me a lecture, reminding me that I'd been in the bush for nearly twenty years on and off and that we both knew the lions would not approach the camp when a fire was burning.
"Anyway, Joan, by the time we get back Japhat will have lit the pressure lamps, so stop worrying."

Sure enough, when we returned, the lamps were lit and after washing Jeni, I put her in the cab and told her to stay there. Japhat shouted that dinner was ready and my mouth watered. I hadn't seen red meat for three months and the supply truck had been the day before, bringing us a packet of sausages. Cecil offered to put more wood on the fire while I dished up supper. I walked into the shelter where the food was waiting in a cast-iron pot and lifted the lid. Oh, the smell of those sausages was utterly divine! I cut a little piece off and had it on the end my fork to cool, when I heard the most dreadful, terrifying sound. It wasn't a roar, it wasn't a snarl, but something of both and I heard Cecil scream out "Joan, for God's sake run!"

Well, I didn't run, I literally flew. Jumping into the cab of the bakkie, I pushed Jeni to the opposite side and made place for Cecil, as he scrambled in.

It had been a very hot day and Cecil had taken his khaki shirt off and replaced it with a white cotton shirt, which was now red with dust. He explained that he was putting the log on the fire when a lion jumped out of the bush at him, so close that the dust from its paws was all over his shirt. Cecil's quick reaction saved him, as he grabbed a burning log and hit out at the lion, which retreated briefly into the bush. We sat in the bakkie for about an hour, Cecil nursing his burnt hands and complaining bitterly about not having a gun in camp. Our sausages sat on the table and went cold and Cecil muttered "I'm getting out to pour myself a whisky. They must be gone by now."
As he poured the whisky into his glass, the lion came tearing from the bush, straight at Cecil, who ran around to my side of the bakkie, literally putting it between him and the beast. I moved up and let him in and promptly burst into tears. "I'll divorce you if you get out again." I whimpered.
Cecil laughed and said "You won't have to, you'll be a widow!"

Again we sat for a long while and then Cecil noticed that a lamp was precariously close to the thatching grass. "I'll have to move it," he said, "because if it falls over and burns that grass we'll be late on finishing this contract and that costs penalties."
As he opened the door the lion appeared, watching us menacingly. Cecil closed the door and shouted as loud as he could to the labourers "Hold your axes and stay by your fire, there's a lion in camp."
You can imagine our dismay when the reply "Mbodsa!" filtered back to us through the dark. Cecil had often teased them by roaring into a paraffin tin, so they didn't believe Cecil and were calling him a liar. Cecil called back and told them not to be stupid and to do exactly as they were told. He explained that he would drive the bakkie into their camp and move them six at a time to the tree. They were to climb the tree and remain there, those who couldn't fit into the look-out post at the top, were to just perch on the ladder until morning.

By this time I needed a toilet so badly and I can assure you it was the longest night of my entire life. We couldn't even remove the mosquito net from the bakkie and as we drove to the labourers' camp, it became entangled in the wheels and was ripped to shreds. As we moved, there was a resounding roar from the lion and this caused utter panic in the men. Everyone tried to get onto the bakkie at once, even trying to push Jeni and me out of the cab. Panic is a frightening thing, but I often wonder if it was perhaps all that commotion that stopped the lion from attacking again that night. Cecil actually hit a few staff members in order to regain control and eventually they calmed down enough to take orders again. From my position in the bakkie, it was like watching a movie. All six men jumped from the bakkie at once and headed for the ladder. When the first chap was about four rungs up, the one behind him would pull him back to get up first. This continued until once again Cecil had to hit a couple, shouting at them, before they climbed the ladder in a somewhat orderly fashion to safety. While all this panic was going on, the lion kept up a grunting commotion in the bush close by. It was a sound that put terror in your heart and it is times like these that make a few minutes seem like hours.

The last eight men stayed in the back of our bakkie for the rest of the night as we waited for dawn and the welcome daylight. Eventually it came and the labourers went to check if the lions were still there, returning quite soon to say "They are gone, Bwana."

I was still in shock from the previous night's escapades and only then realised just how much danger we had been in. I took a piece of rope and tied it around my waist and then around Jeni. Where I moved, Jeni had to follow. At about eleven thirty that morning, a Volkswagen pulled into camp and a couple with two children got out to greet us. "Johnny Uys told us that if we were prepared to brave the track, we would see a lot of game in this area and there would always be a cup of tea and something to eat in Cecil and Joan's camp."

Sitting on the grass and drinking tea, the woman turned to me and said "Aren't you afraid here?"

I told her about the previous night and that I hadn't been afraid until then, but now I was terrified.

"I'm only asking, because there are four lions under that tree over there" she said, pointing to a tree very close to camp. "We saw them as we drove in."

I felt the fear wash over me once again and I knew with all certainty that I had become a coward. "Are you heading back home today, or are you staying in the park?"
"No, we must leave today and get back to Lusaka by tonight."
Without any further thought, I asked her if they could give Jeni and I a lift to Lusaka and she agreed, as long as we took no luggage.
Grabbing three nappies for Jeni, I walked over to Cecil and said "I'm going home. I've lost my nerve and I can't stay here any longer."
He didn't smile and I could see he was upset, but he kissed my cheek and said goodbye. At that stage, I didn't really care how he felt; I just wanted to leave that awful place.

As we left the main entrance of the park, we developed car trouble and only reached Lusaka at midnight. The woman offered for us to stay the night, but she didn't appear to be too pleased at the thought. Don't forget, I was no picture at that stage. When I took the knitting needle out of my hair, it stood at all angles and looked dreadful. I was surprised that they drove a Volkswagen, as their home was on Millionaire's Row. She showed me to a bedroom with an en-suite, but I was too scared to use the bath. I had so much ingrained dirt in my feet and hands and I didn't want to soil the bath in case I wasn't able to get it clean afterwards. I had a quick wash in the basin and did the same for Jeni, who looked somewhat like an orphan. All her nappies were wet by this stage and as I looked around the room, the beautiful bed was all satin and lace and I knew I couldn't put Jeni into it. The floor had a lovely soft carpet and so I decided that we would sleep on the floor. Afraid that she would wet the carpet during the night, I wrapped her in my dress, telling myself over and over again that tomorrow I would be home and it would all be over.

When I looked at my dress in the morning, I was horrified. It wasn't wet, but was so creased and as I looked at myself in the mirror all I could think was Ugh! We weren't offered breakfast, as they were running late for work, so by seven-thirty that morning we were standing in Cairo Road, which was the main road in Lusaka. I remembered the Indian shop where my family had spent thousands of pounds on photographic equipment and I decided to ask them if I could phone my dad. I walked into the shop and I honestly don't know if he realised who I was, but his face was filled with disgust and contempt as he looked at me and said "Can I help you?"

I squirmed and my pride shot up as I retorted "No thank you."

I walked out of the shop, my self esteem having now descended into a minus-rating.

Looking at the Edworks shoe shop, I recalled a gentleman employed there, whom I had found to be a truly nice man. We had once asked him if he would sign a visa for us when we were going on holiday, as the visas had to be signed by a witness. He had been such a jolly man and had even played with the children while we chose our shoes. I mustered up my courage and with tears in my eyes, I entered the shop.

"Please don't look at me; I've been chased by lions." I whispered, looking up at him.

He gently put his arm around me and said "Come through to my office."

He was dialing my father's number when I saw dad's car pull up outside the shop. I ran out as he headed down the street and as I reached him, I touched his shoulder. Turning around, my dad's face was an utter picture. "What the hell happened to you?" he asked in a disbelieving tone. "Get in the car, I'm taking you home."

Without doing any of the shopping he had planned, dad took Jeni and me back to Mazabuka. To my horror, instead of taking us home, he took us to the tea room. My mom and Joyce sat me down and made tea, then began phoning all our friends. "Come and look at Joan."

My saving grace was when Stoffie entered the tea room. She spun round to look at the family and said "Shame on you. How could you keep Joan here, looking the way she does? Come on, Joan, you're going home."

And so I was taken home and Stoffie ran a bath. It did not do much for my ego when she threw an entire packet of washing powder into the bath, ordering me to get in. It did the trick, though, and it was a bath I will always remember.

I have been plagued by nightmares of lions ever since that episode, especially when I am ill or feverish. They are in my dreams every few nights. After my bath, Stoffie cut my hair and then the phone began to ring, each time a creditor looking for payment of accounts. It was early 1962 and the stirrings of unrest were getting worse in the country. People were worried about money and every time I promised "As soon as Cecil gets home, we will pay the account in full."
They weren't satisfied with this promise and just kept phoning me, leaving me feeling helpless and depressed.

A week before the lion episode I had felt the top of my breast start to itch and burn and realised that I had a poetsie there. Having not had an iron in camp, this was bound to happen, no matter how careful we were. All we could do was wash the clothes in the river and then leave them in the sun for a full day and we didn't even wear the article for at least another full day in the sun. At the first opportunity, I tried to squeeze the poetsie, but to no avail. As the days passed, I realised I had a major problem. I must have killed it and the wound was turning septic. It became a hole the size of a two-rand coin and a second hole, about the same in size, developed alongside it.

When I got back to Mazabuka I was not keen to visit the doctor, as we still owed him money. However Jeni was looking rather pale and I was afraid she was starting with malaria again, so swallowed my pride and went to see him. He was furious. "I never asked you for the money," he said.
Just then, Jeni threw her head back and hit me on the septic breast. I nearly fainted with pain and he looked at me, saying "Let me see."
I opened the bodice of my dress and the look on his face told me I was in trouble. "Have you ever heard of cancer? How could you let this get so bad? I should put you in hospital right away, but I know you'll only lie there and worry. I will treat you at home, but you come back every day until it's healed."

I had only been home for five days when George Luden visited and he said, "I'm going up to Tree Tops tonight. I've got the contract to put the water pumps in for the school camp. If you have anything you'd like to send to Cecil, I'll gladly take it for you. I'm leaving tonight after the MOTH meeting."

When George arrived that evening, I was waiting for him on the verandah, Jeni asleep in my lap.

"Where's the parcel?" George asked, looking around.

I stood up and said "Right here, but I'm sorry, it's two parcels. Jeni and me."

He was horrified. "What do you mean? Are you really going back after all that?"

I looked at George for a moment and then replied "A woman doesn't walk out on her man when there's trouble. I'd also rather face the lions than the creditors."

I had only seen the doctor once and knew that returning to the park would mean I would once again have to rely on good old Germolene to heal my breast, but it was already looking better after the doctor had treated it.

We arrived early the next morning and what I saw in Cecil's eyes as he saw me, made it all worthwhile. I had regained his respect. A little later when we were alone, he put his arm around me and said "So you walked out on me, you so and so."

I laughed and said "Yes, but I'm back and I'll stay until the end."

I must admit the fears were no less when evening drew near. Cecil told me that he had gone to Johnny's camp after I left and brought Johnny back to see the lion spoor in our camp. Johnny had said "What I'm doing now, Cecil, is against all park rules, but you and your staff cannot do a proper day's work with this threat over your heads. I'm giving you a rifle and a full magazine of bullets, but please, I'm putting my job on the line here. Don't use it unless you have to."

The lions had remained close to Tree Tops for another two days, when the buffalo herds passed through on their way to the Busanga Plains and the lions followed them.

Once again, the animals were part of my life. I woke up one night hearing a strange noise next to the bakkie. It sounded like a 'coughing' growl. Cecil was fast asleep and I grabbed his shoulder to wake him. "They're back, they're back." I whispered in terror. He shook his head to wake up properly and then said, "Well, if you will get off me, I will have a look."
I hadn't even realised that in my fear, I had climbed right on top of him. With all the noise we made, the animal moved off into the bush and looking at the spoor the next morning, we knew that it had been a leopard.

The camp was nearing completion and we went home to Maz to collect fresh supplies. Ethné and Mike were on school holidays, so we took them back with us to Tree Tops. Ethné slept on the seat of the bakkie, Mike on the floor and Cecil, Jeni and I slept in the back. Talk about a full house! The youngsters were so thrilled with their surroundings that I never heard one word of complaint and they seemed really proud that they were part of the project their dad was doing. They spent most of their time climbing the baobab to sit in the look-out post. One night, just before bedtime, Ethné and I went off for our 'last port of call'. We were always afraid to go in the enclosure at night for fear of snakes or creepy crawlies, so we ran behind the baobab. Playing with Ethné, I said rather nonchalantly "It's so dark and creepy; a lion could be watching us from the bush right behind us."
Before my words were cold, a hippo bellowed from the river, the sound reverberating through the still night air. Ethné was just about to bend down and I put my hand against her chest, pushed her flat on the ground and I took off for the bakkie as fast as my legs could carry me. A few minutes later a very indignant Ethné approached the bakkie and she asked, "Is that what you call motherly love?"
Laughing, I replied, "No, sweetheart, it's called survival of the fittest."

The first bungalows were nearing completion and as the walls dried, I remember hanging curtains and putting little cloths on cupboards that were sent up by Mr Critchley. The first group of school children was due to arrive a few days later. The new lecturer, whose real name I will not mention as my book is not intended to embarrass people, arrived in camp. I cooked a meal for us all that night and I noticed that this man liked his liquor and even worse, he was telling lewd jokes in front of me. My thoughts at the time were that he didn't seem the right type of person to be in charge of children.

The next day I didn't see much of him, as he spent the day fishing and the following day the children arrived. Japhat and I busied ourselves making a big meal, as there was no staff yet and, before long, the children were calling us Aunty Joan and Uncle Cecil, yet they addressed the lecturer by his surname. Next morning he left with the children for the Lafupa River and about two hours later, a young lad came running up shouting for Cecil. With tears pouring down his cheeks, he told Cecil what had happened. The lecturer had taken all the children to the edge of the river to measure the depth of the water. One of the youngsters dropped the measuring stick into the water and he had instructed them to all dive until they retrieved it. Cecil flew down to the river and ordered the children out of the water. It was almost miraculous that no-one had been attacked by a crocodile or hippo. Once Cecil was sure all the children were safe, he turned to the lecturer and muttered "You are relieved of your duties. Pack up and get out of my camp now."
He turned to me and said, "We take over the lecturing as from now."

Faithfully each morning, we would bundle the youngsters in the bakkie with the canopy off. I would sit in the back with them to make sure there was no jumping around and with each animal we spotted, I would tell them the name and they would write it down. In the afternoons Cecil would tell them all about each animal they had seen that day. There were many things we did not know, but we did our best and even arranged for the supply truck driver to fetch the film 'The African Lion' once again. I still have a letter from the teacher who came along with the youngsters on the second trip.

By this time Cecil and I had grown very close once more and worked as a team. At last the buildings were finished and we were getting ready to leave. A message came through from Johnny to say that a chap (once again I will not mention his name, but will refer to him as

Mr Farmer) had sent a message for Cecil to meet him at Chunga on the Wednesday. We made a special trip down and he offered Cecil work. He was a dairy farmer and was keen for Cecil to join him. He promised to increase his dairy herd and eventually wanted Cecil to be in a position where they could have half shares in the cattle. Our hopes rose that life was going to be good after all. We had met his wife on a few occasions, but they were just acquaintances and not people we normally socialised with.

On our arrival in Mazabuka, I threw a small party for the friends who had stuck by us through our troubles. We paid up all our accounts and Cecil was due to start with Mr Farmer on the first of the next month. Mr Critchley wrote Cecil a letter of thanks for taking on the duties of lecturing the children and at the same time, Cecil got a letter from Mr Shenton, offering him a position in the park. He would be responsible for all the buildings in the various camps and also for keeping the roads in good order. After a lengthy discussion between us, Cecil decided not to accept, as he had already accepted Mr Farmer's position and we could only work for six months of the year in the park due to the rains. This was a decision we would regret many times in the years that followed.

We packed up and moved into a little house on the farm. Cecil would start milking at four in the morning and finish at about ten. From there he had to check the fodder and would come home at about two in the afternoon for lunch. However nine times out of ten, Mr Farmer would arrive within a few minutes to let Cecil know that he was needed to do something, such as repairing a tractor, or tending to a sick bull. Afternoons were spent cleaning the dairy ready for milking at four and then cleaning it again for the following morning. He would normally get home at about nine thirty at night, including weekends.

If Mr Farmer was expecting guests, he would pop in and tell me what time I would be expected to be at his home to serve tea. I didn't drive, so was no longer able to attend the WI meetings and Mrs Farmer never invited me to accompany her. We had become their workers, nothing more. I used to ask my family to bring out groceries, as Cecil could never get away, but he was so proud of the cattle and got really good at being a farmer. He injected them, treated them himself for mastitis and ran a highly efficient dairy.

One morning I woke up early and Cecil was sleeping so peacefully, I didn't have the heart to wake him. I crept out of the house, started the car and drove to the dairy to do the milking for him. I might add that I never changed gears once; I simply drove the car in whatever gear it was in. Thank heavens it wasn't reverse. However I was shot down in flames by Mr Farmer, who said I didn't know what I was doing. He and his wife had no children and suddenly he began calling to take Jeni wherever he was going, from about seven in the morning, only to return at five in the afternoon.

To keep myself busy I began making wines. There was a big mulberry tree in the yard and I made a huge quantity of mulberry wine. I was limited to whatever fruit I could get on the farm and even tried mango wine, but this was a huge flop. I had a large glass demijohn and tried molasses beer at one stage. I asked Cecil to taste it and he suggested that I add more sugar. You can imagine my surprise when I added some sugar and the contents began to churn and then shot out the demijohn like a volcano, hitting the ceiling. A week later my home still smelled like a brewery.

We had been on the farm about six months when two gentlemen came to the farm looking for Cecil. They wanted to know whether any of our staff had gone home to their villages during the time they worked for us in the park. Cecil confirmed that they had never gone home at any stage and asked why. The men informed him that two of the men had just died from sleeping sickness. This meant that the camp was not a safe place for children and Tree Tops was closed for many years. Later my brother went to the park and said he went as far as Tree Tops, but that it was completely derelict and was literally taken over by lions.

Months passed and we came to realise that none of the initial promises made by Mr Farmer had materialized. Cecil went down with malaria and was terribly thin. He looked drawn and washed out to say the least. The doctor hospitalised him for three days and when he came home he said "My annual leave is almost due and I was promised a full month, so I think we'll go to South Africa and visit the family."

The day dawned for our leave to start and apart from his three days in hospital, Cecil had not had one day off. Mr Farmer went to Cecil and said "My staff gets twenty one days leave a year and you have already had three when you were sick, so you only have eighteen left."
Cecil was furious and told me that as soon as we got home from our holiday, he planned to resign. The funny thing was that during Cecil's stay on this farm he was awarded the Methylene Blue Cheque for cleanliness every month without fail, but during the eighteen days that he was on leave, Mr Farmer lost this award.

True to his word, as soon as we got back from holiday, Cecil gave one month's written notice to Mr Farmer. He was very upset and asked me why. He wanted to know what he had done to make Cecil resign. I asked him if wanted to hear the truth and he nodded. I then asked him what had happened to the promises he had made us. I also told him that he had worked Cecil to the bone and that I was quite happy that we were leaving and would take great pleasure in once again doing my own shopping, instead of always asking my family.

Cecil worked his notice period and in the meanwhile, John and Nelly offered Cecil a job at their garage, which he duly accepted. Three days before we were to leave the farm, Mr Farmer's father passed away and he asked Cecil to stay on for an extra week while they attended the funeral. Cecil told him to speak to John Hillier, but reminded him that if he worked for John his hours would be eight to five with an hour's lunch. Any other time would be considered overtime. He promised to ensure that we would not lose out and why we trusted his word, I will never know. On his return, he paid Cecil one week's pay at the same rate he had been getting for the past year, which wasn't a good one to begin with.

George Luden arrived the following morning to help us move and he and Cecil left with the first load, taking it to our half-built house on the hill in Maz. When they got back they told me that the water wasn't connected yet, so they drank some of the mulberry wine. After the second load the water still wasn't connected, so more of the mulberry wine was consumed. The third load took everything except one mattress and a few small oddments. Jeni and I waited and waited, but they never came back. Eventually we went to sleep on the mattress and in the morning the two sheepish men arrived, a flask of coffee in hand and full of apologies. They had drunk more mulberry wine while unpacking, then sat down on a mattress to rest and literally passed out for the night. I truly had no idea the wine was that potent and we treated it with great respect after that!

CHAPTER TWELVE

Goodbye Northern Rhodesia, Hello Zambia.....

Ethné and Cynthia, Joyce's daughter, never really got on well. The trouble was that they were not allowed to be individuals and Granny was the main culprit. If I bought Ethné a doll, mom would buy Cynthia the same doll. If Joyce bought Cynthia a bike, mom bought one for Ethné and so on. It was so bad that while they were both in boarding school, Ethné needed shoes and as mom was going to Lusaka, I asked her to get them. She asked Ethné her shoe size, which was a four and then asked Cynthia, who took a six. She returned with two pairs of shoes, both size six and said "Cynthia takes a size six, Ethné, so you can't possibly only take a four, as you are older than her." Poor Ethné slopped around in shoes two sizes too big until I could get her new ones. For all that, mom loved the children dearly and spoiled them rotten most of the time.

Christmas time was always very special and a wonderful occasion in our family. There were always lots of presents on the tree and the whole family would spend this time together. Cecil was usually elected to be Santa for the children and even though they knew who it was, they would squeal with delight when they saw all the gifts. With all the partying and celebrating on Christmas Eve and then the children waking us up at the crack of dawn to open gifts, we decided that we would open presents every Christmas Eve instead. This ensured that we could sleep in while the children played with their new toys and it became a firm tradition in our family.

Life settled into a pattern, with Cecil working as a mechanic and doing a really good job, but he didn't look happy. I believe it was because he was working indoors. John sent him on a welding course and he did all the welding at the garage as well. The country was getting worse politically, but in fairness, there wasn't much violence.

My dad took ill and we could get nothing out of the doctor. He was sent to Lusaka for tests and then put to bed at home. He complained bitterly of pain in his legs and he would ask us to move them, but as soon as we tried, he would cry out as we touched them. Doctor eventually hospitalised dad and Cecil became a faithful visitor. They seemed to have become closer through dad's illness than they had ever been before. One day the doctor called Cecil to one side and said "I think you're the only one who realises how ill your father-in - law is. He has lung cancer."

Dad smoked fifty cigarettes a day, yet still reached seventy five before the disease struck. He battled it for two months before sinking into a coma. After watching his suffering, I passed the comment one day that if one of my family got lung cancer, I would personally shoot them to end their suffering. He was buried in the Mazabuka cemetery and we were told to wait for six months for the ground to settle before putting a stone on.

On the 24th October 1964 independence was declared and we broke away from the Federation. Most of the whites were afraid, as we had heard so much about the Mau-Mau in Kenya and the atrocities in the Congo. Many of our professional men packed up and left for greener pastures elsewhere. Those people who could not get away, wanted to send as much of their money as possible to South Africa, using whatever means they could.

I heard quite a few really strange stories, such as the one whose doctor phoned a South African hospital to let them know that his patient had broken his leg so badly that he would have to be transported to Johannesburg for surgery. He told the hospital that he had stabilised the leg with plaster and they were to charter a private plane to Johannesburg. In actual fact this man's leg was just fine, but well cladded with a small fortune in cash under the plaster.

An Indian man was caught at the border with twenty-one thousand Kwacha in his spare wheel. It was confiscated and he was fined the same amount in cash. Another chap tried the same trick, but he got a puncture and put the spare wheel on, resulting in the cash being churned to pieces.

Security at the airport became more intense, with x-ray equipment and Geiger counters being installed. Today this is the norm, but to us this was all new and rather scary. The only time Cecil and I travelled by air, they put the counter over Cecil and it started to buzz loudly. After being told to empty his pockets, they found that his pipe had a small metal section and it was this that had been detected. People were slipping out of the country supposedly on leave, never to return and without paying their income tax before they left.

Doctor Kenneth Kaunda became president and Northern Rhodesia became known as Zambia. He was a fair man and did his best to still everyone's fears. He appeared on television (oh yes, we had TV ten years before South Africa!) and announced that he was addressing the white population of Zambia. He begged them to stop taking their money out of the country, as this was crippling Zambia. He promised them that their money was safe and urged them to stay where they were.

The black man who became the commissioner in Mazabuka came to see Cecil and said "I suggest, for your own safety, you either get a Rhodesian or British passport. South Africans are not popular here in Zambia."
Cecil replied "I am a South African and will not give up my nationality. If you want me out, I'll go, but I love your country and would be very sorry to leave."
Every time I suggested we leave, Cecil said that he was a true Rhodesian and wouldn't leave unless he had to. "I don't run just because there's trouble where you've had years of peace."

We had a lot of armchair politicians at that stage among the white population, but it never got any further than the armchair. Sadly, many people left at that time. I suggested that we move to Southern Rhodesia, but Cecil felt we would be jumping from the frying pan into the fire. During this time I witnessed bitter hatred and moments of great love between the blacks and the whites. A number of stories did their rounds, some of them true I believe, so I thought I would put them in the book to bring a smile.

A villager met his friend who wore a watch on his arm and he asked him what time it was. Not knowing how to tell the time, he stretched out his arm for the other villager to see the watch face.
"There it is" he said.
Looking at the watch, with also no clue as to how it worked, the villager replied "Ah, so it is!"

The phone rings and a voice asks, "Is this two-two-two-two?"
"No, this is double two, double two."
"I seem to have the wrong number. I am so sorry to have worried you"
"Oh, it was no trouble, the phone was ringing anyway!"

After my dad's death our lives took another turn. In his will he had left his half of the business to Charlie, who became sole owner of the BP garage, the tea room and the two flats upstairs. Joyce got dad's car and Cecil and I were to get his house, but this was heavily bonded and we found ourselves financially flattened while we tried to pay the bond. We didn't want to move mom and our little house at the top of the hill was too small, so we decided to move in with her. It was the last thing I wanted and although Cecil acted the perfect gentleman, I could see that he was devastated. I remember George popping in one afternoon and I said "I do not want to live in that museum, nor do I want to live with my mother."
I burst into tears and ran to our bedroom. Cecil sent George after me and he sat at the bottom of the bed and said "After a few months have passed, you'll find it won't worry you so much anymore. This is one time your mother needs you and she's always been there for you in the past. Now it's your turn."
I felt ashamed and apologised, promising to try hard to make it work. That night Cecil held me in his arms and I realised that we could cope with any problem, as long as we had each other.

Jeni was five when I needed to go to Salisbury for an operation. I dreaded going, as the Rhodesian crowd seemed to hate us, saying

215

that every white should have left after independence, leaving the blacks to muddle along on their own until they would have been only too glad to call us all back. Petrol was rationed in Southern Rhodesia, as it was in Zambia too. We arrived at the border at about three in the afternoon. The men on duty were watching a game of rugby on television and ignored the queue for about half an hour until the match finished. Coming through at their leisure, they began to serve the people in the queue. At last it was my turn and the man asked me where I was going. When I told him, he muttered something about using their petrol, then asked me how long I would be staying. Indicating that I wasn't sure how long I'd be in hospital, he replied "I'm giving you seven days."

"Is that to live or die?" I asked sarcastically.

Giving me a filthy look, he stamped the passport and then told us how much petrol we were allowed. Cecil replied that he didn't know whether it would be enough for him to get there and back and the official turned to him, retorting "Take it or leave it" then he walked away.

I was fuming! I was sick and certainly didn't feel like this sort of problem. I would be staying with a friend of my father and when we arrived she announced that I was to accompany her to a cocktail party that evening. Typically female, my first words were "But I have nothing to wear."

Cecil kissed me goodbye, wishing me well for the operation and I could see the worry on his face. He was anxious about being away from work for too long as well and left shortly afterwards. My hostess and I then proceeded to dress for the party. There were a lot of people, but no-one that I knew, so I found a little spot in the corner, sat myself down next to an elderly gentleman, who said "I believe you come from Zambia? I've been dying to hear how you are all getting on under the new government."

I looked at him and smiled. "We are all doing very well indeed, but your customs officials could learn a few lessons from our border post at Chirundu. They greet us with smiles and ask whether we had a pleasant journey."

I told him all about our episode at the border post and before I knew it, it was time to go home as I was to be at the hospital early the next morning.

On arriving at the hospital, I found a beautiful bouquet of flowers from Cecil with a note wishing me luck. My operation was scheduled for the next day, which was my fortieth birthday. Another bouquet arrived that afternoon, wishing me a happy birthday. The operation was not successful and I still have problems today. I stayed in hospital until Friday, but then my allocated time in Southern Rhodesia was almost up. The doctor indicated that he would have liked me to stay a few more days, but knowing the position, he urged me to rest as much as I possibly could. Mrs Brown (not her real name) arrived and took me back to her home. "You really threw the cat amongst the pigeons at the party, you know."

"What did I do?" I asked, surprised.

"Didn't you know who the man was that you were talking to? He is the aide de camp to Mister Ian Smith, and he has raised merry hell about the way customs are acting up."

Well, going home was a different story and the officials just about fell all over us to be nice. I only prayed that they were not aware that it was me that had started the entire affair! Just before I was due to leave Mrs Brown said that Cecil had phoned to enquire whether she had accommodation for Joyce, who needed to purchase goods for the garage and would be coming with him. I asked her if I could use her telephone in private and when she left the room, I picked up the phone and dialed the garage's number. Nelly answered and I asked her to call Cecil and to ensure that he could speak in private. As he answered the phone, I said "You have two choices. Bring Joyce with you and I don't return to Zambia. I will find work here in Salisbury and you can go your own way or come alone and I will go home with you. I've had enough of Joyce in the past six years."

He must have left Mazabuka immediately, because he arrived at about eleven that night. When we were in the room on our own, he said "You put me in a very embarrassing position, you know."

I didn't feel that his remark needed an answer and simply changed the subject.

When we returned to Maz, I was telling Nelly all about the phone call and she looked at me in a strange way and quietly said "You should be ashamed of yourself. Cecil drove home six hundred miles after dropping you at Mrs Brown, because he was concerned about leaving John alone in the garage. However he was so worried about you; he drove back to Salisbury the following day and arrived while you were in theatre. After hearing from the doctor that you were alright, he left before you even came round after the anaesthetic to get back to work. My reply to this was simply "Shame."

We moved into my mother's home and were once again living next door to Joyce. My jealousy was never far from the surface and the time of Jeni's birth still rankled. Perhaps I over-reacted, but I will never know.

Ethné finished school and found employment on the telephone exchange. One event that still brings a smile was when a villager phoned in to the exchange and said he wanted to book a trunk call. Ethné asked for his number and promised to phone him as soon as she had the other party on the line. He replied that he was in a phone booth and didn't know the number. Ethné explained that he should look straight ahead of him and he would find the number there. After a somewhat silent wait, he suddenly blurted "Oh yes, I have found it. It is 0,1,2,3,4,5,6,7,8,9" as he read out the numbers around the dial.

Ethné worked there for a few months and was then offered a position in Barclays Bank. She was so conscientious in her work and was soon promoted to teller, but she was really young and very inexperienced to handle such a position. Despite this, she only ever made one mistake and came home that night in a flood of tears. "I was eighty pounds short in my takings today." She sobbed for ages, knowing that eighty pounds was a lot of money. Next morning, Mr Kirby phoned from the Salvation Army and asked for Ethné personally. When she answered the phone he said "Yesterday you gave me eighty pounds too much in my wages bag. Thank heavens for honest people and what a relief for the bank and particularly for Ethné.

Mike started boarding school in Livingstone. In his dormitory were three white boys and seven black boys. However after a couple of terms, Mike stated that he was worried about the situation at school. "I don't have a problem with the mixed dormitory, mom, in fact some of the black guys are my best friends. The problem is that there is so much tension with the staff. They are so terrified of offending a black child, that when a white guy threw a pillow at a black guy who was snoring the other night, he was expelled for racism."

This concerned me as well and I tried to find out if there had been extenuating circumstances surrounding this incident, but no-one would talk. Cecil and I discussed it and we decided to send Mike to South Africa where he would live with Bill and Phyllis.

I shall never forget the day Mike caught the train by himself in Maz. He had to change trains in Salisbury and then get off alone in Germiston. As he stood in the doorway of the train, his bottom lip being constantly chewed, he said "You don't have to wait for the train to leave, mom. I will be alright."

Before he could turn away, two huge tears plopped from his eyes and ran down his little cheeks. As I walked away from the train my tears flowed freely and Cecil's face was full of emotion too.

Mike stayed at Germiston Boys High for a year and then we heard about a boarding school in Salisbury and arranged for him to attend this one. No longer would he have to commute by train, he would fly to Salisbury and be fetched at the airport. Life became rather steady with average day to day happenings, with just the odd incident to mar the peace. The first one happened when Joyce asked if I could run the tea room for a day while she went Christmas shopping.

I was busy packing one of the shelves when a black man walked in, looking very dirty and bare footed. He ordered one hot dog. I called to Joseph, our kitchen helper to prepare the hotdog to take away. While he waited, the man suddenly said "One inanimate hot dog." I looked up, then continued packing the shelf and he walked over to me and said "You didn't laugh."

I looked at him squarely and replied "No, I didn't see anything to laugh about."

"I made a joke and you will laugh."

By this time I was actually dying to laugh, but I'm afraid I dug my heels in and said "I only laugh if I want to, no-one makes me laugh."

I got quite a fright when he retorted "I am ... (no name, no packdrill!), a minister in the government and if you refuse to laugh, I will have you deported."

Typically myself, my reaction was "If you are one of our ministers, you are a disgrace to your government. You are dirty, you are not wearing shoes and I suspect you have been drinking. Now go ahead and deport me."

I was truly worried for a few days, expecting the worst, but nothing ever happened and I began to wonder whether he had lied about his position until a photograph was published in our local newspaper of all the cabinet ministers and, sure enough, there he was, all dressed up and smiling for the camera.

The next incident was with my sister in law. She was in the tea room when a smartly dressed man walked in and closed the tea-room door and announced who he was. Once again, I shall not mention his real name.

"I have closed the door and I have two askari's at the door with fixed bayonets, so no-one can get in. What are you going to do about it?"

Joyce, with the courage she could muster, said "I promise you, if you so much as lay a hand on me, I will kill you."

He laughed, purchased a packet of cigarettes and then left the tea room. A few moments later an obviously very upset petrol attendant came in and he was shaking like a leaf. "Oh, Dona, we were so worried about you" he cried, "there were two askari's at the door with bayonets crossed and they would not let anyone in."

Our next shock came when a government official died and was to be buried in the Maz cemetery. There were about three thousand people at his funeral and when it was over, all the graves that had no slabs on, were trampled completely flat, including my father's.

Petrol rationing once again came into force and when Christmas arrived, Hillier's Motors wrote on the windows 'Walk Well, Walk Shell'. Someone was so amused by this that they went home and drew a life-size horse on a board and erected it near the garage, writing on it 'We are once again a one-horse town!'

Joyce and Charlie wanted to go on holiday and I promised to take over the shop with my mom for a few weeks. My mom had very little patience and early one morning a couple entered the shop. The black man was very well dressed and a beautiful foreign woman, whose skin was a lovely golden colour, accompanied him. When our newspapers arrived, we would write on them the names of those who had firm orders and the balance were for sale in the shop. We had sold all the spare copies, but the ordered ones were laid out on a table for collection by the local farmers. All the poor man did was put his hand on one, obviously thinking that they were for sale, and my mother flew at him. "Don't you touch those" she shouted rudely, which was completely uncalled for.
The man turned to his companion and spoke in a foreign language and was obviously very angry, then turned towards my mother. Fortunately, his companion took his arm and said something to him and he stepped back again. Turning to me, she said with utter contempt "You whites make me sick. You think you are so special. You even send your children out of the country to be educated, because our children are not good enough for yours to associate with."

I was afraid that this was getting out of hand and I gently reached out and touched her arm. "Why are you jealous of me?" I asked her softly. "You are so beautiful, look at your golden skin as opposed to my white skin. I don't send my children out of the country, my daughter is at school here in Mazabuka and I certainly don't think I am better than you in any way. I have to work all day to keep food on the table and I can see that you don't work, you are a lady."
Mollified, she asked "Then why is that old lady over there so rude and insulting?"
I smiled and leaned forward, putting my hand against my cheek, as I whispered "She's old and stupid."

She turned and repeated my words in her language to the man, who shouted back at her again and she reiterated whatever it was she had said. With that, she smiled at me and they walked out of the shop. My mom came over and asked what had happened and I just smiled and said casually "I haven't a clue."

The last incident during that period that caused major concern was when Japhat came running into the sewing room to announce that sixteen UNIP youths were sitting on my front lawn and they were instigating each other to make trouble. I told him to quickly make jugs of coffee and plates of sandwiches and biscuits to give to the young men. It is amazing how a full stomach brings with it a feeling of content and it was not long before they were laughing happily. When I walked outside, I was greeted with smiles and "Sikona, dona", meaning 'thank you dona'. Soon afterwards they moved off and we breathed a heavy sigh of relief.

There was also a movement started that was called Instant Justice. Once, when I was in Lusaka, a young boy was caught stealing and he fell to his knees crying, begging us to phone the police immediately. He begged to be put into jail rather than let the Instant Justice get their hands on him. This movement was not against any particular race or creed, they simply punished those who they felt had done wrong, be it black or white. There was a rumour that a white man in Lusaka accidentally bumped a little black girl with his car. She was unhurt, but Instant Justice members pulled him from his car and broke his arms. We never knew whether this story was in fact the truth.

Cecil developed a terrible pain in his side and was diagnosed with appendicitis. He was operated on and came home the following day. A couple of days later he decided to go hunting and the doctor, who was going with him, said "The stitches are still in, but I'll carry all the heavy stuff and walking certainly won't hurt you."
They shot an impala and while running towards it, the doctor fell and broke a bone in his ankle. He could not walk at all and Cecil offered to carry him back to the vehicle. "You can't, you will damage

your wound" the doctor cried, to which Cecil replied "Well, do you have a better idea?"

So, Cecil put doc on his back and carried him half a mile to the landrover, then went back to fetch the impala. On their return, Cecil didn't seem to be any the worse for wear, but little did we know that a few years later, this incident would have serious repercussions.

We went up to Lusaka one day and we always had lunch at the Grand Hotel. On entering the dining room we realised that we were the only whites in the room and everyone was talking at the top of their voices. We sat down and I noticed that Cecil was smiling. I asked him what he found so amusing and he motioned to the buffet table, saying "Watch this."

There was a couple dishing up their food from the beautiful layout of various meals and desserts. They started with meat, then vegetables, then salad and on top of this delicious meal, they spooned their dessert.

"In future we will stop for tea at the little drive-in place near Kafue, because I just cannot stand the noise in here" Cecil complained.

Not only were people seated at a table talking to each other, but they also shouted across to people at other tables and the noise was deafening.

On the next trip, we stopped at the drive-in restaurant, which was what we call roadhouses in South Africa, and were enjoying our tea when a car pulled up next to us with a black family. They also ordered tea and when the wife had finished pouring it, she passed the sugar basin to one child and the milk jug to the other. The little one with the sugar, stuck his tongue into the basin and began to lick up the sugar. Cecil just shook his head and announced that in future we would be taking a flask and padkos with us if we travelled.

I tried to go into the public toilet in Lusaka, which had always been spotless, but I could literally smell them from half a block away. When I got to the door and I saw the floor was covered in stale urine, I turned away and used a quiet spot in the bush on the way home to Maz. So our way of life had turned full circle. At one time in our lives it had been the black man who ate his meal sitting on the back of a truck or alongside the road and it was he who used the bush as his toilet. Now it was the whites' turn to do so and the blacks were all eating in the restaurants.

Now that Kariba Dam had filled, we began to go tiger fishing and once again the adventure appeared in our lives. We drove down to Chipepo for a long weekend with Marie and Attie van Wyk, also very good friends of ours. Marie was quite a tall, big-boned woman, certainly no fat on her and although not really pretty, a certain beauty emanated from her smiling eyes. Attie was also tall and dark, with a terrific sense of humour. Each family took their own boat and Jeni came with us, but Marie's children were in boarding school.

We took along food for the night and each person had a blanket. Sleeping bags were not something one even saw in the shops, so I don't know whether they were in fact in production at that time or not. We also took along our ponchos to slip on when it got cold at night, because being surrounded by water, the temperature on the islands dropped quite a bit. We chose an island that still had a tree on it and Marie and I spent a short while removing the small stones from under the tree, as this was where we wanted to sleep. We sat chatting until about ten that night and then lay down with Jeni between us and fell asleep. At about one-thirty in the morning Cecil shook my shoulder and I awoke instantly as he whispered "There are hippos on the island, get ready to climb the tree and then I will pass Jeni to you."
I looked up at the first branch, which was at least seven feet up and said "I'll never manage it."
Smiling, he replied "Oh, trust me, you will if you have to."
I gently woke Marie and we sat as quietly as possible for about twenty minutes when Cecil called from the boat to say it was alright, the hippos had moved away.

We returned to our bungalow in Chipepo early in the morning and dropped off all the blankets, picked up two folding chairs and rejoined the men to visit another island. We sat close to the water's edge, chatting away, when all of a sudden a hippo burst from the water right in front of Marie. She got such a fright that she threw herself backwards, chair and all, and I honestly don't know who got the bigger scare, the hippo or Marie. He let out an indignant grunt and disappeared back into the water. It was impossible to conceal my laughter as I helped Marie untangle herself from the deck-chair. While on this holiday, Jeni called me to look at a long, thin snake lying against the wall. While we stood looking at it, the snake suddenly launched itself into the air, flinging itself straight at us. We quickly jumped out of its way and it disappeared into the bush close by. On returning home, someone told me that we had been extremely fortunate, as it was a Whip Snake and it throws itself up in the direction of its quarry and bites on contact. This is also something that I never bothered to follow up.

The men had caught quite a few tiger fish, which we never ate, but they were wonderful sport on a rod, even the small ones gave quite a fight. They had also caught a few Vundu. This catfish is similar in appearance to the Barbel, but grows enormous. I have seen them the size of an average man and heard that they get even bigger than that. There was a story of a man who tied a fishing line to his wrist and had hooked a very large vundu, which ultimately pulled him into the water where he drowned, his body being found downstream some time later.

Our annual holiday was approaching and Cecil suggested that to save money, we would holiday at Chipepo instead of going down south. I agreed that it was a good idea and once again the truck was filled with supplies and our car towed the boat. After settling in, Cecil suggested we go for a ride in the boat. He packed in his rods and fishing tackle and said "This is where they stay for the month."
We hadn't gone very far and I was staring in awe at the sunset. The sky was vibrant with a kaleidoscope of colour as the sun slowly disappeared behind the horizon, leaving only a dark void with a multitude of twinkling stars. Suddenly Cecil shouted "Joan, Tiger! Get your head down."
Grabbing a rod, he began casting and I spent the next hour with my head on my knees as Cecil enjoyed the fishing. In his excitement, he stepped back onto his other rod and it snapped like a dry twig. He hooked a very large fish, I don't remember now whether it was a

tiger or a vundu, but as he tried to land it, his rod snapped, leave him with no means of fishing. After a few moments silence, he suggested we get a villager to watch our camp while we drive back to Maz, sleep over and then go to Lusaka in the morning to buy more rods. We did this and Cecil bought three rods and we returned to Chipepo the following day. I didn't have the heart to point out that after this escapade, a holiday to South Africa would have been the cheaper option, but I never regretted our decision, because it was one of the most wonderful holidays I had ever had.

CHAPTER THIRTEEN

An encounter with Rabies....

Cecil was now in his forties and life had lost a lot of the adventure we had been so used to. He was trying hard to come to terms with the fact that our children were growing up and he was nearing middle age. Weekends were no longer spent in the bush, so to speak. He still wasn't happy with the work he was doing and at times he reminded me of a caged wild animal and one could feel the frustration building up in him.

Ethné was still doing well at Barclays Bank and had reached the 'boy' stage. The first boy who came along was a nice chap by the name of Harry, but Cecil still regarded his daughter as a little girl and insisted that she be home before eleven if Harry took her out. One night we attended a dance at the WI and Harry invited Ethné to a dance at the Settler's Club. It was a teenagers' dance and Cecil agreed she could go, telling Harry to have her home by eleven.

We were on the dance-floor, when Cecil looked at his watch and said it's after eleven and they are not back yet. By eleven thirty Cecil was really agitated and announced that he was going to the club to fetch Ethné. I jumped into the car beside him and even I was shocked when we reached the club, only to find it in complete darkness, with a few flashing lights inside. This was the first 'disco' we had ever seen. We checked inside, but they were not there and then Cecil scoured the grounds, but to no avail. By this time he was furious and we decided to go home. As we pulled into the driveway, there sat the two youngsters on the front step. Cecil jumped from the car and shouted at Harry "Get going and don't come back! I don't want you seeing my daughter again."
Poor Harry was gone within seconds and Ethné turned to me and said "Mom, we have been sitting here since eleven o'clock. Dad said I must be home by that time and I was."

Sadly that was the end of Harry.

One night a car pulled up outside and hooted, then hooted again a few minutes later. Cecil asked Ethné if it was someone for her and she nodded. She was almost eighteen, but still horribly under her father's thumb. Cecil told her to call them inside and three young chaps walked in. As they entered the room, Cecil's voice boomed out "Do you guys consider yourself men? No man sits in a car and hoots for a woman. He knocks on the door like a gentleman. Don't ever hoot for my daughter again. Now sit down!"
He turned to a red-faced Ethné and told her to go and make tea and eats for her guests. I think it was only me that saw the twinkling in his eyes, the others were too petrified.

The fishing club was still going strong and one of the best members was a Francois Joubert. A young man, he and Cecil were on first name terms and got on famously. We went to a gymkhana one day and Frans walked over to Cecil and asked "May I take Ethné to a dance tonight, Cecil?"
"Yes, but be back by twelve. Oh, what the hell, Frans, I know you; stay until the end, but just bring her back safely."
I must tell you that thirty years later, we were all sitting at the dinner table when Ethné turned to Cecil and said "Dad, do you remember chasing Harry away?"
When Cecil nodded, she continued "You know, Dad, Harry was a perfect gentleman, but Francois got his face smacked the very first time he took me out."
Frans laughed, but he looked rather sheepish after that comment, as he busied himself with the food on his plate.

It was around this time that Cecil and I realised we could no longer keep up the bond payments and we put mom's house on the market for the amount still owing on the bond. There were very few people wanting to buy property, but the sugar estate that had opened up on the Kafue River made us an offer and in desperation, we accepted and moved onto Bardmony Farm with my mother. Bardmony was owned by a friend and the house was vacant at that stage, so he offered it to us. Graham Pringle, a young chap who worked at the bank with Ethné, came to board with us as well.

Mike was home for the holidays and would often take the rifle and bring back a duiker for the three dogs. Mike was growing up very much like his dad where hunting was concerned. I often wondered if he really enjoyed it, or if it was purely to impress his father, because he spent far too many years of his life trying to be a son that his dad could be proud of, but he was far too gentle to be truly like his father. One day he came running in and said "Mom, Jeni has run away."

I had shouted at her earlier that afternoon and she had packed a suitcase with her colouring book and crayons and her favourite teddy bear. I was terribly worried, as the farm was very remote and full of wild animals and if she got lost in the bush, we would not find her before dark. I asked Mike if he had seen where she had headed and he nodded, pointing towards a pathway leading away from the house.

Jeni had followed the dirt track for a while, then seeing the dust from the approaching bakkie, she had run off into the bush and climbed a tree to hide. Fortunately Mike saw her and we stopped the bakkie and walked over to the tree. Between Mike and I we eventually coaxed the stubborn child out of the tree, where I promptly gave her a good hiding. This was more out of relief than actual anger, because by then I could see the funny side of the situation.

Christmas time on Bardmony was a picture of beauty, with all the trees in full blossom. In the shady spots of the bush grew the beautiful flame lilies, their vivid colours lavishly brightening the otherwise dull bushveld. I used these flowers to decorate the house for Christmas and it was utterly exquisite.

It seemed that we were to be plagued with medical problems for a while; the first incident was when Mike took ill. He had suffered a bout of Bilharzia when he was about six and this flared up again. I don't know if there is new treatment today, but in those days they were not able to kill all the germs when one contracted it, so they would lie dormant in the body and flare up every so often. The treatment in this case was quite radical. Mike was not allowed out of bed, as exercise could damage the heart. At the same time Jeni showed me a patch on her thigh, which was the size of a small cup and red and quite raised. I realised she had ringworm and took her to the doctor as well.

Mike's health improved a few days later and we took him to Eagle's Rest on Kariba. He jumped off an anthill and a piece of grass stuck him in the eye. A couple of days later the eye became very red and he complained that it was painful and he couldn't see properly. Cecil took him down to the doctor, who told us to get him to Lusaka as quickly as possible. The doctor found that a grass seed had embedded itself in the pupil and had started to grow.

Graham Pringle was small in stature, with a lovely honest face and in all the time he boarded with us, I never once heard him complain about anything. He went fishing with a friend and as he was trying to get the hook out of the mouth of a tiger fish, it fell on his lap and gave him a nasty bite on the knee. Before they got back to Maz, the wound had become septic and this wound continued to give him problems for many years.

Cecil had been complaining of abdominal pain for some time and suddenly took really ill. He woke up in the early hours of the morning and he was in such agony that he pulled his knees up against his chest and we rushed off to fetch the doctor, who had been treating him for a stomach ulcer. The doctor called me to one side and said "I believe Cecil's ulcer has ruptured and he has Peritonitis. There is no time to send him to Lusaka."
He ordered an ambulance to take Cecil to the local hospital in Maz and told me to get there as soon as I could. This was early morning and at about eleven he entered the waiting room.
"I'm sorry it's taken so long, Joan. We opened him up, looking for the ulcer, but he has never had one. So, we kept cutting until we reached the bowel. It seems as though his bowel was twisted when they removed his appendix. His bowel was completely blocked and I had to remove about three inches of it, but he is out of danger. He

does have a scar from his chest to the bottom of his stomach, though."

So the memory of Cecil carrying the doctor and then the impala after his appendectomy came flooding back. I went into Cecil's ward and as I looked at this strong, virile man, still drowsy from the anaesthetic and tubes everywhere, I realised that after twenty years of marriage, he was even more important to me than when we first met. He opened his eyes and smiled, whispering "I'm fine."
My heart swelled with love as I stroked back the unruly lock of black hair that always adorned his forehead.

Cecil had just recovered when I was hospitalised with more problems and I came home weak and exhausted. Joyce came over to tell me that Cynthia was getting married and Ethné and Frans, who had been dating for some time, decided to ask Cecil if they, too, could wed. Naturally I said they should wait, as I was not in any position to arrange a wedding. Ethné and I had an argument and she blurted "I'm not asking you to do anything. Granny and I will arrange it all. Mrs Slinger will bake my wedding cake and Mrs Venter will make the bridesmaid dresses."
They planned to marry on the seventh of January, which was only five months away.

Ethné adored her granny and they went off together to get invitation cards printed and to choose a wedding dress. I really felt neither needed or wanted and was also secretly concerned. All the young chaps in Maz were quite heavy drinkers in my opinion and Frans was one of them. I once said to Ethné "You can fight another woman, but you can't fight the bottle." Naturally this fell on deaf ears and quite thankfully, too, as this had been a gross misinterpretation. Frans has been a superb son-in-law and he has never been a drinker since they got married.

In the October, Frans was playing what they called 'Bok-Bok' and he fell, dislocating his shoulder. He came and stayed with us until the injury had healed. Ethné was planning everything and discussed very little with me, until the day came when she realised that promises were not always honoured. Mrs Slinger told her that they were going on holiday, but if I was prepared to bake the three-tier cake, she would ice it. Ethné asked me and I agreed. Mrs Slinger arrived with three wooden cake boxes, together with a recipe for wedding cake. I purchased all the ingredients and began baking. In the first batch, I miscalculated the weights, forgetting that sugar has double the mass of flour and instead added equal quantities of both. The result was a lovely bunch of fruit, but certainly not a cake. Needless to say, by the time I was finished, I felt like quite the professional and the cake turned out really nice.

A few days later Ethné came home in tears, saying that Mrs Venter had taken ill and was going to South Africa for an operation. She had purchased yards of exquisite material for the bridesmaid dresses, which had cost the earth and now had no dressmaker. Once again I stepped in and offered to help. I was not a dressmaker, so made each dress in sheeting first, to ensure that the fit was perfect before cutting the expensive fabric. Once the fit was done, I unpicked each dress made of sheeting and used this as my pattern. The material was terribly difficult to cut, as it was embossed with flowers, but the end result was terrific, barring one dress. I had told the girls to wear the shoes they would be wearing for the wedding for all fittings. The one girl was very tall and had chosen to wear flat shoes, so her hem was pinned and sewn accordingly. However she could not find suitable shoes when she went to Lusaka, so bought a pair of high heels. Fortunately, there was sufficient fabric to let the hem down, but the edge of the original hem showed very clearly on the embossed fabric and there was nothing I could do about it. She was very upset, but I refused to be daunted by this, because it had not been my fault.

In early December I asked for the list of guests and discovered that there were one hundred and fifty. I nearly had a fit. There were no caterers in Maz, so I got really and truly stuck in, baking and freezing every day until the freezer was completely full of goodies. I asked Ethné which bridesmaid was planning her kitchen-tea, but as it turned out, they were both on holiday in South Africa. By this time I was truly enjoying myself and felt wanted at last, with Ethné and I being on exceptionally good terms. I told her I would plan the kitchen-tea and she should invite all her friends for the following Saturday, using the Golf Club as the venue. There was plenty of food for all and it was a pleasant afternoon.

Next on my agenda was Christmas and we still had Graham boarding with us. The festive season went off smoothly and we had a wonderful new year. It seemed that life was just food, food and more food. Although the bride's parents are supposed to supply everything, Frans' family brought twenty roast chickens, small cakes and milk tarts. A few of my friends accepted the task of decorating the tables, arranging flowers for the church and reception hall. I woke up early on the big day and all I could smell was Orange Blossom. All the orange trees on the farm were in bloom and the world smelled and looked beautiful. The morning was spent much the same as with any other wedding. Hair-do's, make-up, last minute arrangements and solving any problems that cropped up.

The wedding was to start at three and I remarked to Cecil that someone could have swept the stairs to the church, as they were full of red sand. The church was full and I was waiting outside for the bride to arrive. As she stepped from the car, my heart swelled with pride. A slim girl, she looked exquisite and the dress hugged her body to perfection. Her dark hair was beautifully done and the white veil only made her big brown eyes seem even larger. I thought to myself at that moment. 'This is the beautiful baby you brought into the world all those years ago and she's gone through the dirty little toddler stage, the demanding little girl stage, the impossible teenager and has now matured into this wonderful woman'.

Jeni, dressed in her full length flower-girl dress, ran forward to greet her sister and accidentally stepped on Ethné's full length veil, ripping it from her head. Jeni began to cry and say how sorry she was. We quickly fitted the veil again and Ethné began to ascend the stairs. Jeni's eyes were still filled with tears and she tripped as she climbed the stairs, falling straight into the red dust. No matter how we tried, the dust would not come off the dress and was sadly there to stay. Ethné was upset because her beloved baby sister was crying and the organ was playing the wedding march over and over. Eventually

Ethné reached Frans, walking proudly beside her father. The minister motioned to Frans to move, as he was on the wrong side of the bride. There was a bit of a scuffle while they all sorted out their positions and the ceremony then began.

I noticed something in Ethné's veil, realising that a stink-bug was crawling in it and I prayed that no-one would notice it. Just then my mom, in what she might have considered a whisper, from a few seats away from me, said "Joan, there's a stink-bug in Ethné's veil. Go and get it out."

I motioned to her to be quiet, but the entire congregation had heard her and all eyes lifted to the stink-bug.

At last the ceremony was over and we proceeded to the hall. I was shocked to find a ladder behind the bride's table and a chap trying to fix lights as we all began to take our places. The first speech was taking place when I got a nudge in my side and from under the table, I was handed a pair of high heeled shoes, with a whisper to pass them on to Frans' mom. A few moments later a pair of flat shoes came back. The bridesmaid could now dance after the speeches were over.

Eventually Ethné and Frans took the floor, circled a few times and then the guests began to join them. We planned for Ethné and Frans to leave at about seven thirty, as they were booked into a hotel about a hundred miles away. Cecil had hidden their car to avoid silly pranks being played by the men. We had a friend whose entire honeymoon had been marred by such a prank, where they put raw fish in his hubcaps and we didn't want a similar incident.

Frans' flat was to be used by three guys from Lusaka instead of them driving all the way back late at night. Unfortunately, someone slipped Frans a 'mickey fynn', which is what we called a concoction of different drinks. In no time at all he was dead drunk and completely unable to drive. Cecil persuaded them to return to his flat for the night and we told the three chaps from Lusaka to follow us home. Cecil drove the newly-weds to the flat and then returned to the dance. We danced a few times when he got back and then several black youths arrived and broke a number of car headlights and then tried to gatecrash the party. Our own crowd was none too sober by this time and wanted to fight. When Cecil saw one of our friends push one of the black boys down the steps, he announced loudly that the party was over and everyone should leave. We packed up and headed back to Bardmony.

The house had four bedrooms, one for my mother, one for Jeni, Graham in the third and our bedroom, which we had given to Frans' parents for the night. We planned to sleep in Jeni's room. Now I suddenly had three extra guests, so before we could think of retiring, we pulled out all the camping stretchers, blankets and pillows and laid them out on the front lawn. It was a beautiful night, so warm and peaceful, and Cecil decided he would join the chaps under the stars for the night, something we often did. I was busy making coffee when Mom went to bed and Jeni was asleep in her room.

I saw car lights approach and went outside to find one of the couples from the wedding with their mother standing on the lawn. Their car was giving problems and they had turned off at the nearest farm, being ours, for place to stay until the next morning, when they could fix the car. I rushed in and woke Jeni, guiding her to the sofa in the lounge. I gave her room to the old lady and grabbed a few more stretchers and bedding for the couple waiting outside. I made more coffee and made sure everyone was settled in for night. As I walked inside, I wished I had another stretcher to join them outside and suddenly realised that there was nowhere for me to sleep. I was so tired by this time that I lay down on the lounge carpet in my wedding finery and slept till dawn.

Frans had asked us to look after his little fox terrier, which he absolutely adored. The day after the wedding, Cecil and I went to town for groceries and on our return to Bardmony, I jumped out of the car and went inside, calling for Japhat to help carry the groceries, when I heard Cecil shout urgently "Joan, fetch my gun."
"What for" I asked, surprised.
"Just get it quickly" he shouted and I knew something was terribly wrong.

I grabbed the rifle and ran outside, but the crisis was over. As Cecil had stepped from the car and walked towards the house, a rabid dog had run at him from the bush. Leaning against the outside wall of the house was Cecil's sjambok, which he grabbed and pushed it into the rabid dog's mouth, in this way keeping the dog at bay from attacking him, while he called for his gun. Our dogs kept their distance, almost as if they sensed the danger in the diseased animal, but Butch, our Bull-Mastiff cross, ran forward and hit the dog with his rump and knocked it away from Cecil. The saliva from its foaming mouth splattered all over my dogs as it shook its head and headed for the bush.

I looked at the dogs and realised that I would have to act swiftly. I bathed each dog thoroughly and only then thought about the fact that I had been dressmaking and by this time my hands were full of pinpricks. My blood ran cold as the realization hit me, because rabies is a definite killer. We phoned the research station to come out immediately, as late as it was. On checking the rabies certificates, we saw that those of Butch and Teddy Puff were still valid, but Shandy's was overdue and I didn't have one for Frans' dog. Not being able to contact them for weeks, I could not take the chance. The inspector decided that Shandy and Frans' dog should be euthanised immediately, together with our four cats. I begged him to let me take them to my own vet in town, but when we went outside to tell his assistant to leave the dogs, he had already shot Frans' dog and my four cats. He told me to visit the hospital early next morning for the first of a series of injections against rabies.

I will never forget my little Shandy as I took her to the vet. I left her there before carrying on to the hospital for my injection. When told to lift my blouse and expose my stomach, I was horrified. The doctor injected me next to the navel and on asking how many I would need, I was told I should return every day for six days. The nurse told me that I was very fortunate, as if they only had the old serum, it would have been fourteen injections.

By the next morning I was dreading my second injection. The first site was now swollen having formed a red, hard lump the size of a marble and was really painful. After my injection, I went to the tea-room to tell Joyce about our rabies scare. While I was chatting to her, my little Shandy ran through the door, her tail wagging happily as she found me. She had escaped from the vet's office and I had the awful task of taking her there yet again. Little did I know that I would hear more of Shandy a week later.

I had four injections and we had decided to go to the Victoria Falls for the weekend. I spoke to the doctor about it and he agreed to let me take the other two doses in a cooler bag and I could get the sister at the Livingstone hospital to inject them each day. The sister at Livingstone walked in and said "Here's number five. Push your stomach up as hard as you can."
I followed her instructions and the needle went in easily and I found the procedure far less painful. "That was easy" I remarked, "Why didn't they tell me to do that in Maz?"
The sister then told me that she had done all her training in India and as they have a lot of rabies over there, one makes sure to learn the least painful and easiest method of administering the injections. Apart from my six marbles, I showed no reaction to the series of injections and after about three weeks my marbles slowly faded away.

We arrived back from the Vic Falls the next day and I got a call from Joyce to tell me that Shandy was sitting under a tree in her front garden. I burst into tears and said to Cecil "I don't care what the vet or anyone else says, I'm bringing her home."
I saw Graham take his keys and leave. Cecil and I changed and then left the farm to fetch Shandy. We were about half-way there, when Graham's car approached us and he motioned for us to stop. As he stepped from the car, his face grave and sympathetic, he said "Joan, it's all over. I took her to the vet myself and held her in my arms while he injected her."

It seems that Shady had escaped once again and had been running around all week. I tried to find out why she hadn't been put to sleep immediately, but the vet said that she had escaped before he could do so. It was, however, whispered in my ear, that Shandy had been given to someone in the compound and ran away from there. I was not sorry that this vet did not stay in Maz very long, being a government vet he was transferred elsewhere and a new vet arrived.

About five months later, we came home one afternoon after shopping and Teddy Puff ran to the car. There was oil on his back and I said to Cecil "Teddy Puff doesn't look well. I wonder if someone has been here and perhaps hit him with their car?"
Before I could pat him, he shot passed me and ran into the house, straight under the couch. I was really worried by now. This was my favourite pet and I ran after him, calling his name and lay down on my stomach to pull him from under the couch. Cecil rushed in, grabbed me by the feet and dragged me swiftly away from the cowering dog.
"Are you mad? Don't you know a rabid animal will cower in dark places?"
"He's not rabid!" I shouted back at Cecil. "He must be hurt."
With that, Teddy Puff ran from under the couch and headed through the front door. Once again I ran after him, Cecil on my heels. As I called to him, Teddy Puff tried to walk towards me, but he appeared to have an injured spine, as his body was contorted into almost a half-circle and he walked sideways. Cecil said gently "Joan, fetch me a blanket."
I did as I was asked and returned, handing the blanket to Cecil, who threw it over my beloved little dog, picked him up and headed for the bakkie. Placing him in the canopied back of the bakkie, we headed for the vet and left him there overnight for observation. The vet phoned me the following morning to advise that Teddy Puff had died during the night and the results of the tests done were positive for rabies. He told me he wanted the rabies certificate, as Teddy Puff should have been safe for at least another year. This was, however, the second dog from that particular batch of serum that had died.

Once again the question of injections arose and we were told that there had been so many incidents of rabid animals that year that they had run out of the new serum and were back on the fourteen day serum. There was my mother, at seventy seven, Graham Pringle who was about twenty five, Cecil and poor little Jeni, who was six.

238

Everyone had to endure the course, except for me. The doctor told me that you can only have two lots of these injections in your lifetime (this may have changed now, but this was nearly forty years ago) and I would only receive another dose if I was actually bitten. I asked if I was not still immune like animals after their injections, but the doctor said that in humans it only lasts a few months. So, the poor family began their ordeal. My heart bled for my mom and my little girl. Jeni would try to run away when it was time to leave for the hospital. I bribed her with sweets, toys, in fact anything, but that tiny tummy just didn't seem to have enough space to get the last few injections in. The tummy around the navel was a mass of lumps and the last injection was actually administered into the navel itself.

Graham was young and always out with the boys and often came home after one drink too many. Doctor told him not to partake in any sport, active games or drinking for the duration of the injections. After his first injection, he went out and played badminton after which they had a few drinks. Next morning he called me to his room and said "I am too sore to move and every gland in my body is swollen."
I phoned the doctor, who came straight to Bardmony, examined Graham and said "You have had a nasty reaction to the serum. We are going to give you a penicillin injection each time you have the serum injection to counteract it."
The poor bloke would lie on his back for the rabies shot and then turn over for the penicillin injection in his rear for fourteen days. At night we would hear him groan as he turned over in bed, but at least after that he stayed away from sport and liquor until the course was over.

CHAPTER FOURTEEN

The beginning of the end....

Cecil came home a few weeks later to say that he had been offered a position with the Central Electricity Corporation, which later became known as the Zambia Electricity Supply Corporation, or ZESCO for short. The only electrical work Cecil had done was to do the wiring for houses he built and the Chikankata Hospital. Apart from that, he knew absolutely nothing about electricity and the job would entail the operation and maintenance of extensive township and town networks at voltages of 88 KV, thirty three and eleven.

On the Mazabuka Golf Club committee was an engineer who Cecil often played golf with and it was due to this man putting Cecil's name forward to CEC, that he was offered the post. The engineer's name was Sid Wormleighton, who was a tall, very stately, middle-aged man. His wife, Alice, was a very friendly, slightly plump lady. When Cecil told Sid that he didn't know enough about electricity, Sid's reply was "Don't worry, I'll teach you. I'll be your senior and I want you, because I know how conscientious you are in everything you do. You are also honest and hard-working."

Cecil approached John Hillier and said "John, I've been with you over five years, but I still may not do any intricate work on the cars, as you have two qualified mechanics for that. I feel that this is my opportunity to get on in the world. Working here, I feel that I'm stagnating. I do appreciate all you have done for me and hope you don't think that I'm ungrateful."
John wished Cecil well and he and Nelly remained our friends for forty years. John died about five years ago, but Nelly is still alive and living in Switzerland.

Cecil joined CEC and became responsible for nearly two thousand square miles of line, including all the farms between Monze and Maz, Kafue and the remote farms that were situated off the main road. In all the years we were with CEC, I watched Cecil's pride return and remain intact from then on. Gone was the quiet, self-effacing man he had been since leaving the Kafue National Park. Working outdoors all day, checking on lines and replacing old wiring, he would have to travel miles into the bush and check the transformers. We started attending the dances again, we entertained regularly and life was suddenly wonderful. We moved into the CEC house, which was situated in the power station grounds. It was only a short walk to the office or the power station itself and we were very comfortable.

We had been at CEC for about six months when we had our first robbery. They stole all the clean washing out of the ironing room and my electric iron. Fortunately nothing was taken from the house. About a week later we both awoke to glass breaking. We both jumped out of bed and went to investigate. Our verandah had a door covered with gauze, which led to the glass door in the lounge. The windows of the dining room also faced the verandah. The thief had cut along the edge of the gauze against the wooden frame and climbed through the hole. He then cut a circle of glass out of the lounge door next to the keyhole, but the glass fell into the house, waking us before he could enter. I had phoned the police regarding the first robbery, but nothing had been done about it, so I phoned them again to report the second attempted robbery.

When the police arrived, I showed them the broken glass and the one policeman said "I'm not interested in that, as it is obvious that he broke it to get in. However," he said with a puzzled look as he held the piece of gauze in his hand, "I cannot understand what he wanted with this."

A few days later Joyce's cook had his bicycle stolen and went to report it. The police told him not to bother them with such trivial matters, as bicycles were stolen every day. They then suggested that he steal one for himself, which he decided to do. The poor chap got arrested and spent four months in prison for his trouble!

The last robbery attempt at our home was so funny that I still laugh when I tell the story. Cecil had started creating a pretty garden and had already strung a couple of wires for the sweet peas. I believe that it was the same robber that had cut the glass, as it was only a couple of days later. We had made a rule that the key never be left in the door until we could get to Lusaka to replace the glass. Mike's cycle was on the verandah under the dining room window, which was very high up. I think that with him finding no key and knowing that if he broke glass again, he would wake us, he decided to try and climb through the dining room window, which was ajar. He stood on the bicycle to reach the window, but the bike slipped and he fell heavily onto the concrete floor. This commotion woke us up and we dashed to the lounge.

The chap had obviously hurt himself, as he was sitting holding the area between his thighs. Cecil shouted "I've got him!"
The key was usually on the television, but it had fallen under the cabinet and as we searched for it, the robber got up and started limping away. Cecil found the key eventually, opened the door and ran after him. By this time, the robber, in his more earnest haste tripped over the wires Cecil had strung and fell into the flower bed. Again Cecil shouted "I've got him this time", then promptly tripped over the hosepipe, going face first into the dirt. I was laughing so at these antics when Cecil shouted for me to phone the police. As I went to turn away, I saw the robber try to jump the fence, which was made from chicken wire. His foot caught in the wire and he ploughed into the cement drain on the other side of the fence with a thud. Again Cecil shouted for me to get the police and as he did so, he went to jump over the fence. The wire had buckled by this time and Cecil's foot caught in it, catapulting him over the fence in a very ungraceful motion. By this time the robber was up and running as fast as his legs could carry him. That was the last I saw as I headed inside to phone the police.

The frustration during that phone call was so immense. I told the constable who answered the phone that the robber was running up the road towards the police station and that they should go out and arrest him. "Hold on" was the reply.

A second voice came on the phone and I quickly explained again, this time even saying "He is wearing a white shirt. Just arrest him; I'm on my way there now."

"Hold on."

A third voice, which I recognized as the chief inspector, then came on the phone and asked "What colour trousers is this man wearing?"

My reply by that stage was "Oh, don't bother; he's already half way to Cape Town!"

Nevertheless my sarcasm fell on deaf ears and I put the phone down, shaking my head with frustration.

About three months after this, Cecil asked me if I wanted to start work. I looked at him as if he was crazy.

"Have you lost your mind? I only have a standard six certificate and after twenty odd years of rearing children in the bush, what could I possibly do?"

"I want you to run the Maz office for CEC. It's only a small town and there will just be you, me and Sid."

The woman who was in the position at that time had resigned because she was expecting a baby. With great trepidation I accepted the position and, just to add to my worries, Zambia changed their currency from sterling, at the same time I started at CEC, to Kwacha and Ngwee. Bearing in mind that there were no calculators those days, I was passed the list of charges and nearly fell over with heart failure.

The rates differed for private homes, shops, pumps and African houses. The decimal point was new to me and my first thought was "Where the hell do I put the dots?"

At that stage there were over four hundred accounts to do and I took work home each night, working until the early hours of the morning. Each account was calculated manually and this took time. The lady from the Lusaka office phoned twice, asking when they would be ready, to which I sheepishly replied "I have lost two Ngwee and I can't find them."

Fortunately for me, she was really sweet and told me to send them up to her anyway. She promised to go over them as well. I dreaded the following month-end, but I soon learned the ropes and we became quite a team in our office.

Sid and Cecil were an excellent pair and went on many of the breakdowns together at first, but eventually Sid was satisfied that Cecil knew enough and allowed him to take over all the outside work. I ran the office while Sid liaised with Lusaka. If Cecil had a call-out in the evening, he would pick up four or five staff and could be out all night, or in some cases, for a couple of nights. I would go to the office, which was very close to the house, and take with me a pot of soup. I would put it on to cook on a hotplate in the back office. Piles of buttered bread and coffee would be waiting for the team to return. Sometimes they would walk in looking so exhausted and I would watch them drink their soup, which seemed to inject new life into them. There were times when they would search for hours before they found the fault and I had such respect for these hard-working men.

When a fault occurred, the phone would ring incessantly. One farmer after another would phone to complain that they had no power and their milk coolers were full of milk. However most were polite and understanding that there were so many miles of line that had to be checked for the source of the problem. A few were rude, especially if it was the wives who phoned. They would moan and grumble and it was up to me to soothe their frayed nerves and assure them that we were doing everything possible to restore the power as quickly as we could. I knew who the difficult ones were after a while and by the time they had announced themselves on the phone, I was already appeasing them as best I could.

So many nights I sat doing office work, as I had to be there to answer the phone, while Cecil and the team were out working. Then I had a brainwave. Although I still belonged to the WI, I couldn't go to their meetings, because I had to be at the office every afternoon. These meetings were very important to me, as I loved knitting, crochet, smocking and sewing. The WI held an annual show, combining the efforts of the entire Zambian membership and the ultimate was to win the Livingstone Cup. For work that was considered outstanding, they awarded silver teaspoons with the WI crest on, together with certificates for the first three places in each category. I asked Sid if I could have time off to attend a meeting and gathered all the information I needed to attempt show work. During the long hours of sitting alone at the phone, I worked on a number of articles and won the Livingstone Cup for 'the most points on the show' in 1969 and 1970, for which I was very proud, as the competition covered every WI in Zambia. During that time I also won sixteen silver spoons, mainly for crochet work. I did try for the cup in 1971, but we decided to move to South Africa that year and I just didn't make the grade.

Also living in Maz at that stage was the world-renowned golfer, Simon Hobday, who got married while we were there and had a little girl. Cecil had quite a few dealings with Simon and they were both very keen on fishing. Also in Maz, we had a man who was in a wheel chair, due to severe arthritis. He had been a very keen golfer in his younger days and was actually the cousin of Gary Player, our South African champion of champions.

Father's Day was approaching and as Miempie, George Luden's wife, had been chosen to shoot at the Bisley in Britain, I invited George for a meal. I bought both George and Cecil a small gift, which I set on their side-plates. George was very touched by this gesture and while Miempie was away, he spent many happy hours at our home.

We took a trip to Lochinvar with him and had tea with the owners. During the conversation, it was mentioned that they were doing massive excavations (for what, I do not know) and they had uncovered a lot of graves. Since these graves had been opened, people had reported having seen what looked like a large baboon wandering around, usually at dusk, but the image disappeared as you watched it. The villagers maintained that it was there because of the desecration of the graves.

Mike suddenly started having nightmares and would wake us, calling out loudly. I couldn't understand this, as he was already a teenager and had never suffered from nightmares before. I went into his room one day and on his dressing table, I found a flat object which was covered in mud. I asked him what it was and he told me that he had picked it up at Lochinvar. I took it to the kitchen and washed the mud off, only to find that it was part of a human skull. Taking it outside, I quietly dug a hole and buried it, saying a little prayer for the soul that it had once belonged to. Please don't think me stupid, but I also apologised to this soul as I covered the hole with sand again. Strange as it may seem, Mike's nightmares ceased from this moment. Coincidence?

Ethné bought a Pekingese and called it Peking. It was a lovely little animal, although my first reaction when she told me was "What, one of those horrible, snuffly, snoring dogs?" He was a pale-beige in colour and Cecil fell utterly in love with it. Ethné and Frans asked us to care for Peking while they visited the Copperbelt on business. When they returned, Ethné walked inside and said to Cecil "Dad, go and have a look in the car."
There, curled up on the front seat, were three tiny brindle Pekingese pups.
"One is yours, Dad, one is for mom's birthday and one is mine."

We named our puppies Chang and Yogi-Bear. They were absolutely adorable and very obedient, making me a Pekingese fan for the rest of my life. Unfortunately our home bordered on the main road and we lost both our dogs within a few months of each other. They dug holes under the fence and both landed up under the wheels of passing cars or trucks. The staff used to laugh at Chang regularly. If they entered the property, he would run up and bite their heels, so they would pick him up and carry him until they were on the other side of the fence again and then put him down.

When Chang died after Yogi-Bear, we decided to find more Pekingese. We managed to find a male and female from different parents and named them Suzi and Wang. They started breeding and oh, those pups were so beautiful, my heart broke to part with them when the time came. Those tiny bundles of fluff would follow me everywhere. A gentleman from Lusaka contacted us, wanting to know how many pups we had at that stage. When I told him that

246

there were six, he replied "They are all booked and any future litters you have are booked as well. Just phone me when you have more."

I came home from work one afternoon to find that a pipe had burst inside the house. The floor was completely flooded in about four inches of water and I was horrified, thinking that the pups would have drowned. I rushed to the room to find Suzi sitting, sopping wet, with all her pups pushed into a cupboard through a door that was just slightly ajar. They were wet, but alive, so after a good drying off and a nice clean bed for them, they suffered no ill effects after their adventure.

We began planning a trip to the Wankie Game Reserve for a two week holiday with Jeni. Mike was in boarding school and Ethné and Frans were holidaying in South Africa. Ethné was pregnant and still feeling pretty ill, but hoped that all the nausea would pass as she got a little further into her pregnancy. The two incidents that stick in my mind from this trip were when we were out looking for animals. There was a warthog grubbing on my side of the road and he was very close-by. I still always made padkos and there was a large tin of biscuits at my feet, with the lid off. Cecil couldn't see the warthog from his side, so I opened my door for him to have a look. Before I could do or say anything, the animal's head shot up and he jumped into the car. I was so surprised that I jumped across and landed in Cecil's lap. Needless to say, as soon as he had eaten all the biscuits, he got out of the car and walked away as if nothing had happened.

The second incident occurred in our bungalow at camp. I opened a tin of bully beef and out of nowhere an animal was standing in front of me. Frozen to the spot, I thought it was a leopard, with the most beautiful green eyes I had ever seen. It snatched the tin from my hands and ran out through the open door. Shaking with fright, I went outside and asked Cecil "Did you see that?"
Cecil started to laugh. "I was sitting here when the damned thing jumped onto my lap and started to purr as it rubbed its face against mine. I was too scared to move for a minute, until I realised that it was a tame Cervil cat, albeit a big one. Suddenly it jumped off me and headed for the door of the bungalow."

It just goes to show how much trust an animal places in humans once it is tame. However I was one human who did not appreciate its love or trust, nor did I enjoy the surprise visit. He actually belonged to the warden of the park.

We left for home a few days later and on our arrival, I was told that Ethné had taken ill in Bloemfontein and had suffered a miscarriage. This was awful news. It was her first child and our first grandchild. She had taken ill in Port Elizabeth and had been treated before they left for Bloemfontein, where they booked a suite in a lovely hotel. It was while they were staying in this hotel that the baby had miscarried. After Ethné recovered they returned to Maz, only to hear that Francois had been transferred to Lusaka.

I received a phone call from a lady who said "I believe you speak Peke language?"
Laughing, I said "Yes, I suppose I do."
She explained that she was moving into an old age home and had no-one to take her two Pekingese.
"They are no longer young dogs, but I have to find homes for them and I only want them to go to a Peke lover. Won't you please take them?"

What a sad day. I went to her home and there were two little beds with their toys in them and two lovely, well-groomed dogs sitting next to the old lady. She was crying bitterly as she fondled them both lovingly for the last time. I put my arms around her, saying "I promise you faithfully I will love your dogs and take good care of them. Give me your address at the home and I will send you photographs of them regularly."
We reluctantly left with the two little dogs and headed back home. They soon settled in and crept into our hearts like we had never imagined. The male was named Tuli and the female, who became Jeni's pet, was Kimi-Lu. She was so tiny and had to be carried in a basket, because her little legs were so short that her tummy scraped on the ground.

Sadly the old lady died two months later, I truly believe from a broken heart. Tuli would diligently follow me to work and lay under my desk. By this time Cecil, Sid and myself were a firm team and, on a Wednesday afternoon, Sid would say "If Lusaka phones, we're on a call out."

I would see the two men load two sets of golf clubs and leave for a few hours. They worked such long hours that I felt they truly deserved this little break each week. Once in a while, when it was very quiet, I would ask Sid if I could go up to the tea room for the afternoon and he would watch the office. Apart from this, we never abused the trust of Head Office and we made sure that the office was run in a highly efficient manner at all times.

One afternoon I had gone to the tea room to talk to Mom and Joyce. Joyce offered to take me home if I waited until closing time. At five we left the shop and as we pulled in to the CEC premises, I saw two askari's standing with crossed bayonets at my gate. Looking across to the gate of the power station, I observed another four standing guard there. I smiled politely at the two standing at my gate and asked if could pass.

"Yes, certainly, Dona." The askari's moved aside and let me pass before resuming their positions. I asked Cecil what was going on, but he had no clue, as they had taken up their posts without consulting anyone.

Cecil went to the substation to check on something and asked the one askari what was wrong, but he told Cecil that he did not know. We turned on the television to see if we could find out, but all I heard the announcer say was "It took me half an hour to get into the building, I wonder if I'll ever get out."

Unfortunately I heard nothing more and we were still completely in the dark about the situation. Cecil and I were sitting on the veranda with sundowners when the phone rang. Sid had forgotten to transfer the line to the house and knowing that it could be a call out, I jumped up and ran towards the office to take the call. Suddenly sensing something, I stopped and turned around. An askari was running towards me, his bayonet aimed straight at my back.

"What the hell do you think you're doing?" I asked.

"Why are you running?"

"I'm going to answer the phone; can you not hear it ringing?"

"Walk. Do not run."

He followed me to the office and waited while I took the call, then escorted me back through my gate. I often wonder if I hadn't turned around that day, whether he would have used the bayonet.

Cecil suggested that we go to the Sugar Estate sub-station to see if that was being guarded. Sure enough it was and so, too, was the Mazabuka sub-station. It was some time later that we heard that President Kaunda had to attend a conference overseas and had heard that someone by the name of Kapepwe was going to do a coup while he was away, so he had ordered that all important places be guarded. I do not know if this was true, but it was certainly one of the moments when I was given a big fright.

Jeni came home from school crying a few days later and told us that her teacher, Mister Naidoo, had shouted at her. (A lot of South African teachers had come to Zambia for better salaries and working conditions and Mister Naidoo was one of them). I asked her why he had shouted at her and she explained.

"There are only five white children left in my class, the rest are Asian and Black. Mister Naidoo called me to the front of the class and asked me what colour I am. When I replied that I am white, he marched me over to his desk and put my hand on a piece of paper, then asked me what colour the paper was. When I told him that it was white, he asked me the colour of my hand. I told him that my skin was flesh-coloured and he then asked me my nationality, so I told him that I am European. He shouted at me and said that I am not white and I am not European, because I was born in Zambia, and that I must never refer to myself as white again."

This teacher really gave Jeni a hard time that year and it was with relief that she went to the next standard in January, to a wonderful teacher by the name of Miss Anderson. A Coloured lady from Cape Town, she and Jeni had a special bond from the start. She rebuilt all the confidence in Jeni that Mister Naidoo had so willingly broken down and was a truly fantastic teacher. She later married the principal of the school, a man by the name of Mister Carlisle.

Cecil was now in his late forties, walking miles every day checking lines and looking for faults. His body was still lean and muscular. He certainly did not look his age and he thrived on the outdoor life he was leading, yet he still yearned for excitement and became voluntary Chief Fire Officer in his spare time. He persuaded some of his friends to join as well and the chief officer from Lusaka came down and taught them the basics. They would all gather at our house after a fire to discuss their mistakes and would end up laughing at the things they had done wrong. The first fire they were called to was a small house with a thatch roof. The thatch was burning and after attaching the hose, not knowing how to regulate the flow of water, they promptly blew the entire roof off. Needless to say the fire was out in a few seconds! There were a few big fires they had to attend to, but the biggest was when a tanker full of diesel set alight just outside the town and actually exploded. Fortunately no-one was hurt in this incident. On another occasion, all the poles in the yard of Africa Farming, where Francois was manager, set alight and the fire blazed all night.

We received a call late one night to say that Joyce and Charlie had been involved in a car accident. Cecil went through to Kafue to fetch them. They weren't badly injured, but were full of small cuts from the shattered windscreen and they were both full of bruises. Poor Joyce moaned bitterly as she got into the bath that night. A week later she came looking for Cecil and asked him to look at the underside of her chin. She said it was very sore to the touch and there was a small, hard lump under the skin. Cecil scraped the skin as gently as he could and saw a piece of glass. Taking a tweezers, he took hold of the point of the glass and began to ease it out as gently as he could. It was triangular in shape and the more he pulled, the more it cut her chin. Eventually he got it out and then cleaned the cut and put a plaster on.

Japhat approached me soon after this episode and told me that after seventeen years of service, he was leaving. He had been offered a job as a carpenter at the management board. I was heartbroken to say the least. He was literally part of the family and we had been through so much together. When he had problems, he would come to us and we would try and help wherever we could. It was Japhat that had been willing to follow us to the game park, leaving his wife and three little sons in Mazabuka. He had also gone with us to Bardmony Farm, his entire family moving onto the farm with him. They had moved from a brick servant's quarters in our yard, with a shower and three rooms, to a little round shack with no facilities whatsoever. It was a good ten minute walk to the river to have a wash and yet they had never complained. He had always said that we were his dona and bwana and where we went, so did he. All of our friends had a similar loyalty from their servants too. Knowing people like Japhat taught me a lot of respect for the black man and this respect is still with me today. When people talk about the crime in South Africa now, I always say that there is good and bad in every nation and in every race.

Life was so good at this time. Cecil was a popular man and we were invited by a couple we had just met to join them for dinner. As we got out of the car at their house that night, we noticed a dreadful smell and Cecil remarked that something must have died close by. However, the nearer we got to the house, the stronger the smell became. The host greeted us with a big smile at the door and welcomed us. After sundowners, he said "You know we are foreigners and we are very fond of 'high game'."
We realised with horror that we were smelling the food we were about to eat. As his wife began to dish up, I told her that I was a very small meat-eater and took just a tiny piece of the guinea fowl. This left poor Cecil in a bit of a spot and he politely took two pieces and placed them on his plate. I noticed when the plates were cleared away by the servant that Cecil had not eaten the cabbage and on the way home that night he confessed the he had hidden the meat underneath it.

While on the subject of strange foods, I recall walking outside one night and finding Jeni sitting under a street light with two little African children. They were catching flying ants as they flew towards the light, pulling off the wings and eating them. She gleefully called to me, saying "Oh mommy, do come and have one. They taste just like nuts."

Her birthday was approaching and she asked if she could have a party. I agreed, telling her to invite ten friends from school. I was surprised when she handed me a list of names, as apart from her close friend, Annerina du Plooy, the other nine were black children. By this stage there were very few white children in the school and Jeni had befriended a number of the little black girls. Unfortunately Cecil went down with malaria and was so ill that I decided not to hold a party. To make it up to Jeni, I promised her that I would buy her a walking doll on our next trip to South Africa. Needless to say, when we went down south, we bought her doll and she was one very thrilled little girl.

Annerina was the daughter of the local butcher, Piet du Plooy. Jeni lost contact with her when we left Zambia, but thanks to the technology of the internet and a certain 'ex-Zambian' website, she managed to locate her again thirty-four years later, just a few days before this manuscript was submitted to the publishers.

One amusing tale remains in my mind regarding her father Piet. He was working in the butchery one afternoon, when a young African came and Piet, without thinking, asked "What can I do for you, boy?" The young chap gave him a lecture for calling him 'boy', as this had become a big no-no with the African people, who were fighting for independence. Rather chagrined, Piet replied "I'm terribly sorry, how can I help you?"
"I want Sixpence boy's meat" was the young man's reply!

There was a knock on the door one afternoon and when I opened it, there stood a little black girl of about eight. Her hair was scrunched up into two of the biggest pink bows I had ever seen. She asked for Jeni, who was out at the time, and I asked her name so that I could tell Jeni she had called.
"My name is Helen Temba. My father is the Commissioner for Mazabuka."
When Jeni returned, I told her about Helen's visit and she replied "Oh mommy, she is a good friend at school."
Two weeks later everyone was talking about the Temba family. It seems that the father was drunk and began arguing with his wife.

253

He beat her with his gun and when the doctor saw her at the hospital, he remarked that all the beatings he had seen on prisoners of war could not compare with this woman's injuries. Her kidneys were crushed and she had massive internal injures. Sadly, she died the next morning. I tried to find out what happened to Helen and her father, but to no avail.

Butch, our cross Bull Mastiff, started to give trouble with passers-by. If he saw anyone on a bicycle, he would bound over to them, knock them off the bike and then stand over them, wagging his tail. Most of our policemen rode bikes and we were constantly paying for new shirts or pants that got torn from falling from their bikes, not from Butch biting them. Eventually we decided to have him put down, but this was a hard decision to make. He was the one who had saved Cecil from the rabid dog and Jeni adored him.

Soon after putting Butch down, Tuli ran out of my office and I heard him yelp, then he came running back inside. He crept under the desk, shaking terribly. A chap came in to tell me that Tuli had run into the side of his wheel as he had pulled into the driveway. Poor Tuli never ate for two days and when I took him to the vet, they found that he had a broken jaw. This is almost impossible to fix on a Pekingese and we decided to put him to sleep. A couple of days later I noticed that Kimi-Lu wasn't well and the vet diagnosed an infection of some sort. He expressed doubts that she would respond to the treatment, as she was very old. So Kimi-Lu also left us and Jeni was heartbroken to say the least, so I promised her the pick of the next litter we had. When the pups were born, Jeni made her choice and she called him Thai Yun, or Thaitjie for short.

A few days later we had friends over for supper and it was quite late when they got up to leave. When Cecil opened the door, Jeni ran out onto the step, but suddenly started screaming. When I got to the door, she was jumping from one leg to the other, with a snake wrapped around the one leg. With all the jumping, the snake slipped off, and slithered away into the dark. How she never got bitten, I don't know to this day.

Ethné was pregnant again and soon gave birth to a beautiful son, whom they named Jacques. The very next night after being discharged from hospital, Ethné, Frans and baby visited us from Lusaka and arrived after dark. As Ethné got out of the car, she screamed as she nearly stepped on a huge snake on the pathway. It slithered into the flower beds and we never saw it again. However it made us realise that walking around barefooted at night without a torch was a really bad habit. Cecil decided to put a torch in the bakkie after those episodes so that if we arrived home after dark, we could see our way to the house.

Our lives appeared to have become quite civilized until we went to Lusaka. On the way home, we came around a corner on the Manali Pass only to find a huge leopard standing in the middle of the road. He was a beautiful specimen, his coat gleaming in the bright headlights. The markings stood out proudly and his eyes glistened as he looked at us. We sat admiring him for at least five minutes, before he jumped onto the bank next to the car and disappeared into the night. We talked about him all the way home and Cecil remarked how few animals one saw on the roads those days. Strangely, three days later, the train from Lusaka was derailed when it hit a hippo. No-one knows how it got onto the line, so far away from water.

Koen popped in to see Cecil and he looked dreadfully ill. He told us that he had been retching blood the previous night and did not feel at all well. We urged him to see the doctor and after having done so, he was later diagnosed with cancer. The doctor said that he needed surgery and I have never forgotten my words to him that day. I said "Koen, don't be half a person if you have the choice to be whole."
He did have the operation, but six months later Cecil and I attended his funeral. A dear friend, he was the first of the three musketeers to pass on and we missed him terribly. Shortly after his death, Stoffie moved away from Maz to live near her children in Livingstone and George Luden decided to move to the Mulobezi Sawmills, so in a way, he passed out of our lives as well, as we only saw him a few times after that. The last time we saw George was when we had all moved to South Africa and he was living in Barrydale. A few months

later he too passed away, leaving us with a deep sense of loss for our best friend.

Life went on and my office was well established by this time. I enjoyed my job and got on well with most of the folks that came to pay their accounts, but there was always the odd one who did not pay and this resulted in us having to cut their power supply. I got a phone call one day from a lady, who said "You have cut my lights, but you don't cut the whites'. You are a racist and I will have you deported."
She slammed the phone down before I could explain that it had nothing to do with colour, only timely payments. Another threatened to get me into 'hot soup' with my superiors.

Most of the farms were on a party telephone line and Cecil and Sid refused to make a call if it was to a party line. They would always ask me to get the person on the line, as they knew it could be a lengthy procedure. A lot of the farms had been purchased by black people and they did not understand that each homestead's phone had a different ring. Every time you requested a particular number, everyone would pick up the phone and it would take some time to explain to them that they needed to replace the receiver so that I could speak to the correct person.

My phone rang one morning and I answered politely. The voice on the other end said "What are you doing on my telephone? Get off my telephone and stop wasting my time."
I pointed out that the call had come from her and she slammed the phone down. I replaced the receiver and the phone rang again.
"Good morning, Zesco."
"You again!" She yelled at me. "You're bloody wasting my time and money. You are going to be in big trouble if you answer my phone again."
I ignored the persistent ringing for a while after that before taking calls again, chuckling to myself all morning. One dear old black man phoned one day and said "Please don't cut my lights. There was too much month left at the end of my money."

At the age of forty three, I began to feel ill and went to the doctor. He announced that I was pregnant and told me to return in a month's time for a check-up. Cecil was devastated. He sat with his head in his hands and said "We are going to South Africa soon and I don't know if I'll get a job there. I'm classed as senior electrician here, but I don't have papers and even the building trade is difficult unless I can produce papers."

Nevertheless we slowly began to accept the fact that another child was on the way and at the end of the month I asked Telly, one of our drivers, to take me to the doctor for my check-up. He had quite a few meters to read on farms in the Chikankata area, so I agreed to drive along with him and when he was finished, he could stop off at the hospital. I knew the roads were bad, but I honestly never gave my age or the complications with Jeni's birth a thought at that stage. We bounced along in the truck all day on corrugated roads and some time later I realised that I was starting to miscarry.

When we arrived at the hospital, a sister came out and said "UNIP have some people here today and we don't give white people preferential treatment. Please stand in the queue and wait your turn."
There must have been sixty or seventy people waiting and I stood there for nearly five hours, feeling things get steadily worse. When I eventually saw the doctor, he said "You are going straight to bed in hospital. We will try and save this baby."
I looked quietly at him and replied "No, doctor. The last baby nearly killed me and I am forty three years old. We are moving to South Africa soon. If I'm meant to have this baby, it will not miscarry, but this time I'm afraid nature must take its course."
Being from the Salvation Army, he was horrified to say the least. He asked me what I intended doing and I said "I'm going home."
He warned me that if I found myself in trouble, I would not get any help from him and I nodded calmly. I thanked him for all his help in the past and asked him not to condemn me too much. I admitted that for the first time in my life I was afraid of the future.

"I'm afraid of starting a new life in South Africa, I'm afraid that another baby will kill me this time, I'm afraid of going where I will have no friends where we must start from scratch again. We don't know if Cecil will get a job and the Zambian government is only allowing us to take eight thousand rand out of the country. We have no home to go to, so I beg you to please forgive me if I seem callous, as I will ask the Lord tonight in my prayers."

By this time my eyes were brimming with tears and I walked out of his office. For two days I lay in bed at home, bleeding profusely and Cecil was worried sick. He was angry that I hadn't stayed in hospital, but I had reached the stage where one says 'enough is enough'. On the third day, I began to feel a little better and by the end of the week I was back at work. I did feel heart-sore about my decision, but oh, the relief of knowing that it was all over.

By this time Cecil was having more and more work thrown at him. Many farms were putting in electricity, which meant more electric lines to be checked, more call-outs and more metres to be read. However, he didn't mind, as it was outdoor work and mostly in the bush. He was still a lovely golden brown and his eyes showed small wrinkles from squinting into the sun. The first few grey hairs adorned his temples, but he was still a very attractive man, with the body of a much younger one. He was somehow starting to mellow in character as well. He was a lot quieter and calmer than he had been twenty five years ago. Mike immigrated to South Africa to stay with his Uncle Albert, who took him on as an apprentice motor mechanic at the garage where he was workshop manager.

It was our silver wedding anniversary and the family gathered to celebrate. I quietly sat and wondered where the years had gone as I watched my family enjoying the evening together. Such wonderful years, yet gone so quickly and it seemed only yesterday that I had stood beside my husband in the church to say 'I do'. One thing the years did for us was to deepen our love for each other. Cecil was still a passionate man and my body held a particular fascination even after all these years. He would pull me against his muscular body and whisper "I love you and tonight I'll prove it."

My body would respond instantly and I would smile as I whispered back "I can't wait."

We notified Zesco that we would be leaving at the end of Cecil's contract in six month's time and began to prepare for our departure. Zesco then begged Cecil to remain for a further six months, which gave us a year to plan our big move. We took some leave and went to South Africa, mainly to take our holiday allowance out and we needed to make arrangements for a place to stay. Cecil had always loved Sundays River, with its two little villages, Cannonville and Colchester.

On our way down, we called in at Bill and Phyllis and also went to the bank, where we had savings of about three thousand rand. We drew a little of it and together with our holiday money, we bought a Jurgens caravan from their factory near Germiston and then headed for Colchester. We parked in a friend's yard and had the use of their bathroom. They lived in Port Elizabeth and this was their holiday cottage.

The lady next door invited me to join her at a ladies tea group and Cecil urged me to go, so that I could enquire about properties for sale. Several were mentioned, but they were quite expensive. One of the ladies, Gloria Rowe, told me about three vacant plots opposite her house and gave me the name of the seller. Cecil and I looked at the plots and realised we still had enough capital to purchase all three. We decided to build on one and sell, then build on the second, sell and then settle on the third. You can imagine our dismay when the bank refused, saying that we were not residents in the country and for that reason, we could not buy them.

On our way home, we went to our bank manager in Johannesburg and told him our tale of woe. He promised to see what he could do, using Bill's address in South Africa. A few weeks after we arrived home, a telegram arrived from him saying 'All's well, one in the bag.' We knew that he had managed to purchase one plot, so at least we had somewhere to go.

We notified the Receiver of Revenue about our intention to leave the country and I phoned the Provident Fund office to claim the money owing to me, which was about eight hundred Kwacha. An Irish lady phoned me and said "I'm sorry, but you won't get any of the money. The people running the fund have spent it all as it was paid in by the companies."

It took three trips to Lusaka before we sorted out our income tax, but at last it was finalized and we were free to leave the country. As our departure drew nearer, we tried to see as much as possible of Ethné, Francois and little Jacques and we both resigned from the various committees.

Zesco sent down an Indian gentleman to take over from Cecil. Sid was so upset that we were going, but said that he planned to stay for another year or so and then they too would be leaving Zambia. A young girl from the Sugar Estates arrived to take over my position, but two days before we left she decided that this wasn't the type of work she would enjoy and left. Head office was worried, as I had shown her how to do the accounts, but she hadn't personally done any, so I promised to get them out before we left. I took them home and spent two days and most of the nights to finalise all the accounts. I really gave of my best and my reference praised all my hard work, making it all worthwhile at the end of the day.

At about eight thirty that evening, Cecil hitched the boat to the bakkie and I threw a pillow slip filled with Tupperware into the boat. (When we stopped later on, it had blown off, so someone found themselves quite a surprise along the road). How sad I felt when I thought back to how much we had packed into our twenty five years in Zambia and now we were off to start a completely new life with so little. By the time we reached Beit Bridge we were ready to face the problems that lay ahead of us. Cecil was forty eight and we only had eight thousand rand and we had to build a house and still eat. I looked into the back of the bakkie, which had a canopy on and smiled as I saw my three little Pekingese sleeping peacefully. We had decided at the last moment to give Polly to Ethné and Frans, because the vet had warned us that parrots were often confiscated at the border post, despite having the necessary permits. We could never have faced some stranger walking off with him, so we said our goodbyes and left him in capable hands.

On the road near Beit Bridge we stopped to go to the toilet and someone had been to that specific spot before me. Lying on the ground before me were three ten Kwacha notes that had been used as toilet paper. The Kwacha had fallen very low and was no longer accepted as currency in South Africa at that stage.

The first thing I noticed on our way to Port Elizabeth was the cold. By the time we reached Pietersburg, we were freezing and I asked Cecil to stop so I could put the three dogs in the cab with us. I felt as bleak on the inside as I did on the outside. We stopped over and slept at Bill's house, wrapping the dogs in blankets and letting them sleep in the cab for the night. Michael had taken two week's leave and went with us from Germiston to PE. We collected our caravan from Eddie and Flo and towed it straight out to our plot. Eddie apologised for not having put up the fence yet. He had the material, but had never got around to fencing the plot before we arrived.

Who knows how Cecil was feeling at that time, leaving his beloved country to start a new life at forty eight years of age? He still had an eleven year old daughter to educate, his trade was French polishing, but it was twenty five years since he had done any and he could see no hope of work in any of the trades he had been working at in Zambia. His smiles were few and far between, but at no time did he allow me to feel his worries or pain. He just became a silent, sombre man.

CHAPTER FIFTEEN

Sundays River.....

Now our new life started on a bare plot of ground, with only a caravan and a boat. Things seemed to go wrong from the start. The brick truck arrived to deliver bricks and accidentally rode over Suzi, killing her instantly. Cecil had two brothers in Port Elizabeth and every Sunday they would arrive with their wives and total of seven children, plus a couple of their playmates. Everyone would stay for lunch and afternoon tea. Not one of the women ever brought any kind of food along to help out and, with feeding so many, Cecil watched his capital going down rapidly. I think they just thought that we were the rich Rhodesians, whereas in reality, they were all far better off financially than Cecil. However, in fairness to them, their brother Cecil had returned after twenty five years and was living in a place where their children could swim and play while they could sit and enjoy Cecil's stories of our adventures in Zambia.

It was at this time that I wondered what Cecil was feeling. He seemed very quiet at times and I knew that he had made this move for Jeni's sake. It must have broken his heart to leave his beloved Zambia behind. I could see no light at the end of the tunnel and I knew that neither of us had ever been so vulnerable. The reason I say that he did it for Jeni's sake, was because of the fact that the schooling in Maz only provided facilities up to grade seven and she would then have to be sent to boarding school. Cecil was not willing to let her attend the school in Lusaka and definitely did not want to send her to South Africa on her own.

The building inspector arrived and told us we could not live in a caravan, even though we were building. However a gentleman by the name of Jimmy Arthur, who had a small shack nearby, offered us the use of his bathroom and toilet and even to sleep in the shack if we wished to. We decided to park the caravan in his yard and only use the bathroom and toilet facilities. This man is still such a dear friend today.

Cecil began to seek employment, but no matter how clever he was and how capable, each prospective employer asked for papers. He had started to build the house, brick by brick himself, but he was worrying himself sick because of all the money we had to spend on building materials and food. I only had the little caravan fridge, so we relied mainly on tinned foods. Unfortunately we were both too proud to admit that we had financial problems and allowed the relatives to descend on us every weekend.

One of Cecil's brothers arrived from the Transvaal and asked if he could use our boat. While he was out fishing, he burnt out the motor on the outboard. He was a wealthy man and both he and his wife worked, but apart from an apology, he offered nothing. When Cecil took the motor in to be repaired, he was told that it had got so hot that the pistons had pulled away from the sides and we could throw the motor away. Needless to say, that was the end of the fishing by boat for a few years, although we often fished from the bank.

Christmas Eve arrived and a family who owned a holiday shack at the river came over with a gramophone and all started dancing on Jimmy's lawn. They introduced themselves as Shirley and Barney Joubert. Cecil and I watched their children grow up and then their grandchildren. Shirley was the bubbliest person I ever knew. She would laugh at absolutely anything. Barney was a much more serious type of man, but he and Cecil got on well together and we always looked forward to their visits when they arrived on holiday from their citrus farm.

We had been in SA for eighteen months and I started with severe abdominal pain. Cecil still had no job and our money was so low that it was frightening. I went to visit Gloria, who had become a close friend and she listened to my tale of woe. She suggested I attend the clinic about twelve miles away, saying that it was free and the doctor was very good. I took her advice and saw Doctor Ferguson the following week. He suspected that I had a tumour and referred me to

263

a gynaecologist in town, saying that I could attend as an outpatient, which was a lot cheaper.

The specialist found a tumour and told me that he was booking me for a hysterectomy. After the operation and ten days recuperation in hospital, I was allowed home. However complications set in, causing me to haemorrhage very badly and Cecil rushed me back to hospital, where I stayed for three weeks. When the hospital account arrived, it was for two hundred and fifty rand and Cecil was terribly worried. I told him to give me fifty rand and I would make arrangements to pay the balance off over a couple of months. When I explained our situation to the accountant, he asked me how much I had on me and I told him that I only had fifty rand. He took the fifty rand, stamped my account 'paid in full' and said "Good luck for the future."

Well, his wish for us worked. The following week the building inspector visited again and told Cecil that there was a vacancy for a second building inspector. He suggested that Cecil apply, which he did and thankfully my sweetheart got his pride back and held his head high once more. At the age of forty nine, Cecil became building inspector for the council and was responsible for a large area. What joy, to see his face alive once more. He spent each day travelling country roads to do inspections, so once again he was outdoors and I knew that he was happy. In fact, he enjoyed his job for the entire seventeen years that he was employed by the council.

Joyce, Charlie and my mom, who had moved in with them when we left Zambia, left the country and settled in Port Shepstone. My mother wrote and told me that she wanted South African citizenship, which I helped her to achieve. I received another letter from my mom telling me that she had brought quite a lot of money out of Zambia. Being over fifty, she was allowed sixteen thousand rand for herself and as Charlie had inherited the business in Zambia, she had made a will and left everything she owned to me. A copy of this will arrived a few days later.

There was not much wildlife at Cannonville, but the Addo National Park was only a few miles away and occasionally we would visit the park. Of course there are all kinds of restrictions, not like when we were in the bush in Zambia and eventually Cecil decided he did not want to go again, because it was like viewing animals in a zoo. We do have monkeys on our sand dunes at the river and we would often sit and watch them from our verandah in the early morning. We also had the odd little buck enter the yard to eat Cecil's vegetables and once we had a skunk under our car in the driveway. Our dog ran up to it to investigate and was promptly sprayed in the face. It was late evening and mid-winter, but we had no choice but to bath him, because the smell was too terrible for words. Not even this really helped and we eventually made a bed for him in the garage. Once, while boating on the river, a leguaan appeared quite close to the boat. Cecil rode slowly beside it until it reached the other side in safety. He had a wonderful way with animals and sometimes had to enter yards for inspections, only to find that their dogs were quite vicious. He would talk softly to them and put out his hand and they would calm down and even wag their tails as they walked beside him. Some owners could not believe how their vicious dogs were tamed in a matter of seconds when Cecil was around.

In the March we received a telegram advising us that Ethné had given birth to a little girl and they had named her Odette. We were thrilled for her and Frans, they now had their pigeon pair and life seemed wonderful. Odette was three months old when Cecil arrived home from work very early in the afternoon, looking terribly upset. He told me to sit down and then said "I have some tragic news. Little Jacques has been killed by four Alsatian dogs."

I was utterly stunned, but tried to mask my own sorrow, when I looked at Cecil's face. I so wished that this man of mine could cry, he was suffering so much. Jacques was our only grandson and so precious, but my thoughts were on Ethné and Francois and what they must be going through. Knowing how important my three children are to me, I could not begin to imagine the pain they were suffering.

The one thing that we could never understand was that Eddie and Flo had received the news telephonically the previous night, but had not come out to the river to break it to us. Eddie had phoned the council the next morning, but Cecil had already left to do inspections. The building section of the council contacted all the traffic officers on the radio to try and locate Cecil, so the news was ultimately given to Cecil by a traffic officer. I think the shock must have been terrific and then he had to fetch Jeni from school and drive over fifty miles to break the news to me.

We were frantic with worry. Our passports had been cancelled when we left Zambia and when we phoned the airport, there were no available flights for two weeks. Once again someone, who was practically a stranger to us, became our guardian angel. Cecil's senior inspector, a Mister Walters, told Cecil to leave it to him. A short while later he told Cecil to go to the passport office, as he had arranged for our passports. He then phoned a friend who worked at Jan Smuts airport in a very senior position and explained the situation. We were booked on a flight for six thirty that evening. It was Tuesday and Jacques had died on the Sunday. We received the news on Monday and by Tuesday night we were flying to Zambia. At Jan Smuts we changed planes and at Gaberone we changed once again, to Air Zambia. What, or how, I packed I do not know, as I had my own terror to contend with. I was terrified of flying (almost a phobia with me) and I also did not know how to handle the situation when we arrived in Zambia. What does one say to these heartbroken parents?

As we approached the Zambian plane, I could feel the panic rising within me. It was so small, as if it had been put together with stiffened calico. Cecil took my arm and coaxed me on board, so closing my eyes, I got into the plane. Once we were in the air the plane was quite steady, but my feet were frozen. One could feel the cold through the bottom of the plane and as I sucked on the sweet that the air-hostess gave me, I silently prayed for a safe journey. Later the air-hostess served lunch, which was a hot meal, although almost cold. It was roast beef, potato and vegetables. It looked very tempting, except for the fact that they had put a piece of fried Nile Perch slap-bang on top of our roast beef. Boy! That takes your appetite away fast.

We arrived in Lusaka on the Friday morning at nine and as far as we knew, the funeral was at eleven. An old friend of ours was waiting to take us to the church, but an official stepped forward and said "You may not leave the airport. You came via Gaberone and there is smallpox there, against which you have not been vaccinated. We have arranged for a doctor to come."

The doctor finally arrived at ten-thirty and gave us our vaccinations. Bea, our friend, drove as fast as she could but by the time we got to the cemetery, it was all over and people were leaving.

When I looked across at the two people I loved so dearly, my heart broke. Ethné looked so vulnerable. She had a terrible lost look about her, but there were no tears. I embraced her and all she said was "Oh, mom, it was horrible." For the first time in my life, I was without words. Ethné stood shivering with grief and I saw Cecil walk over to the grave. What I saw on that man's face at that moment was pain and grief so great, it was tearing him apart, but he could not cry. My heart cried for him yet once again. He had adored Jacques so much.

From the cemetery we went to someone's house, who had arranged the tea and Ethné never once lost her composure. Like her father, she couldn't cry, but was slowly tearing apart inside. At last we got to the farm and Ethné began to tell us what had happened. It seemed that Frans was helping another farmer and had moved onto his farm to run it. The owner had one male and one female Alsatian and two pups. They had been on the farm for about a week and the dogs had accepted them with no problems.

On the Sunday, some friends arrived and Ethné made tea. Little Jacques was playing outside at the time. He came inside and asked his mom for some coke, took a few sips and spoke to the guests, then went back outside. Ethné suddenly heard a terrible noise and asked Frans to go and see what the problem was, as it sounded as though the dogs had got hold of one of the pigs. When he got outside, Frans found his son lying face down on the ground and the four dogs were walking away. The child was covered in blood and had bites everywhere. His jugular vein was severed and he bled profusely from this wound. They jumped into the car and raced for the

267

hospital, with Ethné nursing Jacques on her lap. No matter how she tried, she could not stop the bleeding and it soaked through her clothes to her skin. Jacques was pronounced dead on arrival at the hospital. To make matters worse, the police took the body in case charges were to be laid against the owner, but Frans said "What point? It won't bring my baby back."

So he signed papers for the police and they were able to make funeral arrangements.

We stayed for two weeks, but I don't think our presence helped either of them. Everything I offered to do was met with a polite "No, thanks mom, I can manage."

Ethné insisted on taking care of baby Odette, she told her cook what food to prepare and ran her household as efficiently as usual, but those eyes of hers worried me sick. They were the eyes of someone dying from pain so terrible, it cannot be imagined. Frans, too, kept his composure outwardly, but I knew that for a man to lose his son would be a devastating event and my heart went out to him so much. They had one of Frans' aunts staying there and she had lost her husband a few months before. I think she gave them much more comfort than we possibly could.

Cecil was also worried about staying away too long, as he had only been with the council for three months and did not want to jeopardize his job. We were battling to get a flight out, so we sat at the airport each day, hoping for a cancellation. Eventually a pilot came over and said "I've seen you here on two of my trips. I am fully booked, but my two air-hostesses have offered to sit on the floor for take off, so you can have their seats. We are flying via Blantyre, so you will have to pay the extra, but at least you can get back home. It was quite expensive, but Frans paid and we boarded the plane for home, feeling that we had not really helped at all.

While we were in Zambia I was surprised to see how the country had deteriorated in a matter of eighteen months. Lusaka's streets were littered with papers, but I still loved my beautiful country and always hoped that one day I could return, but I'm afraid I never saw it again.

268

Even now, thirty years later, I still think of it and my life up there, with a sense of loss of something precious.

Mister Walters was a keen collector of semi-precious stones and I had three. One was a piece of amethyst, about twenty five centimetres wide and thirty long, all in its natural shape. It looked like little roofs on top of buildings and was really exquisite. The other was a piece of tiger's eye, about thirty centimetres square and the last piece was malachite, about ten centimetres square. I was so grateful to this man for his kindness to us and I gave him all three pieces, as well as a Kruger Sixpence. I often think of my stones with nostalgia, but never with sorrow at having parted with them, although they were the last link I had with my beloved Zambia. We also bought his friend from Jan Smuts a silver pen and pencil to thank him and I was pleasantly surprised when he sent me a tablecloth with proteas and the air-force emblem on, plus a gift for Cecil for Christmas.

Cecil had managed to obtain a good second-hand motor and he was able to go fishing every weekend once again. On Friday nights he would get home from work, pack his boat with food and blankets and with shining eyes, he would kiss me goodbye and say "I'll see you on Sunday."

Mike moved back home, as he had finished his apprenticeship in Springs. He had turned twenty and decided he had been away from us for long enough. When he moved in, life became exciting once again. He was always trying something new. He bought a CB radio, installed a huge aerial in the back yard and would talk the CB lingo all night long with other enthusiasts. I loved to listen to their jargon and found the name 'ankle-biters', which referred to small children, utterly amusing.

Cecil and Mike used to use one car to work every day to save on petrol and one morning they got half way to work, when the car began to float. It had been raining very heavily and then an announcement came over the car radio that Sundays River was expected to flood. They turned around and headed straight back home, where Mike grabbed his CB radio, which was the only one in the village. He manned the radio all day, keeping everyone abreast of everything that was going on. We often had warnings about the river coming down in flood. By the time Mike tired of his radio and sold it, there were a number of people on the river who had telephones, so communication was much easier.

Cecil bought a generator and when the folk living on the river heard about it, they asked if we could show films once a week at the fishing club. We would run extension leads over three plots to the club and every Friday, we would collect a movie from town. This eventually petered out, as people had varied tastes in movies and not everyone was satisfied with our choices.

I had a battery radio and after Cecil and Mike had left for work in very heavy rain, I made coffee, listening to the news. It was announced that the Sundays River residents should stand by for evacuation, as the river was flooding quickly. I put all the cushions from the lounge suite on top of a wardrobe and then began collecting items that might get damaged, placing them in wardrobes as high up as possible. Cecil and Mike had left early for work and did not return, leaving me alone at home. I was terribly worried, as I don't drive and I had my animals to take with me if the call came through to evacuate. I packed the back of our bakkie with as much as I could and covered it with canvas, then sat and waited anxiously.

At about four thirty a police car drove through the village with a loud hailer, warning residents to get out immediately. I recall the words he shouted "Get to hell out of it! Eight feet of water just left Addo."
Addo is about twenty miles upriver and I realised that it wouldn't take the water long to reach us and I watched residents begin to panic. One poor chap was trying to get his boat out of the water and broke his arm in the panic that ensued.

I put the cockatiel's cage on the back of the bakkie, the cat in a box on the bakkie and the dogs in the cab, then just stood there, knowing I could do no more. A young boy of thirteen ran up to me and asked "Would you like me to drive your bakkie out?"

Looking at him with misgivings, I asked "Can you drive?"
He stuck his chest out proudly and said "Of course I can."
"Go for it" was all I could reply as I jumped into the passenger seat.
There were lots of cars in convoy, as a lot of people had driven from town to save their boats, or items in their shacks. I had packed three flasks and a large container with water, plus tea, coffee, sugar, milk and a huge container of sandwiches. Once again, my Zambian training was coming in handy!

The police signalled to us to cross the bridge and we travelled for about twenty miles before we were allowed to stop. It was quite amusing to hear the comments, particularly from the women whose husbands were at work. One woman was most upset, because they had just bought a new stove and her husband had phoned to ask her what she was doing about the stove. "What did he expect me to do? Tie it on my back?"

I passed tea and coffee to those who wanted, when a car pulled up and Herbie jumped out. He told me that the police had not wanted to let him through, but he had told them in no uncertain terms that his sister in law was alone and he had to get to her. I was really touched by his concern. Cecil and Mike arrived and Cecil's first words were "What did you do with my cameras?"
To my horror, I remembered that they were lying at the bottom of his wardrobe and I hadn't given them a thought. He then asked exactly what I did pack.
"Well, I knew the lawnmower is new, so I took that."
Cecil's face was a picture. Shock and disbelief enveloped his face as he replied "If the water comes up, there will be no grass to cut."
Thankfully, he burst into laughter and said "I sure married one crazy lady!"
So much for good intentions!

Cecil slipped a little something to the lad who had driven the bakkie for me, then said "I'm going home. I refuse to sit out here in the rain all night."
The police tried to stop us, but Cecil was adamant and eventually they let us through. We ate supper and then went to bed. The

following morning we went to the river and goodness knows what happened to all the water that left Addo, but the river never flooded dangerously and in the last few years it hasn't broken its banks again.

CHAPTER SIXTEEN

The Golden Years....

A few weeks later, we arrived home to find Thai-Yun waiting for us at the gate, with his entire bottom jaw torn off. It had happened earlier that day and he had waited in agony for us to come home. We rushed him to the vet and put him to sleep. It seems that a huge dog on the river had attacked him and Gloria had actually witnessed the event. The same dog got hold of Wang some time later and bit him in the face, blinding him in both eyes. The vet suggested that we keep him after he had removed the eyes, as we had bought two females and Wang was an excellent breeding specimen. He seemed happy enough, but when my one female died and Mike wanted the other, I decided to stop breeding. A couple of months later, we found Wang at the gate with his back broken. I made up my mind not to replace any of my Pekingese and so for quite some time, we had no pets at all.

Cecil had loved Wang for his cheeky ways and fearlessness. He was so like his master, always ready to face a challenge, no matter how big. He would stand and face a dog as large as a Great Dane, snapping at its legs, barking threateningly. After his death, I could see how much Cecil missed his little dog. He was now fifty seven years old and we realized that he would not be able to retire at sixty, like most people, but would have to work for at least another five years. He had finished the house and had built it nearly all himself, laying a few bricks each evening after work. During the winter months, when the fishing is not good, he would work all weekend. The house was a large one, with a big lounge, separate dining room and a lovely kitchen. He was so proud of his achievement and immediately set about developing his garden, buying roses as the main feature. Cecil had always enjoyed gardening; he said that he found it to be the most relaxing hobby.

Quite a few people had moved to the river by this stage and we began holding dances at the fishing club. With candles on the tables and little lamps to light up the kitchen, it had quite a romantic air about it, except of course, that the bar was always open and the men would disappear, leaving the women sitting alone at their tables. One Christmas eve, we attended a dance and Cecil landed up at the pub with the guys, until I saw red and walked over to Gloria, saying "When my husband comes out of there, please tell him I said good night."

Our home was only three houses away from the club, so I walked home and it wasn't much later when Cecil stormed into the house. "What the hell do you think you're playing at?" he demanded angrily.

I looked at him and said "I refuse to go to a dance and sit like a wallflower, while you entertain the guys over drinks. In future you can go alone and enjoy yourself."

Strangely enough, soon after that argument, the dances came to an end, so I suspect that there was more than one woman who had felt the same way.

People moved into a shack a few plots away from us and they had a son, Leon, who was a year older than Jeni. It was wonderful to watch these two youngsters every morning. They would meet at about five-thirty and swim across the river, climb the sand dune, rush back home to shower and get ready for school. Leon had a horse and when he and Jeni became friends, we bought her a horse as well. They spent many happy hours riding together, but one day after they had been out riding, Jeni calmly walked into the lounge and said "Mom, I've already been to Leon's mom and phoned the hospital to expect me, but dad will have to take me in; I fell off my horse and I've broken my arm."

She was resting the broken right arm on her left hand, covering it with a jersey and as I moved the jersey away to look at it, I felt quite sick. Both bones had pierced the flesh at the wrist, one to the top of the hand and the other to the bottom.

"Please don't touch it, mom, it's quite comfortable as it is."

Cecil took her in and dropped her at the hospital, knowing that she would need surgery to repair the fractures and she remained there for a few days, missing her final examinations for grade eleven.

Cecil was changing as he got older. I knew in my heart that the life in South Africa was a poor substitute for our Rhodesian life, but he had the courage to accept the fact that there was no going back. He was becoming more gentle and considerate with us all. He would walk into the kitchen where I was cooking, turn me around and give me a fierce hug and kiss. Laughing self-consciously, he would then disappear as quickly as possible. When Jeni or Mike had a problem, he was behind them completely and helped wherever he could. He was always prepared to sit and listen if someone was troubled and, in fact, I would truly describe him as having mellowed over the years.

We got a phone call from Joyce to say that my mom was in hospital as a result of a fall, but she seemed to be okay. I was worried, as she was eighty six already and I asked Cecil if we could drive to Port Shepstone to see her. Joyce said that this wasn't necessary, but I insisted and we left on the Friday afternoon. We encountered mist and the trip took us almost twice as long as it should have and we arrived at about two in the morning. I told Joyce I wanted to see mom right away, but she said that I would not be allowed in at that time of the morning and that mom had been chatting to them the previous evening. At eight I asked again to see mom and Joyce said "Visiting hours are only at eleven. They won't let you in before that."
To pass the time, Cecil and Joyce walked around admiring the garden, when the hospital phoned to say that mom had slipped into a coma. She died about an hour later, not knowing that I had come to be with her. Cecil went off with Charlie and as I got into the car with Joyce, she said "Your mother owned nothing and I'm giving her personal effects to the St. Vincent de Paul Society."

I could have pointed out that according to mom's will, I owned everything. I also didn't point out that mom had personally told me that she had a nice little nest egg for me. I merely looked across at

Joyce and said "I came to see my mother, not to see what I could get from her."

I left with nothing. In my mom's jewellery box, there were quite a few pieces that had been given to me by RAF boys and I had passed them to her when Cecil and I got married. What Joyce and Charlie did with them I have no idea.

Mike moved out and began his married life. They seemed happy enough and had a son, whom they named Ian. Sadly by the time Ian was a toddler, there were cracks in the marriage and a few months later, they divorced and Mike moved back home. He was doing a lot of military service at the time and was usually away for at least three months on each stint. Whether this had a negative effect on their relationship, I do not know.

The firm Jeni worked for went into liquidation and to make matters worse, her horse, Tornese, took ill. Ethné and Francois were on their way to visit Francois' mother on the south coast and they decided to take Jeni along with them. While they were away, Cecil brought Jeni's horse across from the farm where it was kept and began to tend it for hours each day. He bought special high-protein food and kept the horse on the plot adjacent to the house so that he could keep a close eye on it. He handed me a bunch of carrots one morning and asked me to take them to Tornese. As I crossed the road, the horse saw the carrots, jumped the fence and ran towards me. He was black, very big and loved carrots! I panicked as I saw the huge animal thundering towards me, so turned and headed off down the road, carrots in hand, yelling for Cecil to help me. Cecil was shouting something, between his roars of laughter, but I could not hear what he was saying. Tornese quickly caught up with me, grabbed the carrots out of my hand and quietly stood munching away as I stood beside him, shaking in my boots with fright. As Cecil approached, he said "I was telling you to drop the carrots!"

Rest assured, that was the last time I fed Tornese!

Over the next few years Jeni got married to John, had two sons and then twin boys. Ethné had another son and they moved to South Africa, near Cape Town. Mike remarried a lady by the name of

Verna, who had a little girl from a previous marriage. Mike legally adopted her and they later had three daughters and a son of their own. Jeni divorced when the twins were about seven and later married a chap by the name of Dave, who had two daughters from a previous marriage.

At this stage Cecil decided to buy a Staffordshire bull terrier and we called him Buddy. He was a wonderful animal, but had no desire for any other dog to exist and was always getting into really ugly fights. His favourite toy was a forty five gallon drum, which he would push around the yard as though it were a rubber ball. He had learned to open windows and was looking through our French door, when a labourer from the telephone company walked into the yard. On seeing Buddy, the labourer mouthed the word 'voertsak' and motioned with his hand towards the dog. That was all Buddy needed. He opened the lounge window with his snout and it was a race to see who could get to the gate first, the labourer or Buddy. I was screaming at Buddy to stop, but with the labourer running, my shouts were completely unheard. Thankfully the labourer managed to jump over the gate and Buddy stopped short as he did so.

We had Buddy for nine years and during that time both Cecil and I were bitten a few times as we tried to separate him from other animals. Cecil would take hold of Buddy and I would pull at the other dog, trying desperately to part them before too much damage was done. During one of the fights, Cecil broke his arm and had to have a plaster cast on it for six weeks. We were invited to a party at Gloria's home and on the way home, we saw Buddy lying in the road waiting for us. Just then a mongrel appeared and Buddy flew over to it and they began fighting. Cecil muttered "I'm sick of this damn dog fighting" and hit Buddy with his plaster cast, aiming for the body. At that precise moment, Buddy moved and the plaster cast hit him across the face. He let go of the dog, which took off down the road, leaving Buddy standing there moving his jaw backwards and forwards. Upset at this sight, I turned to Cecil and said "You've broken his jaw."
Cecil's angry retort was "I wish it was his bloody neck!"

Buddy looked up at us with sheer disgust, spat out a piece of the mongrel's ear and walked home.

Cecil loved Buddy more than any other dog we had ever owned. Apart from the dog's courage and fierceness, he was a much bigger, stronger animal than Wang and, being a Staffordshire bull terrier, he was robust and full of life. We eventually put Buddy down when he was diagnosed with cancer and Cecil was devastated. I personally believe that he loved and admired Buddy's wild streak.

At this time Bill and Phyllis let us know that they were coming down to open a retirement village. They were living in one in the Transvaal and Bill was friends with the developer, who said that he wanted him to do the honours in PE. We accompanied them on the Saturday afternoon. Phyllis was beautifully dressed and her hair was immaculately styled. I felt horribly frumpy next to her in my white skirt and navy jacket, but it was the best I could afford at the time. Cecil and Bill disappeared during the course of the afternoon and when they returned, I was greeted with the news that Bill had bought one of the units for Cecil and me, on the condition that when we sold our house at the river, we would pay him back. I knew I had said how pretty they were, but no ways did I want to live there. The next door unit's lounge bordered on our bedroom wall, as they were built in blocks of four.

On the way home I asked Cecil why he had agreed to this arrangement and he said "All my life you have followed me and now it's my turn to think of you. I want you to be happy and it's only a short bus drive to town and you can see the shops every day if you want to. Also, if anything happens to me, you will be secure in the complex."

What could I say? I didn't want to burst his bubble of generosity and so, at the end of that month, we moved into the village. Cecil became indispensable as people moved in. Everyone would call Cecil to help with something and he was adored by everyone in the village. The first few couples that arrived got a tray of biscuits and tea to welcome them, but no-one ever returned a call and I felt that I just didn't fit in and certainly wasn't fancy enough. Most of them were wealthy people, who formed their little cliques, so I went to the shops on my own, catching the bus, while the other ladies went in their cars. Cecil was battling to come to terms with living in such confined space, with no privacy whatsoever. If any of the family came to visit, I was terrified the children would disturb the other folk in the village.

I watched Cecil slowly growing old. He only had a tiny garden, which was cared for by a garden service that did the entire complex, so when Cecil got home from work, there was nothing at all to do, except sit. We stayed there for two years and had no offers on our house, which we had rented out temporarily. Then one night an agent called to say that she had a buyer and she wanted us to pop in and sign the paperwork. I realised as Cecil spoke on the phone, that the house was about to be sold and the words just bubbled from my mouth. "Take the house out of the market. Please don't sell it."
Cecil looked at me, then asked the agent if he could call her back. He put down the phone and asked "What now?"
"I have lived in this village for two years, waiting to die. Now I know I'm not dying yet and I want to go home!"
Cecil's face lit up with sheer joy and it was not long before we packed and moved back to our home at Sundays River.

Our biggest problem was that we hardly had any furniture left, as we had sold what would not have fitted into the retirement unit. However it was wonderful to be back with all our friends and I was content in the fact that I had realised that shopping with money is fun, but looking and not being able to buy is pure frustration. Colchester and Cannonville had water and electricity supplied to the area during the time we lived at Somerson and this made life that much easier when we returned home. Before they made water available at the river, we used to have to order a tanker of water from the municipality in Port Elizabeth and it filled two tanks in our yard, at a cost of two hundred rand per tanker load.

Once we had settled in, Cecil bought another Staffie and we named him Jock. He was the most intelligent dog we had ever had and he learned so many tricks. He would give short, quiet barks to say 'please' and he would not touch the food you put down until you told him to eat it, then he would tuck in and enjoy every morsel. He once came in with a bottle top in his mouth and I was afraid that he might swallow it, so I offered him a biscuit in exchange. After that he would search for bottle tops and sit with them balancing on his bottom lip, waiting for his exchange treat. He reminded me of Cecil, as he never looked for a fight with the other dogs, but if he got into one, he certainly could hold his own. This dog became Cecil's shadow and it was a lovely picture to see Cecil in the beach buggy, with Jock sitting proudly on the passenger seat, as if he owned it.

Not long after we moved back, I went to fetch the washing in and as I entered the house with my arms full of washing, I noticed a spider sitting on the top of the pile. At that moment, I realised that something was crawling on my arm and when I looked down, it was spider and there was another one close by. They were rain spiders, absolutely huge and terrible looking things. Well! If you have ever seen a cross between an Irish jig and the Highland Fling, it was done that day. I let out a loud shriek as washing flew across the room and Mike came running out of the lounge to see what the problem was. After he had managed to curb his hysterical laughter at the sight before him, he turned to me and asked "Mom, where is the woman who took all these things in her stride for years in the bush?"
I looked him straight in the eye and retorted "Mike, that wasn't a woman, it was a lunatic!"

At the age of sixty five, Cecil went on pension and the years slowly passed by. Before we knew it, it was our fiftieth wedding anniversary and, as I looked at this man of mine, I realised that he was still just as handsome. His hair was showing quite a bit of grey, he had a few wrinkles around his eyes and a small paunch beginning to show, but those tawny eyes were still bright and shining. His mind was still quick and very alert. He had softened over the years, learned to laugh a lot more and his face showed a certain gentleness.

Ethné wrote a poem about time and our wedding presents to each other being thrown against the wall. She presented this poem to us, together with a set of watches that she and Jeni had bought for our anniversary. Mike came down and brought with him a slaughtered pig, which filled the freezer. I realised how lucky we were to have these three wonderful children and their spouses loved us as much as their own parents. Between the three couples, we had fifteen grandchildren, if we counted the dear little soul that Ethné and Francois had laid to rest and Mike's first child, Ian, whom we never saw again after Liz left Port Elizabeth.

Someone had once asked Cecil if he had ever considered divorce during our lives together, to which he replied "Divorce no, but murder, millions of times!"

Odette, Ethné's daughter, was already planning her wedding and the other grandchildren ranged in all ages, right down to Mike's last baby, who was a year old. They were all with us for our anniversary and Cecil and I were sitting together on the verandah, watching the children frolic together. He suddenly took my hand and whispered "When I asked you to marry me, I didn't expect to produce the results that we are sitting watching right now."
The warmth of that moment will live with me forever.

CHAPTER SEVENTEEN

The fight to save Kakuli....

Cecil's rose garden was in full bloom and it was a most beautiful sight to see. He definitely had green fingers and his gardening and woodwork had taken the place of hunting and photography, which had become too expensive. He had found a quiet contentment in his garden and still enjoyed fishing at weekends. He had sold his golf clubs before leaving for South Africa, because he knew that he would not have been able to afford it anymore and there no courses near Cannonville anyway.

Somehow it was Cecil who always seemed to be the one who encountered snakes. He walked down the front steps of our house with a friend one night and as they stood talking, he felt something flapping against his foot. He looked down and realised that his big toe was on the head of a snake and its body was wriggling madly around him. It was quite a small snake and, without further thought, Cecil lifted his bare foot as quickly as he could and then killed it. No matter how I begged, I could not get him to put shoes on when he was at home. Even when he was gardening, he insisted on being barefoot.

Snakes seemed to be quite prolific at that stage and a few days later Cecil was working in the garden and moved a plough disc. As he put his hands on the bottom of the disc and lifted, he lifted two Skaapstekers along with the plough disc. As he dropped them on the grass, they swiftly disappeared into the long grass at the side of the house.

I developed a hiatus hernia and a perforation just underneath it occurred some time afterwards, making it imperative that I underwent surgery. All went well with the op and I was placed in high care for three days. When I was moved to the general ward,

Cecil came to visit me and he looked terribly tired. I asked him what was wrong and he replied "I saw you being wheeled out of the lift after your operation and you looked so tiny and vulnerable, I thought you were ready to kiss the world goodbye. I don't know how I've survived the past three days; I've been so worried about you."
I had been cut from under the breast, right around my left side and up to the shoulder blade. They had done the operation through the ribs and I was really sore.

I was discharged two days later, much to my surprise. The old lady lying in the bed next to mine told me that morning that she suspected that she was going home, when they suddenly walked in and said I could go home. I left while she was still lying in bed. I actually think that they made a mistake, as they had only taken the drip out of my neck an hour prior to me leaving.

When I got home, Cecil helped me to bed and offered to make lunch. He brought me a little fried snoek, with bread and butter. That evening he told me he was busy with supper and later brought me snoek, with bread and butter. The following morning he came into the bedroom, saying "Don't get up, sweetheart, I'm busy making breakfast."
What did I get? Fried snoek on toast! I must admit he looked very happy when I said "I'm feeling much better now, I think I'll get up and make us some lunch."
I promise you, it wasn't snoek! I was soon on my feet again and felt wonderful until three months later, when I fell and tore out the entire operation. They would not operate again and I have been on treatment for the past fifteen years since that fall.

As a Christmas present to Cecil and me, a couple of friends booked us into a game lodge for dinner. How beautiful it was inside the lapa. They had fires burning in plough discs and a tame kudu was walking from table to table for titbits. The two men began talking to the owner about Zambia and eventually he turned to two youngsters of about seventeen, "As a special treat, take these people in the landrover to the lion camp."

283

The landrover was completely open and had two sets of seats apart from the driving seat. Our friends sat on the high seat, while Cecil and I chose the lower back seat. They opened huge gates after making sure that it was safe to do so and asked us to be very quiet. However our friend would not stop talking and asked so many questions. The one youngster asked him to be quiet after about ten minutes and as we came round the corner, we encountered two huge lions lying on the side of the road. A third lion was standing not very far away. I surmised that these were the only three lions and the youngster kept his spotlight on them. Suddenly, out of the corner of my eye, I spotted a fourth lion stalking us from behind the landrover. All my fears of lions came rushing back and I shot sideways, almost knocking Cecil off his seat. He pulled me into his arms and held me tightly as he said to the driver "Let's go. This lion is looking for trouble."

On our return, we told the owner about our encounter and he explained that the lions' food was delivered in that same vehicle and that they must have thought it was feeding time. Unamused, I retorted "That's fine, but I had no intention of being his evening meal!" Strangely enough, my nightmares returned after this incident, but once again it was those loving arms that supported me through them.

Cecil reached the age of seventy five and I was close behind at seventy three. We were both still hale and hearty, except for the odd twinges of arthritis and my chronic bronchitis. He was still a fine looking man, who still walked tall in both stature and character. He was a well-loved man, mostly because people realised that his word was his honour and I never saw him lose his dignity in any situation. Our love had grown stronger as the years passed and we enjoyed each other's company so much as we aged together. He was a busy man, doing woodwork which was exquisite and very much in demand. He still adored his gardening and I would often wake up in the morning to find a rose on the pillow next to me. I kept busy making dolls, baby clothes and other items for home industries and we were so content.

One morning Cecil rushed into the house, his face completely ashen. "I was so lucky I never got bitten" he stated as he looked at me. "I picked up my throw net, which had fallen on the floor in the garage, and I felt something touching my leg, but I thought it was the rope from the net. When I went to grab the rope, I took a handful of snake, which was entangled in the net, but its head was striking at me as I walked with the net. Anyway, I killed the snake, but I am so lucky that it never managed to bite me. I think it was a Rinkhals." A few seconds later, Cecil said "Gosh, my leg is burning like hell."

As we looked down, we saw the two puncture marks from the snake's fangs, as the blood trickled down his calf. Looking at the wound, his face changed and all he said was "And to think that a bloody nyoka!" (meaning snake).

In retrospect, I believe that he had a premonition regarding the outcome of this snakebite at that moment. With that, he turned away from me. I ran to the phone and called Noreen, a friend of ours, who told me that her son would fetch Cecil immediately. Within five minutes, Rob arrived and rushed Cecil through to the hospital, ignoring traffic lights, as he raced to get him there as quickly as he could. I quickly dressed and Noreen drove me to the hospital, where I found Cecil in casualty with a drip in his arm.

The doctor explained that they no longer used anti-venom, but first treated the symptoms, as so many people are allergic to the anti-venom. They kept Cecil on the drip for four hours and as he showed no breathing problems, which is typical of a rinkhals bite, they told him he could go home, but if there were any new developments, he should come straight back to hospital. When we got home, a neighbour popped over to see Cecil and he told us that he also thought that the snake was a rinkhals. They took the dead snake and buried it.

The following morning Cecil looked ill and was quite yellow in colour. He complained of nausea, so I phoned the hospital, but they said that it was to be expected after a snake bite. The wound on the leg was closing and everything seemed okay, but on the second day,

Cecil cut his face while shaving and we battled to stop the bleeding. Even later that afternoon, long after the bleeding had stopped, it started up again. We surmised that it must have been from the drip they had given him, so we never phoned the hospital again. So much for ignorance!

A couple of times I suggested that we go back to the hospital, but our car was out of action and Cecil didn't want to bother anyone again. On the third day, a lot of folk arrived to visit and Jeni arrived with nausea tablets, insisting that Cecil take one immediately. He seemed to brighten up during the afternoon and even teased the grandchildren like he always did. When everyone left, I was in the kitchen, when Cecil announced that he wasn't feeling well and was going to bed. I was so busy that I never turned around and simply said "Alright, sweetheart, I'll be there as soon as I'm finished."

It had turned bitterly cold and was raining and I suspected I was starting with bronchitis, as I kept coughing. About an hour later I propped up the pillows and got into bed, but I just didn't seem to be able to get enough air into my lungs. I felt Cecil jerk in his sleep and a few minutes later he jerked again, but I dismissed it, thinking that he was probably just dreaming. Ignorance once again!

I fell asleep and at one in the morning I heard Cecil cry out, "My head, my head."

I heard him pick up the box of tablets near his bed and he drank some of the coke. As I became fully awake, I realised that he had swallowed two blood pressure tablets and not headache tablets. I was worried that they could harm him, so I phoned the hospital to enquire. As I was speaking to the doctor, I heard a thud and realised that he had fallen out of bed. I ran to the bedroom to find him jammed between the bedside pedestal and the couch that we kept in the room for Jock to sleep on. I managed to drag the couch away and release his head and then tried to help him up. He was a big man and I just couldn't move him. I kept asking him to help me and he tried hard to get up, but could not.

I told him that I was going to phone Noreen for help and he said "No."

"Then," I replied, "I'm phoning for an ambulance."

Cecil's only answer was "Don't want."

These were the last words he ever uttered to me.

I phoned for the ambulance and told them that I would stand outside with the lights on so that they would find the house. Running to the kitchen, I switched on all the outside lights, but it seemed that with all the rain, water had leaked onto some wires outside and the lights suddenly tripped, plunging the house into darkness.

Neither of us smoked, but I remembered that we had made a braai that day, so matches must be nearby. I slowly walked around the house feeling for matches and whispered a prayer of thanks as I found them. Switching off all the outside lights, I managed to get the trip switch up and the interior lights came on. I phoned the ambulance centre again to tell them that there were no lights outside, but the man who answered told me that they had already left. "The ambulance doesn't have a radio, but it should be in Cannon Rocks within the next half an hour."
My heart froze as I heard these words, as we live in Cannonville, not Cannon Rocks, which is about a hundred kilometres from us. I quickly explained this and the man replied "I have an ambulance that is on its way back from Grahamstown and they do have a radio. I'll contact him immediately."
I took an umbrella and stood at the side of the road in the freezing cold and rain, waiting for the ambulance to arrive. After half an hour, I became so worried about Cecil that I started to run back up the driveway to check on him. As I reached the house, I saw the ambulance drive past, so I rushed back down and waved frantically. Thank the Lord, he saw me and turned back.

The stretcher would not pass through the little hallway and we had to move two chest freezers in order to get into the bedroom. Cecil was still unconscious on the floor and the two paramedics picked him up and lay him on the stretcher. I phoned Jeni and asked her to meet me at the hospital and then locked Jock in the garage, hiding the key so that I could arrange with someone on the river to let him out in the morning.

With Cecil's weight on the stretcher, the men were struggling to get it through the hallway again and poor Cecil was half outside in the rain, as they tried to manoeuvre the stretcher through the narrow area. I suggested that we use the lounge entrance and in my haste to switch on the lights, I accidentally turned on the outside lights, plunging us into darkness yet once again. Not knowing where I had put the matches, I was only too glad that one of the paramedics was a smoker and in no time we had the lights on and they carried Cecil to the ambulance.

Cecil was so wet by this stage, as was the blanket they had put over him, so they asked me to get another blanket for him. I ran back inside and, in my panic and haste to grab the blanket, I forgot that I had a tray full of fabric paints on the table next to the bed and I heard everything crash to the floor. By this time I just didn't care about anything else and I ran back to the ambulance to cover Cecil with the blanket. They were busy putting a drip into his arm and I stood outside, waiting for them to finish. I hadn't brought the umbrella out with me, so I was drenched by the time they allowed me to step into the ambulance. The paramedic told me to talk to him and I answered "He can't hear me."
"Talk to him" he reiterated as the driver began to run the vehicle down the driveway.
I took Cecil's hand in mine and said "Sweetheart, if you can hear me, squeeze my hand." What a joy when he weakly squeezed my hand! I told him how much I loved him and that he should fight with all he could, for I could not imagine living without him. It was half an hour's drive to the hospital and by the time we reached it, Cecil had stopped squeezing my hand as was completely unresponsive.

Jeni was there waiting for me and when I saw her, I think I went into a state of shock, because it was Jeni who took his hand then and it was Jeni who kept whispering to him. I literally just stood there like a zombie as they took blood samples and we waited for the results to come through. By this time, Cecil seemed to be sucking for every breath of air and his lips were very dry. Jeni asked him if he wanted a little water and, to our surprise, he nodded. She quickly filled a plastic cup with water from a nearby basin tap and gently placed the cup to his lips, letting a little water trickle into his mouth, wetting his lips as well. Cecil whispered a very quiet "Thank you" and then slipped back into unconsciousness.

Eventually after what seemed an eternity, the doctor arrived and told Cecil to lift his right arm. After getting no response, he shouted the instruction again and Cecil lifted his arm. "Now lift your left arm" the doctor shouted, but it was obvious that Cecil could not. He tried to get Cecil to lift his left leg, but there was also no response. Turning to us, the doctor said "He has had a massive stroke and is completely paralysed down the left side. I will get a specialist for you immediately."

The specialist was very good and explained that the next forty eight hours were the most critical. Jeni phoned Ethné and Mike and told them she thought they should come immediately, but it was at least a ten hour drive to Port Elizabeth. I could still not register that Cecil was that ill and kept asking her not to make them drive all that way for nothing, as I assured her that by tomorrow he would be alright. However, by lunchtime, Cecil had deteriorated quite a bit and by the time Ethné and Mike arrived late that afternoon, he was in a deep coma.

The one thing I find hard to forgive the hospital for is the fact that, at no time, did the sister on duty let me know how very ill he was and that we should rather stay at the hospital. They had placed him in a general ward and inserted a catheter, then left us sitting at his bedside. After Ethné and Mike had arrived and sat with him for a while, even though he was in a coma, we left at the end of visiting hour and went to Jeni's house for supper. We phoned the hospital after supper and they advised us that there had been no change, so we all went to bed at Jeni's house to get some much needed rest. At two in the morning the sister called Jeni to tell us that Cecil had taken a bad turn and we should come immediately. We were there within ten minutes, only to be told that he had already passed on. She directed us to a private room, where Cecil had already been washed and laid out.

As I looked at my sweetheart at that moment, something inside me also died. I ruffled his hair and walked out of the room. In time I have forgiven myself for not kissing him goodbye. I only realised many months later, just how much shock I had been in. So much so, that I went to a shop to buy a black skirt for the funeral and came out with a red one!

I thought that Cecil's funeral would be a small, private affair and I absolutely dreaded everyone fussing over me after the service. I didn't want to break down in front of people and when we got to the chapel, I went and sat down in the front pew immediately. Slowly the chapel began to fill up and they eventually opened the section where the choir would normally sit, resulting in me having about fifty people in front of me, facing my direction. I tried to sing the hymns with everyone and I kept feeling a tear drop from my cheek onto my blouse. How I ever got through that service without breaking down, I do not know and how I stood calmly while nearly two hundred people came forward to kiss me and whisper words of condolence, I have no idea. Many of the people I had never seen in my life before, they were people Cecil had befriended while he was a building inspector. I was told much later that, although tears ran freely down my face, I managed to smile and greet every person, thanking them for attending the service. I do not remember.

At last that dreadful day was over. Bill and Phyllis had driven all the way from Potgietersrust and Bill was over eighty at that stage. Francois flew down the following day and he, Ethné and Mike stayed with me, as was Bill and Phyllis. I tried to carry on normally, although Ethné kindly took over the kitchen, while I managed to tell her what to cook for each meal. They all tried not to leave me alone for a minute and when Jeni brought Cecil's ashes out to the river, we had a little service of our own and we scattered his ashes over his beloved rose garden.

At last it was time for everyone to say goodbye and I was left alone with Jock in this huge house, with a big garden. Every time she visited, Jeni would ask me what the snake looked like, but I was unable to describe it accurately. I kept telling her that her father and

Mister Nel had said it was a rinkhals. One day she brought a book on snakes to me and as I paged through it, without reading any of the writing, I immediately pointed at a particular snake and said "That's it."

It was a boomslang. Cecil and our neighbour had both been mistaken about the identity of the snake and that is why Cecil never displayed any of the expected symptoms. The venom of the boomslang is completely different to that of a rinkhals. It causes extensive internal bleeding and fatal damage to organs such as the liver. This is why Cecil's shaving cut would not stop bleeding and why he ultimately suffered a cerebral haemorrhage. Strangely enough, there was a small caption at the bottom of the page of the snake book, where they mentioned that a young female boomslang is often mistaken for a rinkhals.

Jeni's ex-husband, John took ill with flu on the day Cecil died and was hospitalised. Within two days he was completely sedated, placed on a ventilator and became gravely ill. He had been diagnosed with some sort of viral pneumonia and, because his immune system was so low at the time, he died twelve days after Cecil from organ failure. Jeni's poor children were now grieving for both their father and grandfather.

CHAPTER EIGHTEEN

The other me....

As the days went by, I realised that I had literally become two different people. There was the real me, who said to everyone "Yes, I'm fine and I am getting over it."
Then there was the other me, whom I will describe in the next few paragraphs.

I wake up early in the morning and go outside to watch the sun rise over the tree tops, while the other me silently whispered "Where is he now? Where are his loving arms, his smiling eyes, his laughter, as we watch the sun rise together?"
I sigh and go inside. The house is quiet. No-one asking for coffee, or calling me to see a new rose that has opened and how pretty it is. What point in cooking for myself? I'll just have a slice of toast. I sit and eat the toast with a cup of tea on the verandah where we always sat together; admiring the rose garden that now holds his ashes.

The house was always spotless, as there was only Jock and I to make any mess. I would go through the motions of dusting and cleaning, trying to carry on, while 'the other me' would whisper "Oh, my darling, how I miss you. I miss your understanding, I miss your love. At this time of day you would ask me to make tea and to sit with you awhile in the shade of the Banksia Roses."

Lunchtime has arrived, but I can't eat, so I go and sit with Jock on the front steps. I hide my face in his fur so that if anyone should walk past, they would not see the tears falling from my eyes and then the other me whispers "Oh darling, how can I go on without you? I had you for fifty four years to make all the decisions in our life". Then the real me says "Get out of this poor little ol' me attitude and do something. Keeping busy will heal the wounds."

I get up, have a shower, change into something nice and then visit some good friends.

We would talk about various subjects for a while and I would be the old Joan. For a short time my sadness would subside and then I would look at the time and realise that I must be overstaying my welcome, so the real me would say "I must be going, but thank you for a super afternoon."

The other me would be whispering "What's the hurry? There's no-one at home to cook for or to throw your arms around and tell them how much you love them. Only Jock is there, looking as sad and miserable as you do. He misses Cecil just as much."

I walk back into the empty house, boil an egg and have it with a slice of bread. I turn on the TV and become acutely aware of the empty chair beside me, where Cecil always sat. I cannot concentrate on any program, so I lock up the house and go to bed, even though it's only seven in the evening. As I enter the bedroom, I see the empty pillow where my beloved's head used to lay and also where I used to find a rose in the mornings. I get into bed and feel the empty space beside me. No loving arms to snuggle into. The real me says "Stop feeling sorry for yourself."

I thump my pillow and say "Be grateful for the years you had together; think of the good times."

But the other me dissolves into a flood of bitter tears as I ask God "When does this awful, tearing agony ever end?"

Colchester had been a small village when we came from Zambia. The residences were mainly shacks and the boats that came out were small, with people like us, who wanted to do a bit of fishing. Cecil had always loved this place. There had also been very little vegetation on the other side of the river, which boasted the most magnificent sand dunes. They were very high and when the sun shone, it would dance on the hot sand and sparkle in its shadows on the river itself. The river is a tidal one and quite wide across. It has always been very well known for its fishing. At night there is usually phosphorous on the water and if you sit on the bank at night with the stars twinkling overhead, the phosphorous shines in all its brilliant colours in the path of the moon.

Cecil had always said "One day, when I retire, I want to live at Sundays River."
Well, he had ten years of retirement before he passed on and he had some wonderful catches in that time. Over the years, we had watched the shacks disappear and mansions being built in their place. What had once been the poor man's fishing spot, had now become the rich man's paradise. Gone were the little fishing boats with tiny motors, anchored in the middle of the river with two men eagerly fishing. Now weekends saw all the youngsters skiing up and down in their luxury cruisers. Outside all the mansions stood expensive four-by-four vehicles and luxury cars. Ten years previously, it had been worn-out bakkies and cars that were at least ten to twenty years old. There were very few of the 'old folk' left; they had all sold their shacks and moved on. In the old days, we had made our own fun as one big happy family, but today you hardly get a greeting if someone passes by, so the entire atmosphere has changed.

I tried to stay on at the river, but as I didn't drive, I felt I was a burden to friends when I had to accept a lift to town to buy groceries. They all refused to let me pay towards fuel, saying that they were going that way anyway. Having been an independent person all my life, after six months of battling against my pride, I made the difficult decision to find a home for my beautiful Jock and move to town. Shortly afterwards I received a call from Jeni to say that Dave had been involved in an accident at work and he had fractured his back. He was in hospital for a couple of weeks and then sent home to recuperate in bed for nine months.

I found a flat and two weeks before I was to move in, I took a bad turn while out shopping with friends from the river. They rushed me to hospital and the doctor said that my heart was under stress. What did they expect? I had lost my sweetheart, my dog and my home in six months. It wasn't only my heart that was under stress.

The children decided I could not live alone and Dave and Jeni asked me to move in with them. Life then took another twist. Jeni had become a decorative artist, doing murals and paint effects and as Dave's salary was a lot less while he was off work, Jeni had to work twice as hard to earn enough money to keep the family going. This meant that she could not be at home during the day to tend to Dave, so I took on the job of keeping him company and making tea and lunch. He has always been a very active man and he found being bed-ridden terribly frustrating.

They were both so good to me, but once Dave was back on his feet, I told them that I was going to move on. They were hurt and wanted to know where they had failed me, but they just did not understand how I was feeling at that stage. I assured them that they had been wonderful, but I was tired of being just mom or granny. I wanted to find Joan again.

I managed to get a flat with the ex-serviceman's housing, thanks to Cecil being in the navy during the war. It was a tiny bachelor flat on the second floor, with one large room, a tiny kitchen and a shower in the tiniest bathroom you've ever seen. However I was grateful, because it was mine. Once again life became difficult for me. I was alone and afraid. I had to make decisions and so many of them were the wrong ones. I didn't want the children to know how lonely I was, but I sat for many hours in the flat, crying my eyes out. I had been there for two months and every week I saw a sign go up saying 'Tea at Paula's, Flat Fourteen, on Wednesday at 3 p.m. All welcome.' I had never been able to summon up the courage to go, until one day when I was returning from a walk. I saw the lady putting up the sign and she turned to me and said "Wouldn't you like to join us tomorrow afternoon? I see you are new here."
I agreed to go, but as the time grew closer, I was terrified and I still don't know how I managed to get the courage to actually attend the tea. I met eleven ladies that day, nearly three years ago and we are all still the best of friends. A few months later a one-bedroom flat became available and I moved down one floor. In my own way, I am happy being with folk my own age and it was wonderful to hear my own name again.

I bought a little book and I have posted into it Cecil's references, his call-up papers, letters of thanks and appreciation to him over the years, the article from the newspaper about how he was bitten by a snake and, finally, his epitaph from the newspaper. And so, in a few pieces of paper, I read of a man who lived by his word, was fearless in danger and who never lost his dignity. Ours was a marriage made in heaven. I gave him all my respect and love and he was always there for me. Never once have I asked myself why, I rather say "Thank you, Lord, for a wonderful fifty four years together."

I still miss him terribly, especially if I see another aged couple smiling into each other's eyes, or just touching hands. That's when the tears well up and I quickly look away. I'm eternally grateful for the good times and the bad. Cecil was the nicest thing that ever happened to me in my entire lifetime and I have always been a better person for knowing him.

Hamba Kahle, Bwana, I love you. One day we will roam the happy hunting grounds, together once more.

A TRIBUTE TO BWANA KAKULI

(Written by Jeni for Cecil's Funeral Service)

As you leave on your last journey
To your final hunting ground,
We know we have to stay behind
We can't follow you on this round.
But you left us with a knowledge
Of the finest man in time;
One that taught his children
To always give of their prime.
You gave us love and comfort,
You gave us courage supreme;
You brought us such great happiness
As you followed all your dreams.
No man with greater morals
Has ever walked this earth;
And this carried across to all of us
A magical sense of worth.
You gave our mom a good life,
With adventures all the way;
Thanks, Dad, so very much,
Is all that we can say.
Your help towards those around you,
And your compassion to those in need,
Has touched the hearts of so many
Who knew you for your good deeds.
Your sudden departure is sorely grieved,
But deep down in us there's hope;
Because your memory will live within our hearts,
Helping us to cope.
From Tree Tops to Luangwa,
From Zambia to SA;
Your name will be remembered,
With honour all the way.

You truly were a legend
Of the extraordinary kind;
Hamba kahle, Bwana,
You're always on our minds.

CAPTURING THE MEMORIES

For those who are interested, we have compiled a presentation of photographs and slides on CD pertaining to some of the areas and people in this book.

Enquiries to:

Jeni Smithies
PO Box 96
GREENBUSHES
6390

Or

Email to: mwkunda@mweb.co.za

ABOUT THE AUTHOR

To be honest, Joan Slabbert is somewhat of an enigma. Those who know her today, see her as a real lady; well-groomed and gracious. Yet if you were to ask her family, we would describe her as one tough woman, who is able to cope with any situation. There is far more to this woman than initially meets the eye.

For many years we begged our father to write a book about his African adventures, but he dodged the task and ultimately, it was too late. It was his death that sparked a need in our mother to put pen to paper and honour his memory. At seventy-seven she began to write her story and, two years later, felt it was ready to be published. It was a story that needed to be told. Anyone who lived in Northern Rhodesia during those years will thrill at the fine description of so many familiar places and probably recall a number of the people mentioned in her book.

As her children, we marvel at the vast expanse of her memory and it is with deep respect and pride that we look on as her book is published. She has many creative talents and has won numerous awards for various crafts. She has the innate ability to cope with emergencies, calming those in panic and taking control of precarious situations. Yet, through all this, she is able to maintain a special sense of grace and poise.

Although she describes our dad as Kakuli, we know that much of his greatness came from the support and love of our mother and we celebrate having spent our lives with her. Those who know her personally, instinctively know that their lives have been enriched. Joan Slabbert has lived a life full of special memories and adventures and has related them with all the enthusiasm that she shows to everyone around her,

ISBN 1-41206156-3

9 781412 061568

Printed in Great Britain
by Amazon